Catholic
Education
in a
Changing
World

Catholic Education in a Changing World

GEORGE N. SHUSTER *Nauman* , *1894-*

Holt, Rinehart and Winston
New York   Chicago
San Francisco

Designer: Ernst Reichl
8654857
Printed in the United States of America

ACKNOWLEDGMENTS   Grateful acknowledgment is made to the following publishers who have so generously granted permission to reprint from their publications:

Fides Press, Notre Dame, Indiana, for an excerpt from "The Meaning of Virginity in Religious Life," by Sister M. Elena Malits, C.S.C., in *The Changing Sister*, edited by Sister M. Charles Borromeo Muckenhirn, C.S.C. (1965).

The Guild Press, New York, for excerpts from *The Documents of Vatican II*, edited by Walter M. Abbott, S.J. (1966).

Harper & Row, Publishers, New York, for an excerpt from *Education and Moral Wisdom* by George N. Shuster (1960).

N.C.W.C. News Service for excerpts from a study by Father Ernest Bartell, C.S.C. (February 18, 1966).

The Review of Politics for an excerpt from "Public Schools vs. Catholic Schools and James McMaster," by Thomas T. McAvoy, C.S.C., XXVIII, 1 (January, 1966).

St. Mary's College, Notre Dame, Indiana, for an excerpt from "The Education of Sister Lucy," by Sister Mary Madeleva, C.S.C.

University of Notre Dame Press, Notre Dame, Indiana, for excerpts from *Catholic Schools in Action: A Report, the Notre Dame Study of Catholic Elementary Schools in America*, edited by Reginald A. Neuwien (1966).

Contents

Foreword

This book is a congeries of concerns, and no more. It is, as a matter of fact, pretty tame. The author does not suggest blowing the educational house down and building a new structure with the pieces. He will appear stubbornly unimpressed with the notion that the world began when the Second Vatican Council ended. If you can resist being bored, you will come upon rather modest suggestions as to how some improvements could be made and certain strengths augmented. But what the book really tries to do is find out how education, particularly religious education, can live with change—so inescapable, so perplexing, and so hard to endure.

First, what do recently completed studies in the area of elementary and secondary education reveal about Catholic schools or, more generally, the training of young people? Several of the more important of these studies have been conducted wholly or in part under the auspices of Notre Dame University. Researchers have assembled vast quantities of pertinent data never previously made available and have arrived at some tentative but interesting conclusions. I shall try to summarize and discuss these findings.

It also seems desirable to talk about the impact of the deliberations and pronouncements of the Second Vatican Council on Catholic education, particularly where colleges and universities are concerned. Some empirical research has been undertaken in this area, but inevitably it is fragmentary. At best, discussion here can be no more than speculative.

Finally, something will be said about the grave and complex

problem of school finance. But one can go no further than the available information permits.

Despite years of hard spadework done by Reginald A. Neuwien of the University of Notre Dame and Father Andrew Greeley of the University of Chicago, the data is less substantial than one would wish. I am deeply indebted to both of them, as the following pages will indicate, and have borrowed freely from their writings. Since I am superimposing reflection and recollection on their findings, however, this book must be clearly understood as discursive and personal.

My thanks must also go to Joseph Cunneen, whose editorial labor on behalf of the publisher has been tireless, and for whose comments I have entertained the greatest respect; and to Father Theodore M. Hesburgh, C.S.C., the distinguished president of Notre Dame, for inspiration and counsel. Let me mention also my secretary, Mrs. Patricia Mello, whose hours of toil on the manuscript have added greatly to her woes. There are many, many others who helped but there is no room here for a catalogue of names. I shall merely append a word of gratitude to all those who have read my case for and against a Catholic university, and have agreed or disagreed.

Catholic
Education
in a
Changing
World

I

Setting
the Stage

This book was first thought of in terms of an obligation. When, in 1961, the Carnegie Corporation made a generous grant to the University of Notre Dame for the study of Catholic elementary and secondary education, it was assumed that I would write a sort of over-all companion volume to whatever studies based on the on-going or completed research were published. It was to be a veteran schoolman's commentary on how well Catholic education in the United States was responding to the challenge of the age. The expectation was that it might even have something mildly complimentary to report about the way things were going. But the research could not be completed in the contemplated time-span—indeed, in one or two respects it is still in progress—and by the time the fourth session of the Second Vatican Council had closed, the world of religion was no longer the same world; and of course the educational system we are considering must live in that world.

Meanwhile, the stage on which the Republic was playing its part in history also experienced a radical change. While the spotlight was on the war in Vietnam, we were all becoming aware that for some time to come our lives would be shaped by a range of basic concerns no previous age had been obligated to think about in the same way. The international scene was a panorama of far-flung struggles for human rights in all their totality and complexity; our own "inner cities" (and doubtless sometimes our outer cities, too) were deteriorating so rapidly that they all but threatened to bring about the collapse of the society as a whole; and the impact of science on human life was growing larger and more problematical every day. Education could no longer be what it had been, if it was to meet the needs of the present age.

Catholic education had been established in order to make provision for the religious formation of the young. We suddenly discovered that what we had once confidently assumed this formation should be was no longer realistic. Indeed, at the moment it appears to make precious little sense. We have got to leave the educational house we have so far occupied and take a good look around. This is not going to be easy. Informed opinion is far, far from being of one mind about the basic significance of the Vatican Council for religious formation, but agreement appears to have been reached at least tentatively on two matters of crucial importance for education. First, the role assigned to the individual conscience has been so heightened that trying to realize what the change implies may well induce something close to shock. The function of education is no longer to protect that conscience by laying down a series of rules, whose rejection could be considered apostasy. The conscience is, rather, to be steeled through a constant process of asking questions and finding answers, of accepting tasks or rejecting them. Second, thought and action are to be directed toward salvation through the practice of a new kind of Catholic citizenship in the world, so complex in terms of discovery and fulfillment that the horizon is still blurred.

Nor are things any simpler when we turn to what we used to call "training for good citizenship"; the old vocabulary now sounds like a bundle of phrases from a McGuffey reader. One may, for instance, entertain a good deal of sympathy for the conviction that what we need is a common language and a common moral climate, and that these are best taught by handing down from one generation to the next "the best that has been known and thought in the world." Certainly Catholic education has traditionally clung to this view. Colleges and many of the secondary schools abandoned the classical languages and literatures with regret, and at least until recently tried to make the "perennial philosophy" a meeting ground for minds. The best-informed deans and principals have now come, often regretfully, to the conclusion that this will no longer be possible. But what will be possible? The "dialogue with the world," which the Council so gravely enjoined, makes it clear, for example, that our obligation is to know our Negro fellow citizens better than many of us used to know the ancient Romans. Not long ago, Americans were content with a bucolic image of Negroes living in Southern shanties, working hard but presumably singing spirtuals by the hour. However tardily, that image has been permanently shattered, and today we all know that what happens to the Negro in Harlem and Watts and South Chicago will pretty much tell the story of human rights in the United States. This is a crucial test, both for American Catholics and the nation, and there are other challenges before us which are equally exciting and dangerous.

While this world of altered human circumstances was thus coming into being, the conscientious reporter had to review what was available in the form of educational evidence. Fortunately, two major studies have recently been completed which describe very adequately at least some of the principal aspects of Catholic elementary and secondary schools.* The first is a study of Catholic schools in action, conducted by a staff assembled at the University of Notre

* See the Bibliographical Appendix to this book.

Dame and directed by Reginald Neuwien. The second is a survey of what graduates of this and other schools report about the continuing impact of religion on their lives. This was directed by Father Andrew Greeley, in co-operation with the National Opinion Research Center of the University of Chicago and was cosponsored by Notre Dame. Both supply a wealth of empirical evidence within agreed-upon areas of investigation. What distinguishes them from other inquiries into Catholic education is that access to a wealth of statistical data was made possible by combining university resources with those of professional organizations of educators, notably the National Catholic Educational Association, and of course also by very generous grants-in-aid from the Carnegie Corporation. The Notre Dame study group conducted far-reaching inquiries into the schools and school systems of thirteen dioceses selected from the total number, and entered into a slow-paced dialogue with school authorities, teachers, specialists in educational research, sociologists, and experts in religious formation. All of this could not be reflected in the published report of the study's findings. Even after taking into account the maxim that what was true yesterday is not necessarily true today, the Notre Dame data constitute a gold mine as yet unworked. The published report does, however, provide a wealth of statistical tables, stark naked and imperturbable, about enrollments, teaching, teacher preparation, religious training, and other important questions. No (or at least very few) personal judgments were made. Though Father Greeley's study is more restricted in scope, it probes into available information about its important topic—the continuing impact of religious education—with care and up-to-date sociological methodology.

Unfortunately, no comparable study of Catholic higher education has been completed. Here the major difficulty is trying to piece together a vast number of inquiries which, though quite uneven in terms of scope and quality, constitute a literature which in its totality is very helpful and informative. Much more work is now being done, so that within a relatively few years a student of Catholic higher education will probably have all the tools he needs. At present, however, there are areas whose surface has hardly been scratched. In a sense, this may be less of a handicap than one might assume. Sociological inquiries are extremely useful, but feeding on them exclusively may lead to the kind of indigestion which blurs the vision. Coping with the evidence currently available is such a chore that no treadmill can quite compare with it, but there is still value in having an observer who can look through his own glasses, however limited their focus may be.

But why should I write a book about Catholic education? To answer my own question, I had to make a candid review of my assets, which mainly consist in the fact that I have been in education all my life. Twelve years spent editing *Commonweal* may seem an interlude, but they were not. Time was found for some teaching—both college and seminary—during these years, and during periods of research in Europe I had ample opportunity to see something of academic institutions there. Then I spent more than twenty years as president of Hunter College in New York; and if there was any aspect of urban living I did not learn about the hard way, I cannot imagine what it could have been. Hunter was educating young people who were intellectually, but not socially or economically, privileged. We also tried to pioneer in the schooling of those who were underdogs in every sense. We did not get very far, but at least we made the attempt. Like many another college president, during the war and postwar years, I accepted government assignments—fifteen in all, I think—and most of them had to do with education in one way or another. Some, especially those having to do with helping to found and direct UNESCO, added to my dim reputation at the time as a "liberal Catholic." The last and possibly the most important thing to say about myself is that I was the product of Catholic education from the elementary school through college and have never given anyone the slightest reason to believe otherwise—or that

I wished it might have been different. It is also relevant that I am a German-American, formed by the German-Catholic experience, thought, and religious outlook. In a country where during most of my life German-American Catholics have been rather supine, I have doubtless sometimes stood out like a statue of Schiller in South Boston. But though the going was often tough, there is nothing I have to retract. These, then, are my assets; anyone who considers them inadequate need read no further.

This book is not a manual of recipes for upgrading this or that part of the Catholic educational effort. Nor is the whitewash brush anywhere visible. True enough, I share with Mr. Neuwien and Father Greeley the conviction that American Catholic schools have been considerably better than their reputations and are doubtless here to stay. But the book is in essence an attempt to identify problems and place them in their historical, social, and educational settings in the hope of stimulating discussion. It takes for granted that education has always been and will remain a mystery, even in an age which can design and refine electronic gadgets to the almost incredible point of perfection that makes it possible to land something or other on the moon. Man is not a gadget but a riddle—a matter of-fact definition which anyone who begins to teach should know, and which everybody who has taught will have learned by the sweat of his brow.

As soon as one tries to outline what some of the principal issues in American, as well as Catholic, education seem to be, it becomes evident that there are crosscurrents at work on almost every level, created by differences of interest and opinion between pupils, teachers, parents, and the public. Despite varying emphases from period to period, one may say in general that until recently conflicts of interest were the rule. Thus, Catholics wanted schools in which their religion could be taught; some Protestants were determined that biological evolution should be kept out of the curriculum; and in general the public hankered after schools which would cost the tax-payer as little as possible and yet serve efficiently as agencies of Americanization.

More recently, certainly since 1945, the basic conflicts (apart from the central one of racial integration) have been those of opinion. Because there is now general agreement that in a modern industrial society education is as necessary as highways and shopping centers, the first major dispute has been over the quality of the schools, and in particular over the objectives of the teacher-training college. The second has had to do with the course of study in the lower schools and the colleges, and has frequently been focused on the question of whether the nation was falling behind in training its young people in natural science and mathematics. Concern with the value of ethical training, growing out of widespread alarm over a reported increase of juvenile delinquency, is the source of a third clash of ideas; and a fourth debate has resulted over financing the schools.

These will be recurrent themes throughout this book. The traditional pattern of Catholic education, and indeed that of public education until past the turn of the present century, laid great stress on the elementary school and the college. The first provided most of the schooling the average youngster received, and the second was relied upon to provide, among other benefits, the supply of teachers needed. In the Catholic system the elementary school was a place in which children were taught discipline—at an earlier stage, rigorously, and later on, persuasively—as well as the rudiments of their religion, while learning secular subjects appropriate to their time of life. The sexually segregated college, which was often an adaptation of a European Gymnasium or lycée to the American environment, was normally conducted by a religious community serving either boys or girls. It was a place in which one was expected to find out how to keep the world, the flesh, and the devil at more than arm's length, in an atmosphere efficiently fumigated against all three. Over a long period of time it was remarkably successful from the religious point of view. The convent-bred college graduate set the tone for exemplary Catholic family life. She was commendably immune to marital aberrations, genuinely dedicated to the teachings of her Church, and prone to rear a large family when that was biologically possible. But she was not likely to covet intellectualism for its own or any other sake. She made Mother's Day a sentimental occasion, but a library was not a prominent feature of her home.

As for the male college alumnus, the astringent solutions in which he was doused in order to bring about a cleansing of anti-intellectual rashes are fresh in everyone's memory. The question as to whether he was a scholar or had manifested a desire to become one was answered again and again in the negative, most recently and notably by Monsignor John Tracy Ellis.• Sometimes the graduate did stray into teaching, only to find that the label "professional mediocrity" had been pinned on him. It is true that after the turn of the century he stopped being the "hired man" of earlier times, who lived frugally on the campus and was often rewarded by accumulating a fund of lore about his clerical colleagues. Sometimes an effort was made to crack the mold, as it was for example by Father James Burns, C.S.C., who during a few iconoclastic years after World War I was president of Notre Dame. He not only sought to recruit competent and scholarly laymen but also started to create the endowment fund which would make paying their salaries possible. But by and large the Catholic academic alumnus was so immersed in teaching that even when he had the desire, there was little opportunity for scholarship and research. It was the graduate who established a place for himself in business or in such professions as law and medicine who became the omnipresent symbol of what the Catholic college for males could accomplish.

Many of these conditions, as we shall see, have been rather startlingly changed. Competent, often brilliant young Catholic scholars are emerging in numbers from all the major universities, secular and

• See *Perspectives in American Catholicism* (Baltimore: Helicon Press, 1963).

Catholic alike, and it is probable enough that in the foreseeable future the ancient question, "Have We Any Scholars?" will cease to have meaning for Catholics. In addition, despite caveats expressed by no less an authority than the Holy See, coeducation began to spread, especially through the Jesuit collegiate empire and the diocesan high schools. But it is the growth of Catholic secondary education which has been the most dramatic event. The great increase in the number of Catholic high schools is attributable to several causes, among them better remuneration, an upgrading of the teacher-training process which has lifted many teachers above the level of elementary school instruction, and the desires of the hierarchy. Still it is doubtless primarily the result of a widespread uneasy feeling that the public high school has become morally perilous. Unfortunately, the surmise was not completely unrealistic, though one must hasten to add that public education was not at fault. Twenty-five years ago an observant city principal could not avoid noticing the innocence of young people in his charge, especially girls, coming as they did from ethnic groups cherishing traditional standards of family ethics. But the situation then changed markedly, at both ends of the social scale. Migrant populations often lost what sense of family solidarity had existed in the rural areas from which they came; and in suburbia steady dating and premarital sex relations reflected a growing moral instability.

This, then, became an America in which the Catholic Church would seek to build as many dikes as it could. Yet we must note at this point a factor to which reference will be made again and again, namely that enrollments in Catholic schools are selective in character. Whereas the public school must admit and cope with all who enter its doors, its Catholic counterparts can and do reject the recalcitrant, who stand as symbols of a conflict between the traditionally cohesive and morally structured family and the public schools. The situation is complex and is alluded to here only because its importance suggests the tentative analysis we shall attempt later.

We have observed that financing education, ensuring quality of instruction, and providing ethical formation (often called character formation) are perhaps the most widely debated issues in the American school endeavor. The elementary school is doubtless the least concerned, primarily because the major part of the burden was assumed by past generations, once the doctrine of compulsory universal schooling was accepted. They thrashed out the principal pedagogical questions, created the teacher-training institutions, and set up the supervisory agencies without whose help the whole effort would bog down. Of course, this does not mean that the "little red schoolhouse" does not need money, or that teachers are easily come by, or that curricula are fixed in place, or that ethical objectives are self-evident. But secondary and higher education are finding the road ahead much more difficult to survey and their current problems far harder to solve because the same amount of preparatory work has not been done.

It must be said that, in both, academic standards have been raised to a peak never before reached in our history, and that Catholic institutions have in general made heroic efforts to keep their places in the line of march. Whether they can continue to make successful efforts is a troubling question. On the other hand, the improvement of quality and the demands this imposes on young people have bred a whole spate of guidance problems, whose existence would have been inconceivable to older generations of educators. Sometimes bilious critics are inclined to think that contemporary American culture adds up to one huge, continuous guidance problem, but theirs is no doubt a nightmarish view.

Just as important and equally troubling is the virtually omnipresent fear of what is called "brainwashing." It is assumed that young people must find the answers themselves and not be "told." This, too, is a complex phenomenon. One who has rather humbly read a great deal of what the social psychologists have to report on the matter may not be convinced that they have found an explanation.

It could be that young people, facing the doom of becoming "organization men," have their individualistic flings until the inevitable happens. It is also possible that vicarious experience with the totalitarians has injected all of us with a caveat against conformity. Some also believe that we are witnessing the greatest triumph so far won by Protestantism in our culture. For is not the question rather than the answer now the important thing? Yet the revolt against brainwashing is taking place on a world-wide scale and seems to be changing even the intellectual climate of Russia.

The countervailing forces of the search for quality and of the quest for a way of escaping from having it stuffed down one's throat have kept secondary and higher education in a kind of vise. More and more relatively affluent parents have in mind for their sons and daughters more and more education. Some parents think of no such goal; and this difference in outlook is currently dividing the nation more drastically than do color or ethnic background. In so far as the Catholic part of the financially solvent population is concerned, it is considered self-evident that every youngster who has the needed ability will be trained for admission to college, complete four years, and then go on to graduate or professional schools. The black sheep in many suburban families is the youngster who cannot make the grade. These prevailing mores compel all forms of post-elementary education to improve faculties, facilities, and curricula. On the other hand, they make demands on the time, energy, and nerves of young people which were not known a generation or two ago.

It is easy to miss the true significance of these demands unless one puts them into the context of the presently existing society. As a result of affluence and leisure time, immense profits accrue to those who can put the two together. Advertising, the mass media, and the exploitation of sport and sex have created an over-all outlook that is extremely pervasive. How understandable, therefore, that the burden placed on young people frequently becomes the springboard for escaping by hook or crook from the academic grind! It is a mistake to assume that the burden is no greater than it will be once the young man or woman settles down to earn his living. The college and the university are compelling young people to harness their diverse energies and their idealism to a task whose outcome can only be that the knowledge they have acquired is like a feather on a peacock.

Few would claim that the huge enterprise of American higher education is presently kept going by a burning zeal for the fruits of intellectual effort, humanistic or scientific. Young people who thirst after these fruits will be the gifted scholars and teachers of the future, but no doubt the great majority of students will be looking for jobs which will enable them to live with the gadgets and glamor the world to which they are heirs demands. Human nature, however, remains unpredictable. Many youngsters, especially boys, want to devote themselves at least temporarily to idealistic service. Some become rebels. And there is a larger group who continue to be so fascinated by the discussion of "issues," to which they become accustomed on the campus, that they turn from it to a workday existence very slowly and reluctantly.

But who is to pay the bill for education, for escape, for adjustment to life? The sums made available from the public treasury for the first are formidable but they are nevertheless far smaller than the gaping maw of education demands. The taxing power of a Communist state is absolute. What the citizen can buy after standing in a queue in a controlled store is all the reward he can expect for his work. The dynamic economies of the Free World provide far more generously for the individual, so that until recently what the private citizen could pay for the schooling of his children, or contribute to his Alma Mater, loomed fairly large in the nation's educational budget. Now, increasingly, the tax dollar pays the cost of the enterprise. Catholic education, however, has relied primarily on the sacrifice of the religious community. Here, too, the few have wrought nobly for the many. But these few are not enough, and financial stringency has become a grave consideration. We shall have occasion to consider this point again, although a warning must be given in advance that the empirical basis for conclusive analysis remains inadequate.

It is evident, of course, that the problems of money, teacher-training, and perhaps business management are important. But they must be solved in such a way that young men and women will be helped to learn what it means to be a Catholic, a cultivated person, and a citizen of a democratic society committed to its welfare. Catholic education has long realized that these three goals must be conjoined, but each of these goals now needs to be seen in the framework of the difficult present—difficult because it is pregnant with new life. For the time being, we will look at these in only two dimensions: freedom and modernity.

Freedom was a term which the Second Vatican Council placed on its masthead but did not define. Perhaps it was providential that it did not do so, for it is in the living out of freedom that its definition will be found. But we can catch a glimpse of what is in store for Catholic education from this statement of Father George P. Klubertanz, S.J., one of the ablest of contemporary American Catholic philosophers: "An overprotective attitude would incline one to say: the student must never hear about ideas that conflict with his basic natural and Christian commitments. But the flowering of critical intelligence cannot allow such ignorance in principle; and of course in practice the attempt to shield the student from all anti-Christian and anti-rational ideas is foredoomed." •

This is a far cry from the not-too-distant days when a prefect of religion would scan the new acquisitions in the library and discard those of which he disapproved. Now on some college campuses the recipe for an effective course in religion is to begin with Nietzsche

• "Knowledge and Action," as quoted in J. Barry McGannon, *Christian Wisdom and Christian Formation* (New York: Sheed & Ward, 1964), pp. 28–66.

rather than St. Thomas. *Aggiornamento* may occasionally mean something more akin to *tabula rasa*. The defense of positions which Catholic instruction not long ago thought must be fought for has become a meaningless enterprise. It has suddenly become unorthodox not to believe in ecumenism or to cling to forms of scriptural exegesis rooted in centuries of tradition.

Now a word about the dimension of modernity. We must see what Catholic education can do with the principle of movement which has now, by order of the Church, been built into its philosophy. One could not do better at this point than to quote from *Pacem in terris:*

> It is our opinion, too, that the above mentioned inconsistency between the religious faith, in those who believe, and their activities in the temporal sphere results—in great part if not entirely— from the lack of a solid Christian education. Indeed, it happens in many quarters and too often that there is no proportion between scientific training and religious instruction; the former continues and is extended until it reaches higher degrees, while the latter remains at an elementary level. It is indispensable, therefore, that in the training of youth, education should be complete and without interruption: Namely, that in the minds of the young, religious values should be cultivated and the moral conscience refined, in a manner to keep pace with the continuous and ever more abundant assimilation of scientific and technical knowledge. And it is indispensable, too, that they be instructed in the proper way to carry out their actual tasks.*

What the Pope says may seem rather innocuous on the surface but it is in some ways one of the most revolutionary of all his comments. That religious education is to keep pace with the development of scientific and technological knowledge can only mean that there be an interpenetration of methods used to attain knowl-

• Vatican Polyglot Press (April 10, 1963).

edge. Perhaps the difficulty can be made clear if one points out that the traditional form of seeking a rational approach to religion and revelation has been deductive. But if the scientist has accomplished anything of significance in terms of philosophy, it has been to point out the necessary limitations of the deductive method. Dessauer, Popper, and many others have pointed out that this process moves from the statement of a hypothesis—sometimes called a "brilliant guess"—to its verification. Young people, necessarily immune to the anthropomorphic religious imagery of the past, expect to find verification of religious assumptions in their personal lives and in history. "Existentialism" is one attempt to cope with the problem, but it may well be, at least in the forms which have been presented to date, not wholly convincing or satisfying. At any rate the quest is on and what it will lead to is the central question about the future of religious education in America.

The conclusion is inescapable. Older forms of criticism of Catholic education are for the most part outmoded. To be worth its salt, comment must henceforth be concerned not with what is static but with what is dynamic in that education. Nevertheless one must not get so far from the school and the everyday, practical realities of teaching that one can see only what ought to be and not also what is and has to be. In short, a book about schools, the teachers in them, and the young people who come to them must be honest, even if this sometimes means clipping the wings of poets and deflating philosophers. This book will try to do just that.

2

The Sources of the Catholic Educational Commitment

Ancient Roots

The purpose of the discussion which follows is to set Catholic education in the United States in its context. Statistical data about this educational effort are (when one looks at them for the first time) likely to induce surprise or maybe even shock.* It is a sizable operation in every sense. But it is only one part of a world-wide mission which, while not uniform in concept or execution, rivals publicly supported schooling in the Free World. Though it has been suppressed in most parts of the Communist society and to a considerable extent in Moslem states, it flourishes on all the continents and is indeed sometimes more vigorous than ever before. There is a network of Catholic schools at all levels in most Latin-American countries. Australia and Canada are both centers of bustling Catholic educational activity. Even Europe, which still for the most part

* Some of the data are included in the Appendix.

fosters denominational elementary schools, has witnessed a surprising growth of specifically Catholic education, notably in France. In Africa the "mission schools" of yore have suffered some setbacks but have held their ground better than might have been anticipated. In the Philippines, Japan, India, and Southeast Asia, Catholic education has an exciting past and present. In short, this adds up to the most important and absorbing of all the activities of the Church, except for the pastoral care of souls.

Catholic education in the United States is, however, unique in several important respects. First, there is the quite materialistic fact that it has to so large an extent been privately financed. To be sure, everywhere in the Free World some Catholic institutions are funded in the same way. Nevertheless, the total amount of private contributions to Catholic schools and, until recently, the virtual absence of support from the public treasury have set our country apart. The sources of income would not have sufficed, however, had it not been for the teaching and administrative services provided by religious communities. In this respect the United States has been not unlike an African mission territory. To be sure, there are teaching communities in all countries of western Europe, but their participation in the total educational process is proportionately small, for reasons which have grown out of historical developments in the various countries. The tradition of privately supported education, at all levels and under the most diverse auspices, is so well established in the United States that although the Catholic system is unusually large and diverse it is not an isolated phenomenon. Moreover, American philanthropic support of education, notably on the part of foundations, is not duplicated in other countries except on a relatively small scale.*

* The literature about Catholic education elsewhere in the world is varied and extensive, although there is little which the average reader can easily acquire. It includes a vast number of essays in educational and other periodicals; a solid array of unpublished dissertations; and the records of parliamentary debates in which Catholics have argued the case for their schools while others have pre-

For the present, we shall pass over the matter of finance and instead ask these questions: What are the reasons underlying this world-wide activity of the Church? From what sources does it draw strength? The reasons and the sources are so closely interwoven that they should be considered together. A principal source of strength has been the religious community dedicated to scholarly teaching. In the premedieval world there was little Christian educational activity in any formal sense, but during the period which followed the collapse of the Roman Empire, Benedictine monasticism became a highly significant agency for keeping alive both learning and education. It was the monk, living in his abbey or answering the call of princes and bishops, who became the teacher of his time. He went, for example, as far eastward as Regensburg and Vienna, founding schools along the way; and in Alfred's England he was also the hub around which the life of the mind turned. For the first time in Christian history the educational mission had been placed on a par with other missions. The monk found in his rule a short and simple formula: *work and pray*. This enabled him also to rescue from oblivion basic technological arts—farming, animal husbandry, medicine, architecture, and the making of books. It was a dramatic moment in the history of the West, ushering in a time when Christian culture was to be closely intertwined with Christian commitment to a transcendent faith.

Other religious orders—among them the Augustinians, the Premonstratensians, the Dominicans, the Franciscans, and the Capu-

---

sented briefs for the opposition. Fortunately a recently published book, *Catholic Education in the Western World* (Notre Dame, 1967), edited by James Michael Lee, includes well-informed chapters outlining the situation in five European countries—England, France, the Netherlands, Germany, and Italy. Considerable research has been done on Catholic education in Latin America. The reader with a knowledge of Spanish will find *Mensaje*, a review edited and published by the Jesuit Centro Bellarmino of Santiago, Chile, a valuable source of information in this area. Commendable also are the publications of the Centro de Estudios Educativos, Mexico, though they do not concern themselves exclusively with Catholic education.

chins, to name only some—also took up the educational mission, though this may not have been included in their original purpose. No doubt St. Francis of Assisi, who preached to the birds and talked with the Sultan, would have been greatly astonished if he had been told that one of his disciples, Duns Scotus, would come to be known as the "Subtle Doctor." The aristocratic Spaniard who established the Dominicans in order to blunt the sword of heresy would likewise have rubbed his eyes if a prophet had whispered to him that the greatest of his friars (to be born just four years after his death) would divert Christian thought from its historic moorings by professing the doctrine of the pagan Aristotle. It was certainly evident that education had become of the highest importance in the life of the Church and of almost all its monastic institutions.

It is very difficult, even in a time which is heir to brilliant historical inquiry, to evaluate the influence of St. Thomas, not only on the disciplines of philosophy and theology, but on Christian education as a whole. He brought to a close a period when the main stream of the life of the Church was fed on Scripture and Stoic inspiration. In a spate of remarkable books he bound the intellectualistic wisdom of antiquity together with the gospel; even some of the mysteries of the faith were restated in Aristotelian terms. A good illustration of his surviving influence is the fact that, despite the defection of the Tudor monarchs from the Church of Rome, Aquinas remained until after the close of the eighteenth century the fare of Oxford and Cambridge students and of young Americans attending colleges formed in the style of Cambridge. But approval was by no means universal. The churches of Italy also witnessed an effort to surround the altar with triumphs of resurrected Greek art. Not everyone was reconciled with such novelties. Could the pursuit of culture mean abandonment of the Cross? Were not the new art forms secular? Was not the constantly increasing dexterity of scholars manipulating syllogisms merely a new version of ancient sophistry, displayed in a Christian setting? Grumbling and heart-searching were the order of the day in some northern monasteries. Out of them the Lutheran Reform was born, and its first great achievement was the translation and dissemination of Scripture, not of Greek texts.

Before considering what happened to Catholic education in several countries after the Reformation, we may profitably glance at what was done to assist the education of women. By and large, until well after the dawn of the Renaissance, girls were trained at the fireside. Still, convents for women became centers of culture early in the medieval period, though the emphasis was strongly on religion. Thus Radegone, a princess who escaped from her tyrannical and presumably pagan husband, founded a convent in Poitiers, France, and is reputed to have inspired the poet Fortunatus, author of the great hymn, *Vexilla Regis*. The nun Hrosvitha sought, in her German convent, to supplant the plays of Terence by writing comedies with a spiritual import. Great mystical writers such as Hildegard of Bingen were products of convent culture. But the growth and development of religious orders specifically concerned with the education of women did not occur until society became convinced that their education was desirable and even necessary.

The Counter Reformation restored the influence of some of the older orders of men, notably the Benedictines in Southern Germany and Austria and the Premonstratensians in Hungary. Their influence is still felt in our own time at such centers as Ettal and Metten in Germany, Vienna and Salzburg in Austria. But it was the Society of Jesus which revived Catholic education after the Council of Trent, and its example has continued to exert great influence in areas as diverse as Madagascar, Japan, and Colombia. The crusade they undertook to spiritualize culture was unrivalled until the rise of secular science to its position of dominance in modern education. It was a magnificent adventure which would take them across the seas in quest of the "natural man"—the "noble savage"—whom they would try to transform into the "new man" of Christ. They fought on all the fields and on each left their dead. Who could live long enough to draw from the chronicle of their effort all its substance or meaning? That meaning is especially significant in education. The Jesuits created humanistic poetry and drama, shared in the development of science, and did much pioneer spadework in exploration and archaeology. They also experimented with new methods of pastoral care and religious teaching.

Discipline, the conquest of the self, was the basic characteristic of their educational effort. But a Jesuit did not triumph over the ego for the sake of extinguishing it. At a later date, Teilhard de Chardin would say to someone who had asked him for advice, "There must be nothing which dehumanizes, under pretext of super-humanizing." That was the core of the Society's tradition at its best. Of this maxim the Roman College founded by St. Ignatius in 1551 was the first great illustration; on every page of its early history there is a reflection of some mood of modern man. Thus Christopher Clavius, Galileo's friend and (to the best of his ability) protector, was a prophet of that concern with science which Cardinal Newman would later strongly advocate.

But, at least in Europe and subsequently in the United States and Latin America, the flock to whom the Society addressed itself were the socially and culturally advantaged. This gave their effort a special, highly individualized stamp. Others assumed the task of giving religious instruction, at least, to the common family of the Church. It was Charles Cardinal Borromeo, Archbishop of Milan (1538–1584), who in this respect proved to be the greatest innovator and organizer in Catholic history. To him is due the idea behind the Confraternity of Christian Doctrine of providing religious education for all Catholics, young or adult. During the centuries which followed, communities of men and women were established by great churchmen and teachers. Only a few of their names can be mentioned here—St. Francis de Sales, St. John Bosco, St. John Baptist de La Salle, Adolf Kolping, Gabriel Moreau, St. Angela Merici.

They were often exponents of the pedagogy which found memorable non-Catholic advocates in Comenius and Pestalozzi. To them and to many others who followed in their footsteps we owe the Catholic elementary-school effort, with its rewards and burdens.

Catholic education is anything but monolithic in conception or practice. Every religious group which has served it has sponsored its own mode of formation, its tradition, its philosophical outlook, its special spiritual color, its aspirations. To understand it one must to some extent break it up into its parts. Only then can one grasp on the one hand its richness and diversity or discern on the other hand some of its sources of weakness. Just one example will be cited here. The vigor of the University of Notre Dame has been rooted, I think, in a remarkable willingness to accept challenges, take risks. The leader of the small band—priests, brothers, sisters—who came from France as members of the Congregation of the Holy Cross opened the university's history by settling during 1840 in a part of Indiana still largely the haunt of Indians. When the first sizable college building, on which he had set high hopes, burned down, the leader promptly put up another and larger one and capped it with a dome which may well have reminded him of that atop Paris' Hôtel des Invalides. One could hardly have thrown down a gauntlet to the future with more gusto.

Each teaching religious is formed by the common spiritual life of the community as well as by the educational resources it can command. At times a price must be paid for this separateness. Not all communities are equally fortunate. Sometimes leadership is missing, or men on whom great hopes have been placed wither and die. But the sternest challenge is presented by the fact that the work of the community is necessarily institutionalized. It must have property and manage it. There must be friends who can be relied upon. Often enough frugality, to the point of austerity, will determine the mode of life. A community may even be caught up in the meshes of ecclesiastical bureaucracy. Being institutionalized may revive the old, never banished dichotomy between culture and faith. Are the counsels of perfection to which a man or woman subscribed in the days of ardent youth truly to be reconciled with the routine of educational administration and instruction? Is the gospel mandate to go forth unto the nations fulfilled by teaching mathematics or logic to young people who would rather be doing almost anything else?

And conversely, as educational plants expand and larger and larger numbers of laymen are added, as is currently the case in the United States, the work of the community ceases to be like a "family business" and takes on the character of a corporation. Though ownership and management of the enterprise may remain in the hands of the religious, intellectual leadership may pass to laymen. This can be true of the educational endeavor at any level, from the elementary school to the university. Therefore the question may be raised—and often enough is on smaller campuses or in public discussion—whether the religious vocation is now pertinent at all. Why accept the limitations placed on one's freedom of action by the life of religion when one could do the same work equally well as a layman or a laywoman? It would be unrealistic not to admit that this question has become important and disturbing.

Today the redefinition of the function of the religious community in education is certainly of crucial significance. One should try to see first of all what would be lost if it were to disappear from the educational scene. Our sample hypothesis will be: A college will be organized and administered by laymen, and within it there will be established an academic parish designed to foster a rich liturgical and pastoral life. The pastor chosen to guide it will be a priest with great charismatic gifts who is also, as Newman was, deeply interested in the scholarly life and able to think it through. There can be no doubt whatsoever that such a college could be established. But if one is to consider it an example to be imitated widely, in short, a kind of model, it will be necessary to inquire where such pastors are to be found and trained for their tasks. Perhaps one could then assume the creation of a central institute of theological studies—a Woodstock College with a special orientation; this would become at the outset a place to which a variety of religious orders would send their best men to form the corps of professors. Such an institute would certainly be interesting, and something akin to it might also be proposed to train chaplains currently so badly needed on secular campuses.

But it would not be a religious community. One may recall that Newman, when he began seriously to consider what his role in the Church of Rome might be, established a branch of the Oratory, which St. Philip Neri had founded to provide more flexibility for its members than older monastic orders did. Unfortunately, at least in Anglo-Saxon countries, the Oratory has not been sufficiently cohesive to achieve the formation and fruitful interaction of its members. Viewed empirically, the religious community accomplishes a task of importance in this respect. Yet to a layman who has contemplated the scene for some time, it often seems as if canon law and the superior had conspired to maintain the educational effort in a state of dishevelment by keeping teaching religious, particularly administrators, constantly on the move.

Not a few religious communities in the United States seem afflicted with an excess of virtue. They consider the biblical statement that the harvest is ready and the laborers few, and then proceed to chase their members in pursuit of a stray grain of wheat. Often, to be sure, there will be other motivations. In general, communities strive to respond as favorably as they can to requests from bishops. If they did not do so, the Catholic Church would have become quite a different institution. Sometimes, however, bishops are not very reasonable in making demands. Or again—and this is certainly often a temptation—a measure of imperialism may have crept into the community's concept of its mission. Certainly it is not difficult to see why many communities are now making the kind of careful evaluation of their structure and of the individual member's place in it which we shall discuss in detail later on in this book.

When all has been said, however, I fail to see how the direction of American Catholic education can be transferred from religious communities unless one of two things is done. The system of denominational education might be adopted, in which Catholics are appointed by the state to teach in Catholic schools. In this case (let us make no mistake about it) the real direction will be transferred to a state department of education, just as in European countries which have such schools, authority is always lodged with a ministry of culture. While it is fortunately true that the state educational authority in the United States is less rigid and arbitrary than it often is in Europe, no guarantee against change can be given. Or one could revert to the pattern of the bishop's schools in pre-Reformation days, which have often been considered successors of the grammar schools of Roman days and precursors of those of our own time. Classical examples are the schools which Charlemagne established with the help of the Irish monk Alcuin. Such a system of schools might well be beneficial from a financial or managerial point of view (though there is currently little evidence to support the contention), but it would probably prove less creative, less spiritually satisfying, and less human.

At any rate, one should bear in mind that the underlying problem throughout Christian history has been the fusion of religion and culture. This has always been difficult. It is still more difficult today. Even if one accepts Teilhard de Chardin's idea of the Noosphere in which everything discovered or thought about, in terms of either science or literature, is a sort of check made payable to God, one will still find the issue troubling; and it has once again become a central theme for discussion. As we shall see later on, it is now quite possible to visualize a kind of Catholic (or Christian) education in which emphasis on religious concern would become quite peripheral. But in so far as I have been able to make up my own mind, such a development would seem bound to prove fatal to the whole enterprise.

The American Experience

We shall now look at Catholic education in the United States. This will also provide an opportunity to discuss the second source from which the effort has drawn strength, the needs and desires of the people. Of course it is true that upon occasion Catholic schools have been created by the fiats of bishops. We may also observe that not infrequently a religious community has staked out a claim in the hope that the public would enable it to prosper. But there can be no doubt that a desire for Catholic education by parents has been a constant prod to the building of schools. If we can see more clearly what it was they have wished to have, our understanding of both the past and the present will be improved.

In 1840 there were two hundred Catholic schools in the United States. These were instruments of Catholic mission activity in a country which was overwhelmingly Anglo-Saxon and Protestant. Alexis de Tocqueville's remarkable commentary on life in a country which pushed westward with great vigor from a rather narrow eastern colonial base makes it clear what principles and standards were dominant: "The Anglo-American relies upon personal interest to accomplish his ends and gives free scope to the unguided strength and common sense of the people; the Russian centers all the authority of society in a single arm. The principal instrument of the former is freedom; of the latter, servitude."•

Some Catholics who came to this country subscribed wholeheartedly to this platform of action; for example, New York's Friendly Sons of St. Patrick, an affluent association of Irish-Americans, Catholics or otherwise. But the great majority who arrived on these

• Phillips Bradley (ed.), *Democracy in America* (New York: Alfred A. Knopf, 1945), I, 434.

shores before and after 1840 were not in revolt against kings, as the
Puritans of New England happened to be. They were in quest of
opportunity, and sometimes this quest swept them away from their
spiritual moorings. There were, to be sure, groups of early American
settlers who had made very heavy sacrifices for their faith. These
included English gentry of the kind which settled in Maryland (on
the basis of a charter granted to the Calverts), Irishmen, and Germans. They wanted schooling which would keep their spiritual
tradition alive in the hearts of their children. It was frequently difficult to satisfy this desire. But after the revolution against the
British Crown had succeeded and the Constitution with its Bill of
Rights was adopted, bishops took an interest, as did Bishop John
Carroll of Baltimore. If religious communities were available, steps
could be taken to make Catholic education possible for at least a
few children. In spite of Thomas Jefferson and Virginia, the pattern
of schooling throughout the country was prevailingly denominational. It was therefore not at all strange that Catholics should foster
educational activity; indeed not infrequently Protestant parents sent
their children to Catholic schools, either because nothing else was
readily available or because these schools seemed the best at hand.
This happened despite the waves of antipapist sentiment which
sometimes swept through the streets of growing and relatively un-
civilized towns.

Then immigration began to increase including a large number of
Catholics. Men, women and children endured long, dreadfully un-
comfortable and dangerous sea voyages; estrangement from old habits and customs; and economic privation, due to hardship in getting
established or to general financial upheavals.

The Irish tumbled in pell-mell during the 1840's, as a result of
famine and the closing down of segments of the textile industry.
They had been buffeted about in their own country, beaten, curbed,
and subjected to proselytizing. Here they were huddled into shanties
and offered employment on the worst terms which a nascent capital-

ism could draw up. Hawthorne wrote a detached, impersonal account of what an Irish "town" looked like to an observant son of New England; Emerson recommended that the college boys to whom he was offering good advice be tolerant of the "Negro, the Irishman and the Catholic." In such towns the sensitive, gifted Irish, who spoke the language of England with a special accent and savor, grouped around priests who recalled to them with fervor what it had meant in Ireland to keep the faith, and outlined what would be needed to do likewise here.

New England already had its system of "common," later "public," schools. It was tinkering with various expedients for making a once theocratic Congregationalism sit down side by side with fashionable forms of Unitarianism and Transcendentalism. The best available compromise brought it somewhere between Anglican doctrine and Deist absence of doctrine. Nevertheless the King James Version of the Bible and the Our Father with a doxological verse attached seemed, in the flux of change, two boulders on which everyone could stand and remain as respectful of Christianity as was possible in so busy and freedom-loving a world.

But neither of these stones offered anything on which an Irish Catholic priest could stand. English clerics of an earlier generation had gone to the Continent in order to make a Douai version of the Scriptures freed from the alleged errors and corruptions of the King James edition; and to repeat the doxological verse was akin to eating meat on Friday or marrying outside the Church. It is in some ways strange that these two fairly simple recipes for preserving the Christian faith in the hearts of youth should have led to so drastic a parting of company between Catholics and the public schools. Today we are on the verge of having a Bible translation which will serve both Catholics and Protestants; and the American branch of the Church of Rome, perhaps the most loyal of all the branches, is often singing an adaptation of Luther's hymn, *Ein Ein' feste Burg ist unser Gott*, as the priest leaves the sacristy for the altar. But we are always more aware of the things which lie behind than of the things ahead. The Irish immigrant was a great deal closer to Queen Elizabeth and the shattered Spanish Armada than he was to the Second Vatican Council.

Efforts were made to effect a compromise which would save the public school as an instrument of Americanization. Its role in assimilating immigrants into the American culture was crucial, but it was frequently given too large a halo. Catholics also tried to secure public support for schools which were conducted under their auspices. But there were always too many Protestants who, at the very mention of the papacy, ran to look for the enemy of their liberties, and too many Irish who recalled the battle of Fontenoy with belligerent pleasure. The controversy was resolved by the establishment of Catholic parish schools wherever possible (though some dioceses held out against the trend) and the gradual extirpation of the King James Version in public schools, except for polite readings on festive occasions.

The Germans, for their part, planned their great migrations methodically. They tried to know in advance where their people would settle and what provisions could be made for their spiritual and educational welfare. They wished to preserve their language, and one earnest seeker after the kingdom of heaven had an ugly "ism" attached to his name* because he advocated a German hierarchical organization in the United States to serve the immigrant population. It was doubless unrealistic of the Germans to lay such great stress on their mother tongue, when the odds were so definitely against its survival. But their religious outlook and practice were characterized by a methodology which had proved its usefulness during a long period of struggle with both Prussia and European liberalism. They had their own vernacular liturgy, the *Singmesse*, which had distinct

---

* Peter Paul Cahensley (1838–1923), founder of the St. Raphael Society, which planned the religious case of German emigrants. The society also ministered to Italian seasonal workers in Germany.

advantages over what has more recently been offered American Catholics. They also had their own social doctrine, formulated for the most part by Jesuits, and forms of devotion such as the Corpus Christi procession, which they correctly judged superior to anything they were likely to find at hand in the New World.

Soon there existed in the Middle West a large number of Catholic elementary schools staffed for the most part by sisters from the home country, who often carried out their work under the most primitive conditions. Before long they were finding recruits in both cities and the countryside. Theirs was the first functioning Catholic school *system*. This was, whether one looks at it kindly or not, remarkable. There was order in the German parish and school, although often achieved by methods of which we no longer approve. But this went hand in hand with a certain *Gemüetlichkeit* which frequently brought the parish priest close to the home, though normally the teaching sister's out-of-school association with the world was through the piano lessons she gave to the children of faithful and heathen alike.

Occasionally, smaller immigrant groups, the Belgians in particular, also planned their settlements. Others did not. The Polish immigration (which brought more than seven million Polish-Americans into the main stream of our national life) began early in the nineteenth century and continued through the years after the Second World War, when, tragically, veterans of that conflict could not return to their homes. But the peak came toward the close of the nineteenth century, ending for the most part in mill and factory towns. The Poles, too, created an ethnic Catholic school system, whose main purpose was the preservation of their language and traditions. Unfortunately, no history or interpretative account of these schools has been written, so that comment must derive from the most cursory kind of observation. Nor do we have even relatively adequate information about the Hungarian, Slovak, or French Canadian experience. I have known some of these groups, their schools, and their ideas concerning religion and culture, but this does not suffice for an analysis or an evaluation.

Meanwhile some important things had been said by the American hierarchy acting as a whole. For a number of years that hierarchy had convened in Baltimore as a plenary council to discuss matters of moment to the Church. In 1884, resolutions were adopted, two of which read as follows:

> That near every Church a parish school, where one does not yet exist, is to be built and maintained in perpetuum, within two years of the promulgation of this Council, unless the Bishop should decide that because of serious difficulties a delay may be granted.

> That all Catholic parents are bound to send their children to the parish school, unless it is evident that a sufficient training in religion is given either in their own homes, or in other Catholic schools; or when, because of a sufficient reason, approved by the Bishop, with all due precautions and safeguards, it is licit to send them to other schools. What constitutes a Catholic school is left to the decision of the Bishop.*

Despite the fact that a measure of latitude was granted, this language clearly indicated a demand for the speedy building of more schools and an obligation on the part of parents to send their children to parish establishments.** And yet the thirtieth anniversary of the Third Plenary Council dawned before some dioceses had made a serious effort to carry out that council's bidding. There was, by and large, no apparent unwillingness on the part of parents to choose a Catholic school for their children. But many of the clergy and the laity doubted the ability of the faithful to provide sufficient financial support. Would not children who attended pub-

* Reginald A. Neuwien (ed.), *Catholic Schools in Action: A Report, the Notre Dame Study of Catholic Elementary Schools in America* (Notre Dame, Ind.: University of Notre Dame Press, 1966), p. 9.
** See Francis P. Cassidy, "Catholic Education in the Third Plenary Council of Baltimore," *Catholic Historical Review*, XXXIV, 257–305, 414–436.

lic schools have better facilities, better teachers, and therefore a better education?

In a remarkably illuminating contribution to the as yet largely unwritten history of American Catholic education, Thomas T. Mc-Avoy, C.S.C.* demonstrates clearly that in the 1870's it was not the American hierarchy but a rigorist lay convert journalist, James Mc-Master, editor of the *New York Freeman's Journal and Catholic Register*, who supported the doctrine that "every Catholic child should be in a Catholic school." McMaster was persuaded that the public schools were largely staffed by anti-Catholics, who were "working towards bringing to this country the calamities France has been suffering, and preparing torches for American cities such as have laid *nearly one third of Paris in ashes*." The reference was of course to the Paris Commune of 1871. So effective was McMaster's doctrine in Rome that the Holy Office addressed a letter of inquiry to the bishops of the United States (April 10, 1874), calling for answers to a number of questions. Since it seemed impractical to summon all the bishops in a special meeting, the archbishops conferred in Cincinnati during May and formulated a reply which was very moderate in tone.

Their letter softened criticism of public schools, pointing out that many Catholics taught in them and enumerating the great difficulties which would be encountered if an attempt were made to erect schools of equal quality; and it was sympathetic with parents who for good reasons sent their children to the public school. They agreed as a matter of course that having Catholic schools for all children would be preferable, if it could be managed. Rome replied by sending, in 1875, a decree of the Holy Office which, while considerably more temperate than McMaster would have wished, was nevertheless sharply critical of the public schools and insistent on the creation of a system of parish schools as soon as possible. This

* Thomas T. McAvoy, C.S.C., "Public Schools vs. Catholic Schools and James McMaster," *The Review of Politics*, XXVIII, 1, 19–46 (January, 1966).

decree was not promulgated in the United States, but undoubtedly formed an important part of the background against which the Baltimore Resolutions of 1884 were adopted.

Father McAvoy concludes his comment on the Roman *Instruction of 1875* as follows:

*Nevertheless, it is most unusual in the history of Catholicism in the United States, partly because the decree seems to have been brought about by the laity and the moderates were the archbishops and bishops of the country. The whiplash was in the hand of a convert lay editor. Catholic schools increased in number before and after the Third Plenary Council, but its decrees on the parochial schools, never translated from its glacial Latin text, had an effect on those priests and bishops who wanted such an incentive.**

On this subject the Catholic press of the country was not tightly controlled. There were marked differences of opinion about the alleged "godlessness" of the public schools, and many queries were raised concerning the practicability of the Catholic educational enterprise. It was the Code of Canon Law adopted in 1918 which imposed upon the Church everywhere the obligation to foster religious schools, that for a time virtually stifled discussion. The era of change ushered in by the Second Vatican Council has reopened that discussion. It is bound to continue, and it will have had a preview during the second part of the nineteenth century.

At any rate, discussion reached a dramatic climax with an address which Archbishop John Ireland delivered in 1890 to a convention of the National Educational Association meeting in his See city of St. Paul. The Archbishop, in many respects as gifted a man as has ever presided over a diocese in the United States, was then considered an eloquent spokesman for the "liberal" or "Americanist" position. That is, he believed, as had Tocqueville, that there had been a fortunate transfer of Anglo-Saxon traditions and political know-how to

• *Ibid.*, p. 45.

this part of the New World. While European prelates and theologians, especially in France, were fighting a tenacious rear-guard action for monarchical institutions, even in their more autocratic forms (they sometimes fancied that the altar could not survive without the throne), Archbishop Ireland was convinced that in the United States the Church could be free of the shackles of squabbles which had nothing to do with its mission. But like everybody else who has a new idea, he was destined to find that being out in front was lonely.

What he said to the convention would not seem especially bizarre today because the Catholic public has become accustomed to pleas for federal aid. But in 1890 it was news when a prominent member of the hierarchy publicly approved of the public school, recognized that the state had the right to establish it and provide for its needs, and declared that the parochial school was a creature of necessity. He seemed to undermine every educational principle to which some Eastern dioceses and the German-American Catholics of the Middle West were committed. For not infrequently these did not so much as admit that the state could force parents to send their children to school. To be sure, Archbishop Ireland was a firm believer in religious instruction. He held that the American school ought to provide it for the children of all citizens, Catholic or non-Catholic, who desired it. After all, these citizens paid their share of the taxes which made public education possible.

In his view, either of two solutions of the problem was feasible. First, the parochial school might be reimbursed for most of the expense it incurred in caring for the children entrusted to it. This was not at the time a novel idea but one which had actually been tested in Faribault and Stillwater, Minnesota. One parochial school in each of these cities was supported by the public authority. Second, compensatory fees might be paid to the parochial school for each child enrolled. Several other countries had adopted this method of assisting private education.

The experiment petered out, largely because of non-Catholic and Catholic opposition. By this time the conviction that the public school was a unique community-forming institution, able to carry out the "Americanization" program which many believed indispensable in a time of mass immigration, had a strong grip on American public opinion. And so Archbishop Ireland's proposal was widely held to be simply a well-camouflaged plea for "separatism." On the other hand numerous Catholics, including some eastern bishops but especially the German-speaking faithful of the Middle West, were bitterly opposed to the Faribault plan. It seemed to them that the parochial school for which they had made so many sacrifices was being threatened. Other immigrant groups, Poles, Italians, Hungarians, and French Canadians among them, also wanted schools conducted in languages other than English.

At any rate it had become a principle some twenty years later that the public schools would not provide the religious training which the Catholic Church held necessary if youth was to cling to the tradition of its forebears. The slogan now became: "Every Child in a Catholic School." No one can tell on the basis of the available evidence just how strongly lay public opinion supported what was in essence a hierarchical demand, but at least one can assert without fear of being in error that in very many instances when a parochial school was built the problem was not how to attract pupils but how to keep the enrollment within bounds. Until quite recently Catholic elementary and secondary education was dominated by the belief that the calling to the life of religion was the highest vocational objective. Indeed in many areas, urban as well as rural, Catholic parents identified higher education with seminary training and usually the elementary school was thought of in terms of "the sisters."

It is fair to say in passing that the immigrant equation between higher education and the calling to a life in religion was an important cause of the now-well-known dearth of Catholics dedicated to intellectual pursuits. A celibate clergy, moreover, produced no children to turn to secular scholarship, as did the Protestant ministry or the Jewish rabbinate. But when Catholics grew more affluent, and when college and university training became normal aspects of living in the twentieth century, the situation quickly changed. Perhaps Greeley's published prognostications are too optimistic, but it appears safe to assume that in the years ahead there will be a different story to tell. One by-product of changing social conditions, however, is, the emergence of a generation of college-graduate parents who are critical of Catholic schooling. They have brought into being a literature of criticism—and beyond that a climate of objective evaluation —which cannot be ignored. For the first time in the United States lay opinion about education is vocal. A wave of legitimate concern for the quality of the education provided is sweeping over the terrain and it is salutary. If Catholic authorities are wise they will reckon with this as if it were a gold mine. Should they be unwise, however, they will consider it a nuisance.

Possibly the greatest mistake of the recent Catholic past is the failure to take into consideration the opportunities for the religious mission provided in public education. It was already apparent decades ago that "every child" was not going to be in a Catholic school. Though generalizing about practices throughout the length and breadth of the United States would be a foolhardy enterprise, there is no doubt that it was far easier for a child to be admitted to a Catholic school (a) if his parents were active in parish affairs and (b) if he himself had a measure of intellectual endowment and was a "good citizen." Otherwise he was likely to end up in a public school; and there is nothing in the record to indicate that his bishop's permission was normally required. And what happened in the public school? For many reasons which cannot be analyzed here, the number of sincere Catholics teaching under public auspices was proportionately large in several sections of the United States. They and many of their Protestant and Jewish colleagues were by no means indifferent to the religious education of children. Many volunteered their services in what came to be known for a time as the Sunday schools, now (as far as Catholics are concerned) generally conducted under the auspices of the Confraternity of Christian Doctrine.

Numerous members of the clergy and a not insignificant part of the diocesan press were grandiloquent on the subject of "godless public schools." It was true enough that forms of agnosticism or religious indifferentism were gaining (or recovering) some ground in the United States; but in the effort to make "secularism" the scapegoat at every communion breakfast, vocal priests and laymen alike forgot that the Christian mission is to bear witness to the gospel before all men of good will. That the "secularist" might conceivably be a man of excellent intentions was a fact sacrificed to a slogan.

The Challenge of Higher Education

Higher education has presented the most dramatic challenge to Catholics. Sixty years ago collegiate and university education were largely preprofessional endeavors; and since those who could afford to try out their talents in this way were few, the average, relatively intelligent boy or girl thought rather in terms of some sort of apprenticeship. Thus one would keep one's feet on the ground and not waste time being "impractical." One worked or learned in a factory, a business, or even a law office. There existed a rather widespread distrust of college-educated youth. Newspaper editors frowned on young men who had diplomas, and the average businessman gloried in the fact that he had started at the bottom and worked his way toward the top.

Three agencies of social change altered the pattern. Demobilization following two wars into which every able-bodied young man was drafted returned to civilian status more men than could be reabsorbed into the work force immediately; the college therefore became a place for some of the surplus. This was of course much more striking after 1945 than it was in 1918, but the increase in students after World War I was significant.

We have no way of measuring accurately the manner in which Catholic young people were affected, but it would appear on the basis of some samples of the urban trend to college that it was not until 1945 that Catholic boys and girls were attracted in large numbers. This led to a swelling of student ranks in existing Catholic institutions and also to the creation of new ones. Many of the new institutions were small liberal-arts colleges. But these could by no means absorb the tide. More young Catholic men and women entered state and municipal institutions or private secular colleges and universities than went to Catholic institutions. When the second demobilization was completed, the total enrollment of Catholic boys and girls in a single state university of the Middle West was greater than that of Notre Dame and its neighboring St. Mary's College combined.

The second agency of social change was the great economic depression which began in 1929 and ended, or nearly, in 1940. Its impact was felt particularly in urban areas by families which had just begun to emerge from immigrant status into a condition of relative prosperity. Children could no longer be absorbed into family businesses or find the kind of employment which it had been thought would be available to them. Many applied for admission to whatever college offered free, or relatively free, tuition. In New York's municipal colleges, for instance, the clamor for admission was so great that it led automatically to the raising of academic standards. This was the only way in which some kind of dam could be erected against the press of numbers.

Generalizations are always perilous. But it seems likely that a precedent was thus set for a practice which has since become commonplace. Colleges set standards of admission which are relatively difficult to meet. Many states have therefore made provision for junior or community colleges to which young people less well prepared can apply with some hope of transferring to a four-year institution at the end of the Sophomore year. This has confronted Catholic higher education with an unsolved problem. If the hope is to maintain standards which are equivalent to those in effect else-where—and it is clear that such standards must be maintained—logic would demand the creation of junior colleges as well. There are a few, but as yet the problem has scarcely been discussed.

As a matter of fact, the more highly developed religious communi-ties have long since grasped the importance of quality—and there-fore of relatively high admissions standards—because of their ex-perience in the area of secondary education. Since its secondary schools charged tuition fees, often sizable, the community quickly learned that institutions had to compete, sometimes even with schools operated by other communities, in order to attract students. It could not, therefore, draw any other conclusion about its colleges. Some recently established institutions are, to be sure, rather flimsy and may deserve the criticism levied against them by Father Neil McCluskey, S.J., and others. They seem upon occasion little more than places in which a given community can train its own teachers and thereby create for itself the illusion that it is saving money.

But perhaps the Catholic college can compensate for deficiencies in resources and scholarship in another way. Everyone now knows that there may be an astonishing lack of correlation between the scores obtained in College Entrance Board examinations and a student's actual performance in college. This does not mean that these examinations are not useful—indeed almost indispensable—as indicators of how well a young person has done in high school; nevertheless, a poorly motivated student, for example, may not per-form as well as he could. I think the import of Greeley's studies may well be that such a student's motivation can be fostered in the better Catholic colleges. At any rate the studies seem to indicate that it may be a mistake to overestimate quantitative factors like the size of the library and the number of instructors with doctorates from elite institutions, and to neglect the resources for encouraging intellectual and spirtual growth which are undoubtedly latent in an institution dedicated to a religious commitment.

With the third social change we are only too familiar. A sizable population increase, affluence, and automation have created a state of affairs so baffling in its social implications that it would be preposterous to say that one had grasped its significance. A school dropout today is unlikely to be another Horatio Alger hero. At least in urban environments, he may well be destined for unrelieved failure. Research in deprived areas draws an even grimmer picture of the dropouts's potentiality for addiction to narcotics, to sexual promiscuity, and to meaningless idleness. There is no economic spur either. Where is the job? And what could it offer that one cannot equally well obtain by going on relief?

In so far as higher education is concerned, the conclusion Catholics must draw and by and large have drawn is that their qualified sons and daughters need to find a college or university opening somewhere. They cannot drop out of the training process at this point. Only a portion of them is able to enter Catholic institutions. Therefore they must apply elsewhere. They are applying elsewhere. But this fact annuls in a startling fashion one of the basic assumptions of the traditional Catholic philosophy. Cardinal Newman, restating and refining the traditional educational outlook of Oxford, held that science and literature were autonomous disciplines, but that theology, and with it the religious life, gave them universality, luminousness and depth. To be sure, it has taken the Catholic university in the United States a long time to grasp what is meant by the autonomy of the scientific and literary disciplines. But on many other campuses there is no place for religion except in a perfunctory and peripheral sense. Somehow or other a different kind of role for it must be developed for Catholics.

We can therefore draw a set of highly suggestive conclusions. It is impossible to go back to where Archbishop Ireland was and create a place in the public school system specifically for Catholics. Or for Protestants and Jews. It is equally impossible to abolish the Catholic-school system. Despite the criticism directed at it by a new group of Catholics, it is too deeply rooted in the respect and affection of the vast majority of the Catholic people, and in the dedication of religious communities. Third, it will be impossible to put all Catholic children into Catholic schools, particularly at the critical level of higher education. This presents to Catholic leadership in this country a totally new configuration of problems. We are living in a time which nobody could have foreseen, but it is here and one must take a candid look at it.

3
How to
Look at
Catholic
Schools

Growth and Reform

Some questions about Catholic education are now in order. What are the schools, including the colleges and universities, really like? Who enrolls his children in them and why does he do so? Who teaches in them? How are they administered? What do parents and pupils think about them? On the basis of research that has been undertaken, it is now possible to answer these questions with a measure of certainty. Before we deal with them, however, it is important to see more fully the degree to which Catholic education in the United States has consistently recognized the need for change. However constant its basic religious and educational assumptions, it was never content to rest on its laurels, but saw the desirability of adaptation and the possibility of further improvement.

Two important questions were asked during the pioneer period: who was to do the educating, and how could the spiritual life of the religious communities be fostered? The academy, as an academically oriented boarding school was then called, offered a fairly simple answer. Pupils who came to it normally paid tuition; the relative financial security this provided freed the religious for the task of education and also for the responsibilities of community life. The parochial school was quite another matter. In Middle Western villages, two or three sisters might live in a log cabin—later usually a brick convent adjoining the school and the parish church—and during the academic year they kept unruly urchins under control with straps they were not averse to using with vigor. In the shiploads of religious who braved the long journey to our shores and the hardships to follow were cultivated persons who could have, and sometimes had, taught with success in European lycées and Gymnasiums, but many were really little more than manual workers.

The human resources available were therefore of uneven quality, nor did they suffice in terms of quantity. In some schools children were taught by lay people; the religious had begun the quest for lay teachers very early. In the feminine academies these were often widows, women of some cultivation in art, music, and literature particularly; and quite a few of them eventually entered the communities they served. The men teachers in boarding schools or "colleges" for boys were normally bachelors, though by no means always so, and they shared in the struggle to survive, making no inordinate demands in terms of salary and sustenance. There was also frequently a greater sharing of experience with parents than might have been anticipated. In many a town or city it was a parent who brought about improvement through his protest against untutored or indeed sometimes cruel conduct by poorly prepared teachers. There was also a good deal of frontier-style comradeship which frequently blurred the lines of clerical-lay distinctions, unlike the more professional relationships which were to prevail later on.

Each community had a rule of life—laid down by a founder with ecclesiastical approval, or adapted from a traditional cloistered community such as the Order of St. Benedict. A great many of the communities which sent "missions" to the United States had been established in western Europe after the Revolution and the Napoleonic wars, when Chateaubriand's *Genius of Christianity* helped to set in motion forces of religious restoration. Older models continued to have their appeal—for example that of the Benedictine school, especially in Austria and Germany, which had realized that a shorn lamb in the form of a boy could be harmonized with the wind. Many of the new rules emphasized the teaching apostolate; and those who wrote them would have been astounded had someone told them that in the twentieth century a distinction would be made between "education" and "evangelizing." Indeed, some of the rules were stern, or at least had not been tested in terms of life in the world. Nevertheless, many of these religious had absorbed the pedagogical principles of the post-Pestalozzian time.

The differentiations between one community and another, clear enough in the light of the European cultural climate, were blurred in the American context, and so when we look back it is difficult to see very clearly how and where one group parted company with another. Yet anyone who wishes to understand in some depth the character of Catholic educational development in the United States should try to pick his way through this part of the story. In general he will find anonymity, relieved here and there by the emergence of a strong personality, much as would be the case if he were to study the chronicle of medieval builders and artisans.

The demands made on the religious were often exorbitant. Parents, usually poor, expected that the parochial school would cost no more than the public school. Not infrequently pastors tried to remedy their economic situation by asking parents to pay a small tuition fee, but as a rule the children were thereupon sent to public schools. The financial record has not yet been studied in detail, and the burden still remains heavy in our time. In earlier days it could be crushing. The incidence of disease, particularly tuberculosis, among teaching sisters was pronounced. This is part of the record of my own family; and it was only gradually that observant writers, among them Father Arthur Barry O'Neill, one of the editors of the old *Ave Maria*, urged sunshine and recreation for teaching sisters.

During this period a reform movement was clearly under way, identified with those whom today we would term "great teachers." They encouraged better classroom performance, improved textbooks, a diversity of activities. But in so far as young people in school were concerned, the emphasis was strongly on discipline and sexual segregation, though all this did not then differentiate Catholic education greatly from public education. For reasons of economy the average public high school outside of New England and some states to the South became coeducational. The sisters, often following the French pattern for which *gardez votre poule* was a maxim deemed both sacred and commonsensical, kept their fledglings from within a mile of boys. Institutions for young men often tried to do the same, but were naturally less successful. So far as one can now tell the first authentic experiments providing sex education were conducted by parish priests, who sometimes blundered by bringing boys and girls together for instruction, shocking both, and surprising themselves with the discovery of how innocent their charges were.

Catholic America was at that time still simple in terms of spiritual outlook, given to accepting without much ado the words of its clerical teachers. It was morally rather puritanical and convinced that a vocation to the religious life was the greatest of blessings in this world. Of course there were many rebels, from Theodore Dreiser on down. But as I look back over the years, it seems stranger and stranger that some people in Europe should have talked during the nineteenth century about an "American heresy." Catholics there, when they did not live in peasant enclaves, were being torn from their moorings. Just why some French clerics should have screamed for the scalps of Archbishop Ireland, Father Isaac Hecker (founder of the Paulists), and others must remain one of the unsolved mysteries in the history of the Church. The "American heresy" accusations hampered the development of Catholic education in the United States for decades. Fortunately nothing could halt the growth of the social conscience or the habit of generous giving by the American people.

The Catholic citizenry in general doubtless never realized what was happening to the "heresy." Their country seemed to be becoming one of the most Christian, even if anti-Catholic, countries in the world. This was an illusion for which Protestantism was largely responsible, for its evangelizing processes deceived even the elect. As a matter of fact, had it not been for Methodism, which by 1900 established almost 54,000 churches throughout the country, the ecclesiastical scene, particularly in rural areas, would have been exceedingly bleak. Even today, when joining a Church has seemingly become almost as popular as owning a color-TV set, forty per cent of the population shies away from any recognizable religion. It would seem at least a tenable proposition that if John Ireland, the eloquent spokesman for the "American heresy" (whose ideas we have already discussed), had been able to enlist Catholic and Protestant support for his version of how religion and public education could go hand in hand, there might now be a different story to tell.

At any rate, there remained as a legacy of the "American heresy" the Catholic University of America; and around this the second great "reform" movement developed. It set in motion, with the assistance of the genial, courteous, and cultivated Bishop of Peoria, John Lancaster Spalding, an endeavor to reconsider both the philosophy and the methodology of American Catholic education. Memorable names soon became associated with the work—those of Thomas Shahan, Edward Pace, George Johnson, and Frederick Hochwalt in the forefront. The movement was complex and dialectical. Studying it in detail will be no easy task since it will require a careful evaluation of the periodical literature inspired by George

Johnson in particular,* the story of the founding and subsequent development of the National Catholic Educational Association (1904), and the impact of the school planning fostered by the hierarchy. But doubtless it found a kind of synthesis, in so far as educational theory for the lower schools is concerned, in *Guiding Growth in Christian Social Living*, by Sister Mary Joan, O.P., and Sister Mary Nona, O.P. (Washington, 1944). This book's purpose was to indicate how the course of study could be an introduction in the wholeness of the life experience. The school was therefore to be "child-centered," in the sense that the youngster's gifts of imagination, intellect, and will were to be used in order to bring him into a harmonious relationship with his own self and with the reality surrounding him. He was to enter into confrontation with the physical world, the society of his fellow men, and above all, with God. It was the most effective statement of Catholic educational purpose made up to that time in this country, and implicitly recognized indebtedness to what was then "modern" educational thinking, that of John Dewey and others. Critics have, to be sure, noted a certain lack of contemporaneity in the underlying philosophical position. The fact remains that if Catholic education generally had absorbed this doctrine and used it as a basis from which to move forward, it would have overcome some of the uncertainties of purpose and methodology which subsequently lamed its efforts.

It did not do so, and the reason was clearly that so many who directed or taught in the schools simply did not have the time or the preparation to undertake the task. The load carried by the communities of sisters had been too heavy. (The communities of men had meanwhile begun to concern themselves exclusively with secondary schools and colleges.) The question therefore became: How can one train the sister-teacher, how can one organize her day's work, so that full advantage can be taken of her ability both as a professional per-

* See, for example, *The Catholic Educational Review*, which he edited for years with distinction.

son and as a specially chosen servant of God? These questions were asked with mounting frequency as more and more sisters took advantage of teacher training or of university study.

A sort of initial climax was reached when Sister Mary Madeleva,* C.S.C., described "The Education of Sister Lucy," (a "hypothetical high school graduate") in a paper for the National Catholic Educational Association in 1949:

> She wants to be a teacher. To realize her desire on any level she knows that she will have to have a Bachelor's degree and a teacher's license. She plans on all of this under whatever difficulties and demands of time and money. She expects to fulfill the minimum professional requirements for teaching. Any other procedure would be a sort of treason disqualifying her for the things she wishes to be and do. Before she begins her preparation she finds that she would rather be a teacher for God's sake then for two hundred dollars a month. She enters the novitiate of a religious community dedicated to education. She is simultaneously on two thresholds of one life. She is to be educated to be a teacher. She is to be formed to be a religious teacher. The two trainings are completely compatible, complementary, and can be perfectly synchronized.
>
> For six months Lucy is a postulant and has no status save that of hope and anticipation in the community to which she has come. Her Superiors, with wisdom and foresight, logically let her have her first semester of college preparation for teaching. Some Superiors may give her the entire freshman year. At the end of her academic period she receives the holy habit of the community and begins her canonical year of preparation to be a religious teacher. No secular studies can intrude upon this important work. However, young Sister Lucy

• Sister Mary Madeleva, C.S.C. (1887–1963), was president of St. Mary's College, Notre Dame, Indiana. Trained at the Universities of Wisconsin and California, she was both mediaevalist and poet, as well as the author of many books. "The Education of Sister Lucy" was published in pamphlet form by St. Mary's College but is now out of print.

does study religion, Scripture, apologetics, dogma, Church history, perhaps.

At the end of her canonical year of formation she still has one year before her first vows and three additional years before her final profession. These are, I believe, the regular canonical periods and are fairly uniform in all our active orders. She still has three years and a little more of college preparation for her degree and her license. These are as important to her honest professional training as her canonical years are to her religious formation. We need not evade this by arguing the superiority of religious over secular subjects. We do need to face the fact that the religious habit does not confer infused knowledge in any field nor justify the violation of the commonest requirements for teaching preparation. So let us give Sister Lucy these least qualifications.

In the second year of her religious life proper she should be allowed to take her regular sixteen hours of college work each semester. Good planning and budgeting of time can make this possible with an enrichment of rather than an intrusion upon her religious life. During summer session she can take an additional six hours. By the time that Sister Lucy makes her first vows she will or she can be a junior in college. Both her religious and her academic preparation are synchronously more than half completed. There still remain three years before her final profession. With less than two of these plus summer schools she will have finished her work for her Bachelor's degree and will have over a year to go on mission as an unprofessed sister.

On the day of her final profession her religious superiors and her community can receive her as a sister completely prepared by her religious training, her vows, her academic education, to begin at once to carry on the work to which she is dedicated. . . .

I need not tell you that Sister Lucy does not exist. But I know that we all should insist that she must exist.

The Sister-Formation Movement did not flow directly from the spring which Sister Madeleva had opened up, but the objectives were similar. The movement was, however, much more concerned with elementary-school teaching because it was such teaching that the majority of sisters then did. Two questions were being asked everywhere in the United States by school administrators, professors of education, parents, and the teachers themselves: Was elementary school teaching really a profession, and if so what kind of preparation was required? It was not until the mid-1940's that a truly serious effort was made by public school authorities to answer these queries. Certain presuppositions had been popular. First of all candidates for the job, usually young women, were supposed to be taught how to teach. The normal school did offer some instruction in what we generally term the liberal arts, for lack of a more precise term, but what it provided did not add up to much. Second, it was pretty well taken for granted that most of the young teachers would get married soon anyway—which was indeed what nearly all of them fondly hoped to do. But the day came when parents thought they detected in their offspring a marked inability to read, write, and reckon. The most obstreperous parents began to wonder, probably unjustly, whether this was because the teachers could not do so either. Just why it was that the elementary school generally got bogged down in "activities" more or less vaguely identified with the "learning process" is a mystery still not clarified. Many school administrators had grossly misread John Dewey and were convinced that only what was "useful" was worth teaching—a conviction which is meritorious if held for the right reasons, but a manifestation of adult delinquency when the explanations are muddleheaded, which they often were.

But as is customary in the United States, things began to improve as soon as the lights were turned up high enough. The solution, it was rightly held, was to be found in part through making elementary-school teaching a profession. This meant the teacher was to know something about his subject and something about how to get a little of it into young heads. I should like to underscore the second "something" with a comment on higher education. So scornful had the American academician became of anything smacking of pedagogical method that getting ready to teach in college may be described as follows. So much more was now known about nearly everything that the "young scholar"—for no one else can possibly give instruction in a college—was expected to stake out a claim on two or three square feet of research terrain and raise as big a crop of footnotes as he could. But when he proudly emerged in the classroom he was often without the foggiest notion of how to proceed. I have seen very promising, able, and genuinely scholarly young men throw in the sponge because they could not stand the polite boredom of the classes they met. A semester or two of reasonably skillful teacher training would have made all the difference in the world. Harvard is now lighting the way to improvement. I need not stress the fact that it is much harder to teach young children than it is to "confer" with college Sophomores.

At any rate, efforts to reform the situation in so far as the elementary-school teacher is concerned got up steam in 1946, at which time only fifteen states had made the bachelor's degree a *sine qua non* for getting a teaching certificate. By 1961, forty-four states had fallen into line. Yet even today a substantial number of public school teachers do not measure up to this requirement. Catholic elementary-school teachers were for a time by and large sisters. They did not intend to quit after a couple of years to get married. Nor would Mother Superior emancipate them, except for the most awesome reasons, from attending summer schools so as to improve their value to God and the community.

Sister Formation was first of all a movement designed to bring teaching religious to a point where they would be as well trained professionally as were their counterparts in public education. It had a remarkable leader in Sister Mary Emil, I.H.M., who led a tireless, intelligent, and spiritually motivated crusade. She was and is an earnest and persuasive speaker, and listening to her during the 1950's was always a heartening experience. Unquestionably she did more to induce religious communities to give their sisters an opportunity to become truly professional than all the clerics of the country combined. If the objective had been reached, the religious generally would now be better educated than their counterparts in the public schools. It was not reached and the principal reasons have already been indicated. Sister Formation also wished to bring professional training into a better relationship with religious formation. This was to a certain extent—indeed, probably to a remarkable extent—accomplished. There is no better criterion, constructive or destructive, of the real accomplishments of the Sister-Formation Movement than Sister Mary Emil herself, and so the interested reader is referred to the chapter she has contributed to the Notre Dame report. Because many commentators on the Catholic schools are blissfully ignorant of the manner in which sister-teachers are actually prepared, a passage from Sister Mary Emil's contribution to *Catholic Schools in Action* will be useful.

The standard acceptable program for the training of Sisters is now a five-year program consisting of various combinations of postulancy, novitiate, a juniorate (or "scholasticate"). The most common patterns are one year of postulancy, two years of novitiate, and two years of juniorate. During this five–calendar-year period, four academic years, leading to a bachelor's degree are covered. The extra calendar year, which is that of the canonical novitiate, is devoted largely to spiritual training. The five-year period usually includes a number of summer sessions, so that most of these programs total more than the number of credit hours usually considered minimal for a bachelor's degree. •

When one thinks of the many young ladies one has known during the years of their quest for a bachelor's degree and a teaching certifi-

---

• See Reginald A. Neuwien (ed.), *Catholic Schools in Action*, p. 116. The text cited here is taken, however, from the pre-edited version.

ate, one's admiration for sisters willing to endure that kind of preparation rises. The sole ominous question is: Can anybody henceforth induce a sufficiently large number of young women to embark on that kind of training for the religious life, granted the character of the society in which we live?

But admirable though the vigor of Sister Formation was, and great the leadership given it, life does not stand still. We shall see that other and perhaps more radical forms of community preparation for the task of teaching have been proposed. These are not necessarily better forms, but they have the advantage of what one might perhaps term two-way adjustment. On the one hand they are efforts to associate community tradition, always characterized by intense loyalty to the *magisterium* of the Church, with the much more diffuse authority which has been established by Vatican Council II; on the other hand they are attempts to provide a greater measure of liberty in carrying out the religious mission in today's complex and changing world.

The Over-All Situation

When the Notre Dame Study of Catholic Education was begun, the meaning of the program of *aggiornamento* which Pope John XXIII sponsored could not be imagined, let alone grasped. Hence the announcement that the Carnegie Corporation had made a generous grant to support the study raised more eyebrows and hackles than the Duchess of Windsor did in her time in Great Britain. Even though the director of the education department of the National Catholic Welfare Conference had announced complete co-operation with the inquiry and had agreed to be one of the three members of the consultant group to administer it, none of us knew whether the dioceses and schools would open their doors and furnish the data without which any survey would be a relatively meaningless inquiry. It was at a crucial meeting in the offices of Albert Cardinal Meyer, then archbishop of Chicago, in the presence of the archbishop of Baltimore, now Lawrence Cardinal Shehan, that a pledge of hierarchical endorsement was given. All dioceses except those of New Jersey later on honored it. The abstention of Trenton and its "dependencies" was regrettable, as well as inexplicable, but as a matter of fact it mattered relatively little. Some data was available for that state, although they could not be controlled with the requisite rigor.

A distinguished advisory committee was organized, on which non-Catholic as well as Catholic educators served. This group did not, as a matter of fact, function as well as had been hoped because its hierarchical members were so deeply involved in the affairs of Vatican Council II. There were other disappointments. The first director of the study, Dr. William H. Conley, resigned to take a post as president of a newly established university. It took some time before his associate, Reginald A. Neuwien (whose experience had included years of service as superintendent of schools in Stamford, Connecticut and in the direction of educational research), could master the new situation although, fortunately, he was able to do so more rapidly than was expected. One source of information was a questionnaire sent to all the schools, administrative officials, and teachers in the United States. We had to rely on the co-operation and honesty of the Catholic teaching profession, which as things turned out, was forthcoming in a measure no one could have predicted.

But it was evident that such a harvest of statistical data would not suffice. We therefore agreed that a number of diocesan school systems should be studied "in depth." This meant that schools would be visited, teachers, parents, and pupils talked to, and agreed-upon measurement data collected. We knew that any cross section of dioceses should be as representative as possible of regions of the country, of big cities and comparatively rural areas. We also tried to select dioceses in which the "authorities" would probably co-operate. As it turned out, one of our problems soon became finding ways of placating dioceses not included in the thirteen more or less arbitrarily selected. Obviously the desire for a constructively critical evaluation was widespread.

The answers to the nationwide questionnaire poured in. Literally tons of paper were deposited, first at the offices of the National Catholic Educational Association and then on the doorstep of Notre Dame's computing center. Admittedly this information is already somewhat dated. The Catholic school system of the United States in 1967 is not exactly what it was in 1963. Nevertheless the broad outlines are the same, and a thorough examination of them, even on the basis so far established, would be a long and time-consuming process. More than a hundred specialists—educators, sociologists, and theologians, Catholics and non-Catholics among them—took part in visiting the schools. The "studies in depth" took in a broad range of questions. For example: Catholic schools are like any others in that they offer instruction in standard subjects. How well do they manage? But of course the key question was: Since the principal reason why Catholic schools exist is because they are dedicated to religious formation and instruction, how well do they succeed in fulfilling this purpose? Here the study necessarily had to pioneer. There were no tests which could be relied upon to unearth the needed information. In addition our investigators tried to find out what parents expected of the Catholic schools to which they had sent their children and what pupils thought they were getting. Everything possible was done to secure maximum objectivity. But of course when a goodly number of qualified visitors look at what is going on, a brimming measure of individualized conclusions can also be anticipated.

In terms of over-all statistics, the study pretty well confirms what had already been surmised. The often declared demand that every Catholic child attend a Catholic school has not been met. The Notre Dame Study, using baptismal records as a base, reports that as of the school year 1962–63 52.21 per cent of Catholic children in the United States were enrolled in Catholic elementary schools—

4,342,273 of a potential enrollment of 8,315,555. It may be noted in passing that not all children born to nominally Catholic parents are baptized, and that some Catholic schools in urban areas have sizable enrollments of non-Catholic pupils. The number of unbaptized Catholic children is not known. And in consonance with the idea of the "missionary" parish advocated by the late Cardinal Meyer, dioceses and religious have often elected to keep in operation schools in neighborhoods affected by ethnic change.

But the over-all statistical data are not substantially affected by these considerations. In 1961, Catholic elementary schools were served by nearly 110,000 teachers. The number had been 66,525 in 1950.

The study likewise concludes that during the same school year 32.22 per cent of eligible Catholic children were enrolled in Catholic secondary schools—1,009,081 of a potential enrollment of 3,131,574. As of 1961, 46,623 teachers were employed in these schools. There had been 27,770 in 1950. The increase is in the amount of 67.9 per cent, which is substantial indeed. Can one note a trend toward stressing the secondary rather than the elementary school? The study report provides illuminating comment on this question, which we shall consider later on. Very probably the marked growth in certain dioceses has affected the total picture.

To round out the statistical image we should note that in 1961 the number of religious teaching in the elementary schools had also risen from 61,778 in 1950 to 78,188 in 1961, while in the secondary schools it was 34,153 as compared with 23,147 in 1950. The lay staff had grown meanwhile, too, and at a very fast pace. In 1961, the figure for the elementary school was 32,723 (it had been 4,747 in 1950) and for the secondary school it was 12,740 in 1961 (it had been 4,623 in 1950). In other words, the number of lay teachers had grown approximately four times as fast as the number of religious at the secondary-school level, and nearly twenty-three times as fast at the elementary-school level. We shall consider some implications of these data under the rubric of school finance.

This statistical growth, it must be repeated, does not represent any advance toward realization of the old maxim, "every Catholic child in a Catholic school." In addition, it may be noted that during the period between 1958 and 1962 the religious communities of sisters recruited a number which seems to lie somewhere between 13,000 and 25,000, but the actual net increase in the number teaching in schools appears to have been 4,952. We have no way of accounting for the disparity. It may, however, be surmised that training for teaching was the principal factor. As of 1962–63, the "median" preparation of sisters at work in the elementary schools was a B.A. degree. Of course, one must take into account that some states do not require more of teachers in the public schools. Moreover, since the Sister-Formation program is of quite recent origin, one may assume that in the not-too-far-distant future sisters whose training includes the master's degree will be "fed into" the system. At present it is of special interest that as the age level of teachers goes up the number of degree-holders increases. This means of course that many have been "upgraded" through faithful attendance in summer schools.

In general, sisters spend more years in teaching than do teachers in other schools. But one finding of the report is that rumors concerning a prevalence of the blind, the lame, and the halt in Catholic elementary schools are grossly exaggerated. As the age of sisters advances, so does the amount of training. To some, this may suggest that the inmates of convents are chained to a treadmill. This could be the case if a particular community is unwise, but in general it is not. The one glaring weakness is that young sisters are sent out on mission before they are adequately prepared.

The "median" of preparation in the secondary schools for sisters is the same as it is for brothers, namely the bachelor's degree. But there are a substantial number, 47 per cent, as a matter of fact, who have higher degrees. This level of achievement places the teaching sister at the top grade of preparation, in so far as Catholic secondary schools are concerned. Note, moreover, that these are national "medians." What is taken for granted in New York or Boston may not be the rule in other parts of the country. Two comments are, however, in order. First, the improvement of educational opportunity will inevitably bring with it a desire to move up the educational ladder. Young people who develop interests akin to scholarship will wish, if they plan to go into teaching, to find a level they consider commensurate with their gifts. The market for educational services being what it is, they may well be able to satisfy this desire. It would be surprising if some similar kind of escalation were not coveted by religious too. Second, once the bishops transfer their affection to the secondary school, it is probably inevitable that the religious communities will respond. No one can tell at the moment whether this is a good thing or not. There are competent people who believe that in terms of the Catholic "system" the elementary schools should be abandoned if a choice is necessary. There are others who remain convinced that the secondary schools are "all right" for the Jesuits, perhaps, but less serviceable generally to the Church. No results obtained by the Notre Dame Study cast much light on this difference of opinion. The question will be considered in depth later on.

We may conclude that the situation in which the teaching sister finds herself is far from being as dark and beclouded as has sometimes been assumed. There is also ample justification for believing that it will change for the better during the coming decade. The grounds for optimism are sound. The great diversity of the structure of the Catholic educational organization has permitted a large measure of opportunity for gifted and vigorous educators. There are about five hundred separate administrative units in the Catholic school system. Some of them operate in humdrum fashion, but others are alive to the human situation in which all youth now finds itself. The Notre Dame Study, wholly dedicated to the task assigned to it, avoided every temptation either to compare Catholic with public schools, or to isolate any single institution for comment. But of course so much inquiry necessarily led to the discovery that a number of Catholic institutions are very good, indeed, as good as any in the country. In these full advantage has been taken of all efforts to coax out of experimental activity every potential ounce of improvement. There are also both elementary and secondary schools of satisfactory quality. But one can also find poor schools, set in their ways, sometimes governed by persons whose rank in the Church cannot be questioned but whose competence as educators is not evident. The great task therefore is to promote the acceptance of model schools as norms. Perhaps one may also venture the opinion that the central problem of Catholic education is to spread awareness that times have changed, that religious dedication, while having its own radiance, is not enough, that society is moving rapidly to goals of weal and woe which could not have been foreseen at the turn of this century, and therefore that the thing which matters most is to give the Church, which is the family of the faithful, the dynamism that alone can render its mission productive.

New Problems and the Monastic Tradition

The Catholic schools are served, notably on the secondary level, by priests, brothers, sisters, and laymen. They all have about the same median preparation, though as we have seen, more sisters teaching in the secondary schools have been educated beyond the master's degree than have priests or brothers. However, the percentages differ only slightly here. But when a comparison is made with the preparation of laymen and laywomen the variation is marked. The percentages are (again in terms of the master's degree): for sisters, 17.8; for laymen, 6.7; and for laywomen, 4.8. The medians are comparable in the elementary schools, but the data shows plainly that whereas the preparation of the sister-teacher is steadily upgraded through in-service programs, that of the lay teacher is not. Accordingly the lay teacher may be one of the major unsolved problems of contemporary Catholic education.

The Notre Dame Study is a gold mine of information about this situation not merely because of the statistical data provided, but also by reason of the extensive interviews which were conducted with lay teachers and with religious about such teachers. To a considerable extent these data await further analysis. The conclusions which will be reached here are substantially the same as those of the study, but also reflect a fairly extensive correspondence on the subject. They are four in number.

To begin, there is the difficulty that entering the Catholic-school system does not offer the same kind of career opportunity as do other systems. The real "plums" in the educational enterprise are administrative positions, such as principal, assistant principal, or department head. The study learned that in the elementary schools only forty-nine lay teachers had been assigned to full-time or part-time administrative duties as of 1963. In the secondary schools the number reported was thirty-five. When one considers by way of contrast the career opportunities which open up in the public schools, he becomes aware of a major stumbling block in the creation of a solid lay component in Catholic schools.

Also, there is the problem of turnover. This is not only an issue for lay teaching strength. Because of the canonical rule that a religious superior can remain in office for six years only, shifting of principals is routine. Religious also are normally sent from one mission to another at regular intervals. But in the case of lay teachers, it is the absence of career opportunities which leads many, and frequently the best, to conclude that they have no abiding home in the Catholic school. As a result it is difficult to weld the staff together, even when there is ample good will on the part of the school administration. Transients are seldom malleable.

A third conclusion is that there often seems to be no rationale for the employment of lay teachers, other than that resulting from a computation of pupils and religious, which then leads to hiring as many laymen or laywomen as are needed. The most deplorable consequence of this is that poorly qualified teachers are sometimes employed at the last moment, which may lead to tarring the whole lay staff with the substandard performance of individuals.

Finally, salaries are prevailingly lower than the national average, and fringe benefits unobtainable. However, there things do not dissuade some very able teachers from casting their lot with the Catholic schools—men and women who wish to spend their lives exemplifying a religious commitment, or who prefer the "atmosphere" of the Catholic classroom. In not a few secondary schools, moreover, a change is setting in. Teachers are being paid at rates prevailing in the same town or city, and there is a presumption of tenure. Nevertheless, the absence of competitive financial rewards is a major handicap for the system as a whole.

One may make two additional observations. It is difficult for a community to live and work side by side with groups of laymen. Of course a religious may greatly respect the character and the ability of a lay person, may discover in her or him a friend, and may also often feel quite sincerely that "exemplification of the Christian life" is more effective when the exemplar is a layman. But each community has its own rule, its process of formation, its over-all objectives in terms of the teaching mission of the Church. The in-service program it adopts is designated to associate intellectual formation with a deepening of spiritual dedication. In other words, the teaching community absorbs the *whole life* of its members; and those who cannot be so absorbed usually leave. It is therefore almost as difficult for religious to think of their schools as being administered by laymen as it is to imagine a time when their community would have a lay superior.

We may now ask the question: What does the teacher in a Catholic school do with his or her time? The director of the Notre Dame Study probed into the situation with painstaking thoroughness, partly because the most telling of all criticisms aimed at Catholic education by the "new laity" has to do with class size. So brainwashed have we all become about class size, in the belief that the smaller the number of youngsters the teacher has to deal with the more signal will be the prowess of each one that the query looms large in many minds. Will a child "do as well" in a Catholic school as he would in a public school? As a matter of fact, it may be a question of seeking something akin to a golden mean. For instance, as classical studies lost their appeal, it often happened during recent years that a college professor had no more than three students in his class. Descriptions of the ensuing boredom are a matter of record. Nobody can lecture effectively, day after day, to that kind of audience, and discussion will be similarly hampered. On the other hand, if the crowd is too large, it will be difficult, if not impossible, to handle. No one has been able to establish with finality what a happy theoretical medium might be. Some teachers can do better with larger numbers than others. Perhaps—this is said tentatively—the sister-teacher ordinarily can, because her dedication to a religious mission will support her in circumstances which might induce any other mortal to collapse. Yet sisters are human and get tired, too, and there are many public school teachers whose dedication to their profession is equally exemplary.

No attempt will be made here to digest the Notre Dame Study statistics. They show that in the elementary school the median class size is inordinately high, largely reflecting the perplexity of pastors faced with deciding whose children are to be admitted. In despair they often let everybody in who can be accommodated in the available space and close their eyes to what happens to the teachers. As a result there are still some horrendous class-size situations, although these have fortunately been localized. In the secondary schools, difficult to survey because it makes all the difference in the world whether the teacher is giving instruction in French or telling girls how to jump up and down in gymnasium classes, the total situation seems more satisfactory. The study's data indicate that the secondary school is better off in this respect than the elementary school. Yet the likelihood certainly exists that the student load in both branches of education is too heavy. The report permits the reader to draw his own conclusions.

A still more important project for potential reform (in my opinion) is that of defining with relative accuracy what the over-all duties of the teaching staff should be. It is clear, of course, that the sister-teacher will not go out on dates or sit up nights playing bridge with her friends. But she must have some recreation, and in addition she is obliged to conform to the rule of her community in regard to liturgical and spiritual activities.

It is high time that attention be given to these matters. They are more important than class size. One cannot pretend that the report of the Notre Dame Study suggests answers good for all time, but there is a great deal in what it has to say. We may conclude that Catholics have come close to draining their human resources in the rather wistful hope that the sister-teacher, or the brother-teacher, at his level, is something like a hypothetical rubber band to be stretched from here to the moon and back again. This is no doubt also one reason why there are so few full-time principals in Catholic schools, why so little secretarial help is provided, and why scarcely any "follow up" of graduates is possible. Sisters carry these chores into after-school hours, and somehow or other a few of them get done. Whether ample opportunity is afforded for the reading necessary to keep the intellectual hearthfires burning is another matter.

The situation in higher education has changed with almost startling rapidity. Scholarship has created an ever increasing demand for specialization in every field of intellectual endeavor. Mousetraps of quality come these days from the laboratory and the library. The religious community in the generic sense cannot possibly cope with this situation. Of course nothing prevents a priest or a religious from becoming an excellent scholar. A good many actually are just that. But the demand is far too great to be met by seeking to combine on a large scale the religious vocation with the calling to carry on exacting research. Therefore the quest for creative, truly academic laymen is today perhaps the principal characteristic of Catholic higher education. Nor can the need for the improvement of administration any longer by-pass the layman. Even the smaller colleges now frequently entrust important administrative responsibilities to men and women whose business or academic experience was not gained in Catholic institutions.

In higher education, there were further developments in 1966, when Fordham and Notre Dame announced the appointment of laymen to important executive positions. Until this time, deanships were the highest positions they had held. Then, early in 1967, Notre Dame, Portland, and St. Louis Universities announced far-reaching reorganizations of their governing boards. When these are put into effect, responsibility for the affairs of these institutions will have been transferred from the religious community to a group of predominantly lay trustees. At Notre Dame provision has been made for maintaining the University's Catholic character, but in every other respect the Congregation of the Holy Cross will have relinquished ownership of the distinguished institution which has been in its charge since 1842. The change of course reflects the dominance of the lay faculty in terms of both numbers and scholarly achievement, and the ever increasing requirement for budgetary resources. But above all, perhaps, it takes cognizance of Vatican Council discussion of the religious life and of the role of the laity in the mission of the Church.

But if the institutions in question are to remain Catholic in character and dedication should their presidents be either religious or respected members of the secular clergy? For what does it mean to say that their purpose it to exemplify the intellectual life of the Church? It is true that the basic academic disciplines are and must remain autonomous—there is, as has so often been said, no Catholic

calculus or metallurgy—but nevertheless the institution exists because its objective is to manifest the Christian faith in a special
mode. It is, however, dedicated to Christian *experience* and not to
Christian *formation*. Its specific reason for being is to prepare men
and women for all the professions requiring scholarship in the genuine sense. This is a difficult task indeed, and like all such tasks it
must be defined and understood. A truly professional person may of
course become an apostle later on. That is, he may dedicate himself
in whole or in part to corporal and spiritual works of mercy. But
while he is at the university, while he is being trained, he must try
without stint to acquire knowledge about reality (which seems a
better formulation than saying he must seek after the truth, because
this phrase, so often proudly used, overlooks the fact that truth *may
and does seek after him*). Still it is probable that being "dedicated to
Christian experience" implies that the institution is served, and in
all probability led, by men who have themselves had a genuine religious formation.

As has been said earlier, monasticism is the ultimate source of
that formation in the Catholic sphere. Proceeding now to freedom,
we may appropriately note that this too is best assured within the
Church itself by a living monastic tradition. One cannot have any
kind of freedom that is to be taken seriously unless one also has some
form of certainty. To use a very simple example, one cannot be at
liberty to plan to go to Florida during February unless one is certain
about having enough money to pay for the trip. You cannot enjoy
the freedom of being a historian unless you are sure that you know
how to be one—that is, how to find sources of information on which
you can depend. Freedom in the Church also presupposes that one
has a reasonable, personal certainty about the Church and about
one's relationships with it. How could the situation be other than
this? For when we assume that we are "in the Church," but are not
at all sure why, or aware even of what the Church actually is, the only
thing we are really free to do is to look for answers to some questions.

We are not at liberty to live and move about in the Church as we would at home.

Historically considered, monasticism is also *Christian formation* in its essence. All other kinds of formation are imitative, as the seminary is, or are spurious. For instance, the assumption that a Roman congregation could set up a watchtower and, with the assistance of a number of purple-clad sentinels, determine who at any given moment was "thinking with the Church" obviously belongs to a hardly-too-happy past. It may be pertinent to adduce a convincing demonstration. For many years Father John Courtney Murray was bedeviled because he had made the commonsense observation that a literalist interpretation of certain papal pronouncements on religious freedom was outdated. If the appropriate congregation had been functioning in an earlier period of history, Father Murray might well have shared the fate of Savonarola. Fortunately, it was not so functioning. The Council, which provided an opportunity for university scholars to oppose successfully the views of various sacred congregations, then decided to remove from the books forever the assumption that what used to be called the Supreme Sacred Congregation of the Holy Office could deny to anyone freedom of religious conviction.

But what has often escaped detection is the fact that Father Murray is a Jesuit, that is, a man trained in a tradition at least semi-monastic. The Society of Jesus was designed to be a community of militant academicians and missionaries. Like all fighting units it has discipline. Some recent commentators have seemed to suggest, in the name of freedom, no form of obedience should be required of religious communities, or indeed, of the Catholic faithful. Father Murray, of course, had no trouble on that score. No doubt other Jesuits, and members of the Church in general, have been sorely tried. Even so, a religious belonging to a reputable community, who is certain about the Church and what his relationship with it should be, is, I think, as free as anyone, clerical or lay, who respects no orthodoxy save that of his opinions. The fact that Catholics, for example, have overstressed the equation that missing Mass on Sunday equals mortal sin should not lead one to conclude that training in obedience is no longer a necessary part of spiritual life.

The overriding value of monasticism lies in its conjoining of obedience with diversity of intellectual points of view. If, for instance, someone assumed that Thomism was the only tenable Catholic philosophical position, he had to reckon with the Franciscans, who have sturdily professed the sovereign importance of Bonaventure and Scotus; the Benedictines, who have a special Platonic orientation; and several other orders. As a layman, I could conceivably announce that I had discovered a new avenue to truth in fresh theological terms. But I doubt whether I would have much luck unless in some monastic group or other there was an echo of what I had to say. This does not mean that the monks—however one may define them—are always right. Sometimes, like all other human beings, they are glaringly wrong. After all, they can be expected to know with some certainty the answer to only one question: What must I do to become holy? But it seems to me improbable that a group of laymen, even those with considerable training in seminaries, could do any better. Of course, we have all known priests who supposed that the gift of prophecy is given automatically to those who have abstained form serious scholarly effort. My conclusion is that it may well be better to entrust the destinies of a Catholic university or college to a priest with some kind of reputable monastic formation than to a layman.

Practical considerations are also in order. Very few laymen, and it may be doubted that they would be selected for administrative responsibilities, would care to accept the role which would necessarily be theirs. For the president of a Catholic university must be someone who can give symbolic expression to an effort which in the very nature of things cannot succeed. Not all the students who are matriculated will automatically become or remain exemplary

Catholics, or indeed retain the faith of their childhood. To contend that such a result could be, or indeed would have to be, achieved is deplorably restrictive. The Church itself has clearly not accomplished anything of the kind; and it is one of the profound mysteries of the New Testament that the Savior, who could raise Lazarus from the dead, was irritated to the point of anger by his inability to soften the hard of heart. It is only when one erroneously conceives of the university as an instrument of Christian *formation* that one can be misled into entertaining so unrealistic a view. In this area the university should act even as the Church itself does. It should respect, indeed entertain affection for, all who wander in the shadow of doubt or negation. These should be wrapped in a mantle of hope which they themselves neither feel nor see. This is the cross which the president of a Catholic university must know how to bear. The man who is the symbol of what the institution professes to be will bear it, even when he must meet the disappointment and wrath of parents or the hardly veiled derision of the public.

Such is the conclusion to which I have come, returning after many years of mature life spent elsewhere, to look at a Catholic campus from within. The only rules such a campus should impose and enforce are those which may be assumed to be guarantees of the special task assigned to it. It must set high standards of academic achievement and maintain the order which is necessary in its kind of society. One characteristic of these standards and order is academic freedom, which is just another way of saying that within appropriate limitations, "life, liberty, and the pursuit of happiness" are to be assured. But the relationship between the Catholic university and freedom is paradoxical. By its very nature such a university is committed to the conviction that freedom is within the Church. The truth that is Christ makes us free—free from demeaning and selfish passion, free to keep other men in the grasp of one's affection without constantly expecting perfection from them, and free to believe that one is more than a spark in a meaningless cosmic conflagration. Nevertheless, in another sense the Catholic university is not free as some other corporate institutions are. It cannot believe at the same time that the principal, life-giving purpose of the Church is to make it possible to pray to God with Christ, and that it is quite all right not to subscribe to that purpose. And so there are bound to be ways in which a committed university enters into conflict with a university which is not committed. The president of a Catholic institution must understand this and know how to cope with it. On the one hand, he must reckon with ecclesiastical authority, which is likely enough to feel that the conflict has been narrowed to the point of virtual extinction. On the other hand, he must not fail to recognize and if necessary frankly state the vital points at which the university he represents differs in outlook, let us say, from a great publicly supported institution.

I am persuaded that the right kind of religious can do all this more effectively than any but an unusual layman. There may be such laymen about, but for my part I am sure that I would have rubbed myself raw. But when the phrase "the right kind of religious" is realistically considered, in the light of what actual experience has revealed, one may nevertheless come to the conclusion that sooner or later lay presidents will be needed. Very likely a number of religious communities ought to begin to reckon seriously with this probability. This can only mean planning. Potential lay candidates obviously must have administrative experience. But they should also have good training in theology, obtained if possible in a superior graduate school.

Similar considerations present themselves at the secondary-school, or even the elementary-school, level. But they are nevertheless quite different in character. The schools exist in order to prepare young people for advancement to the next rung of the academic ladder. What that rung is to be becomes a matter of importance. If for reasons which are quite legitimate, parents seek, for example, to enable their sons to enter "prestige" colleges, it may well be that a secondary school presided over by laymen will be highly successful. As a matter of fact, such schools now exist and are fulfilling their missions with a good measure of glory. All one knows about them also justifies the belief that they make ample provision for religious instruction. But since their tasks are clearly defined and do not include sharing in the extension of the frontiers of knowledge, they are not obliged to reckon with problems which are of profound moment to the university.

4
Raising
the Sights

Defining Objectives

To return to elementary and secondary education, one of the most important trends revealed by a study of the statistical data is the current rate of increase in the number of secondary schools and of the enrollments in them. This results from several situations which mesh with one another. In some dioceses, notably Bridgeport, Connecticut, the bishop fostered secondary education vigorously. Also, a large number of secondary schools, though by no means all, are "privately" conducted, which means that they are owned by religious communities. These communities staff elementary schools at great financial sacrifice to themselves. Secondary education is no bonanza either but, to some extent at least, it does make possible a better balance of community financing. Another factor is that as teacher preparation improves, the number who prefer to teach in the upper schools increases. This is now important because older methods of exacting religious obedience have given way to increased consideration for individual wishes.

But though these things are significant, they do not by any means suffice to account for the change we are experiencing—a change which, though it has special implications for Catholic education, is far wider in scope. Here I shall not attempt to review the literature but will rely on my own experience and reflection. We may begin with a simple statement of fact. The pattern of adolescent behavior in our society has altered, and every one of us can draw up a catalogue of particulars which would no doubt include the following: greatly increased leisure with which greater permissiveness has generally gone hand in hand; no work experience, except in some rural areas and smaller towns and cities; the fact that the "audio-visual aids" (TV, the radio, and the phonograph) are the unifying influences in the urban home; and the "peer group" in the schools which now seems to build the young community. The character of the schools has also been drastically altered. Not only has the course of study become permissive and growth-centered, but in the city at least there are young people who have a wholly different kind of orientation, if they have any at all.

And so the American family, with a tradition reflecting the mores and religious or ethical aspirations of the parents (some of which admittedly must be termed middle-class), is at odds with the prevailing educational environment. The network of private schools, especially at the secondary level, has never before been so large and flourishing. They assure the "structured" family of a route of escape from a process which they find not only alien but hostile. It is not "integration" as such that they are trying to avoid (witness the ever increasing number of scholarships which the private schools provide for Negroes and other "aliens"), but the total urban educational climate created by the influx of the "dispossessed." The private school has become on the one hand an antidote to "permissiveness" and on the other, a barrier to alleged "demoralization."

Quite a number of Catholic commentators find in such families a manifestation of disinteredness and callousness. Being dedicated to the concept of the "Christian mission" to the "inner city," these commentators may consider any attempt to escape from the full implications of that mission quite irresponsible. But little support comes from within the family. Just as thoughtful and orthodox parents once made sacrifices in order to avoid the risk of proselytization by a dominant Protestant majority, so their counterparts in our day try to box in their children against influences they consider perilous. It is of course true that the only dependable safeguard in the long run is the transformation of the "inner city," but the father of a family sees his responsibility as an immediate one; and we may add that often he is himself a Negro, a Puerto Rican or a Chinese father, who looks at the problem no differently than do his Caucasian neighbors. The social moralist may contend, in terms of Catholic schools, that siphoning off so many priests and religious for service to the "structured" family is hardly, if at all, to be justified. But there are forceful counter-arguments, and the growth of Catholic secondary schools would appear, at least at present, to support them.

We confront another situation in suburbia, which provides a setting for sex relations—doubtless as important an issue as any in contemporary America. We seem to have developed a methodology concerning these relations which in some respects is akin to insanity. "Methodology" may be too discreet a term. We are hemmed in on the one hand by the disappearance of ancient tabus, and on the other hand by solemn and indeed often agonizing queries as to what indulgence may do to the psychic lives of young people—queries which currently are still hidden under the not-too-reassuring mantle of psychoanalysis. The scarecrows of a bygone age frighten few people any more, despite the high incidence of venereal disease. Syphilis, once a bulwark of sexual morality reduced to its lowest—but still quite effective—terms is as puny a scourge as are the mumps. A girl who offers intimate companionship to a boy friend can easily find out what the "pill" will do; and so widespread has the use of the diaphragm become, owing to maternal solicitude, that it can be advertised to one's peers as the safest of devices. Should everything else fail, somebody always knows (or thinks he knows) how an abortion can be safely and expeditiously managed. Accidents still happen, of course, and there are foundling hospitals to take care of them. And so it is not at all surprising that premarital sex relations are now, as a matter of cold fact, often no more than a normal concomitant to being young. Add the prevalent forms of addiction to alcohol, narcotics, and violence, and one has ample explanation of why secondary schools should seem so important to "structured" families, of which Catholics have perhaps more than their share. But in this respect they do not live in isolation. Nor do their pastors and hierarchical shepherds. In this area there is a remarkable "ecumenical" concurrence of views.

But can Catholic secondary education accomplish what is expected of it? Attitude studies provide some evidence, which will be considered later on. Using sexual morality as an object of study (though it is probably no more important than are other forms of ethical conduct, and may be less so, if one accepts the Dantean scale of values), we shall try to see what the outlook and the teaching of the schools might be. It is not an easy task. To begin with, the *frein vital*, which once governed Catholic attitudes, has lost its significant strength. That sexual relations can legitimately be resorted to only when the procreation of children is their object is a doctrine to which only a very few rear-guard moralists subscribe. Psychological insights have made it plain that in man—and to a lesser extent in the higher mammals generally—most intimate companionship between the sexes, whether physical or not, is colored by sexual enjoyment, however sublimated. And so most Catholics now believe that in marriage the coming together is one of persons, not primarily of bodies. Despite the gains achieved by the positive nature of such insights, teen-agers are nevertheless terribly vulnerable to the pressures of a vulgarized popular culture that would transform the Johannine emphasis that God is love into a spot commercial.

If this is the situation in which the secondary school finds itself, what is it to teach? What kind of "formation" will be its objective? These questions are worth considering because the answers to them provide at least a sort of index to the value of these schools, and also give a clue to what the re-formation of ethical teaching in our post-Conciliar period might be. If I understand the moralists correctly, the first motivation springs from a deeply realized sense of order in the world, an order rational and therefore ordained (for what is rational cannot result from chance but must be ordained) on which the welfare of the individual and of society necessarily depends. Whether one conceives of it in Thomistic terms, that is, of "natural law," or in terms of the framework of evolutionary dynamism, as Lecomte du Noüy or Teilhard de Chardin have, one will find it difficult to avoid the conclusion that right order in the moral sense is peculiarly a function of the human conscience. It does not impose itself. It must be recognized, understood, willed, and served. Morality and religion are concepts of order; and so they must always be thought of in terms of effort and aspiration. It is only the self which can be disorderly in terms of the moral order. The relationship between the sexes is therefore properly a relationship between consciences; and so it is when the lover and his beloved experience a commingling of persons growing constantly more unselfish. Casual relationships, hardly more than resemblances of the embraces of animals, are necessarily selfish. This, of course, is not saying that there cannot be quite moral relationships outside of matrimony. A man and woman prevented from marrying may manage to live together in unselfish and therefore impeccable union. It is at this point that Christian and more specifically Catholic teaching makes its scripturally based insistence on the indissolubility of realized love relationships.

The definition of order as ideally unselfish can surely be shared by Catholics with other people, particularly those teaching in public schools, and is so shared even in this time of ethical disarray. Far too frequently, however, "sex education" is little more than an exposition of physiological data. This exposition is of course needed, as is every other means of leading a child from a state of innocence to a knowledge of good and evil. But what if he is led to equate the two? Since Freud has taught us to ferret out the infamies that the alleged innocence of infancy tries to cover over, it is easy to believe that the claim that one can know the good is only a profession of ignorance about oneself. Those of us who have lived close to the scene of moral disarray, whether as physicians, educators, journalists, or confessors, too often resignedly think that, seen in its totality, human nature is beyond redeeming. The scene, as Newman said, dizzies and appalls. Unless the culture to which we pay lip service at least professes that evil is what man moves away from when he comprehends his nature, and that good is what he then moves toward, it must indeed become morally meaningless. All this does not indicate the perversion of youth, but rather the impact on it of so much that is blatantly sexual, violent, selfish, and irreligious.

Nevertheless the Christian commitment in its total context is immeasurably more. Many of us have commented on John Gardner's phrase, "the pursuit of excellence." The Christian in all truth longs for greatness of spirit—in contemporary terms, for the evolution of the human intelligence toward the task of bringing the world "to the Father." It has been said, and I believe rightly, that anyone who has discerned the presence of Christ in another Christian, and doubtless even the presence of God in another human being (for instance an Hasidic Jew), need no longer trouble himself about arguments for the existence of God. This is certainly the rock of conviction on which the ecumenical program of the Vatican was based. To cling to this simple fact is of course not to deny the value of natural theology. Yet the immemorial liturgical prayer does proclaim that Christ is he in whose manhood the Divine One has shared so that all men may partake of his divinity. One accepts the order of brute creation as one finds it but does not identify man with that order completely. In loving all the things which are, loving them because of the glory of God's love, which throws the light of beauty and reason on them, one expands the horizon of the self unselfishly. Surely trying slowly, humbly, laboriously, with both good humor and affection, to bring about this kind of realization is reason enough, it seems to me, for a Catholic secondary school to exist. But no one can tell whether the effort will succeed.

All this does not mean that public educators are indifferent to the problems indicated, or that all the schools over which they preside are sources of peril to youth, or that, as a matter of fact, many Catholic parents do not confidently send their children to public high schools. Those in charge of such schools for their part confront efforts to preserve the ethnic or other standards of given neighborhoods. But it is true that they must accept and try to educate all children who apply for admission. And it is precisely to the "all" that the "structured" family objects.

But perhaps—I do not feel any certainty about this—the Catholic school cannot successfully accomplish the task it has assumed without the assistance of lay teachers whose attitude toward the problems under discussion is at once more realistic and more intelligently sublimated than that of the clergy or the religious can be. But if one says this, and it needs to be said, the whole problem of the lay teacher in Catholic schools is again immediately raised. If he or she is to be of genuine service in the secondary schools— from the point of view of adjusting young people not only to the problem we have been discussing, but to the whole gamut of difficult moral and social relationships which are inevitable in the shift from rural to urban, industrial society—he must undoubtedly have training in the moral and social sciences. Too often lay Catholic teachers are pious amateurs, although some may chop their wood to the tune of utilitarian requirements. It would, in short, greatly enhance the total contribution of Catholic schools to the culture of the country if the lay people who serve them could have some serious spiritual formation.

In general, a lay teacher, living in the contemporary world on a small salary, must confront problems of social ethics and social compassion. He does not have the freedom of a priest or a religious. His commitment to a wife and family is an overriding one. His paycheck really hems him in. An increasingly large group of priests and sisters has been commendably concerned with racial justice and a great variety of other good causes. Some of them may have said and done things which people generally do not like, or may have embarrassed their superiors, but at least they have been trying to find answers to explosive questions. It is still by and large true that even if the lay teacher, for example, had found a way of going to Selma, public reaction to his going, within and outside the Church, would have been relatively unfavorable. This lack of freedom in terms of moral responsibility hampers the layman, or even the laywoman, and to some extent at least dims the example each might otherwise give. Nevertheless it seems to me that in being thus hog-tied the lay teacher may be demonstrating the basic plight of modern man, curbed on the one hand by his indigence and on the other by the weight of the moral challenge which society presents to him. This is why, no doubt, St. Benedict founded his community.

We come to a quite different problem, namely admissions policies and school performance. The comment is often made that Catholic education serves "nice" middle-class boys and girls. To a certain extent, due allowance having been made for the pejorative quality of the adjective, this is true. The average Catholic-school youngster, apart from a few exceptional diocesan elementary and high schools, has a better family background, a higher IQ, and more learning motivation than does the average public school child. This does not mean that the Catholic population has a greater share in the good things of life than does the rest of the nation. Far from it. The situation arises because not all who would like to attend Catholic schools can do so. As we have seen, on a nationwide basis little more than half of Catholic youngsters of school age get admitted even on the elementary-school level. What would you do if your job was to weigh pleas for getting children into your school? You haven't a chance in the world to go from house to house and corral the delinquent. No, you must choose from among many, and naturally you end up by accepting children from families to which you are most indebted. The parents will have performed their parish duties efficiently. They put filled envelopes into the collection box and participate in the social and charitable activities of the parish. To sum up, if a choice has to be made between Michael, the bright and engaging son of parents who go to communion every Sunday, and Oscar, the offspring of wayward folk who show up occasionally and toss a nickel into the basket, you will be sorely tempted to reward virtue here and now.

But, alas, Michael, granted his good family background, a home where there is a crucifix on the wall and grace is said before and after meals, with maybe a rosary one night out of four, might well (in spite of what his parents think) emerge from the public school with a big halo around his head, while Oscar might go to the devil. The problem thus presented is quite a terrifying one, and there are not a few who suffer anguish because of it. At Notre Dame we conducted a few isolated bits of research, under a program not affiliated with the study, and seemed to find that in communities which on the surface appeared likely to make a much better showing twenty per cent of Catholic children of school age were receiving no religious instruction at all. We did not find that Catholic educators were devoting much thought to the problem. They were much too busy to do so, even though when it was called to their attention they were as troubled as anyone could have wished them to be.

A few parenthetical remarks may be introduced at this point. We have all been concerned with finding answers to the question, why have Catholics not taken their proper part in scholarly activity? It is already forty years since I myself offered a contribution to this discussion.* More recently, Monsignor John Tracy Ellis outlined the situation in a fairly blunt and convincing way, so that a great deal of attention has been given to it.** Father Andrew Greeley took up the argument and on the basis of data collected with considerable sociological skill predicted that a change was in the offing and that relatively soon Catholics would have more than their proportionate share of intellectuals.*** At the moment a considerable number of other research workers are analyzing evidence related to the situation.

But the problem which now looms up as at least as formidable is this: by reason of the structure of its schools, particularly from the admissions point of view, the Church in the United States may be in some peril of becoming an intellectualized Church and of losing what for lack of a better term we may call the working class. One of the great glories of the Church in the United States is that it did not lose the industrial worker—as distinguished from the peasant—to Marxism or irreligion; however, if the children of the working class receive no religious instruction of any kind, or very little of it, they may well turn out to be the key to the "leakage" of the future.

If I were a Catholic parent who thought that my sons and daughters should prepare for a learned profession I might well make a beeline for Catholic secondary education, perhaps as far up the ladder as the college. For despite all the handicaps under which it operates, this education, largely by reason of the selective character

* George Shuster, *The Catholic Spirit in America* (New York: The Dial Press, 1927).
** See "American Catholics and the Intellectual Life," *Thought* (Autumn, 1955), XXX 351–88; and *American Catholicism* (Chicago: University of Chicago press, 1955).
*** Andrew M. Greeley, *Religion and Career* (New York: Sheed & Ward, 1963).

of its enrollment, provides a superior academic background. Of course there are other forms of education which do likewise, but it is doubtful that they do much better. I have of course said "Catholic education" and not "Catholic school," because one can certainly pick out some in the second category which are decidedly inferior.

But if one thinks of further education one must bear the times in mind. The bugaboo that Catholic schools are "authoritarian" and therefore not in tune with the truly intellectual life has not been dispelled. It may be that some of them brainwash too much, but it is equally true that very many young people generally are not brainwashed enough. We who look at the social scene through the curious camera of age are at a disadvantage because the opening of the lens widens, making it possible to take in much more terrain but greatly reducing sharpness of focus. Nevertheless one knows from experience that just as it is possible to feed a girl on mental pabulum so that even after she is safely married and pregnant, she still does not know that she is going to have a baby, so one can rear her so that at the age of fifteen she has had experience with even the most degraded vices. One need not be in favor of either method in order to express a preference for the first.

But there are some ways in which Catholic schools do brainwash, and it is well to consider them frankly. I have sometimes said that if a teaching religious had to choose between denying that two and two are four and saying that one could miss Mass willfully on Sunday without serious sin, she would prefer the first negation. Like every other great religion, Catholicism professes a code of personal and communal conduct. Its code is not as strict as is that of Orthodox Judaism, and it makes more provision for the forgiveness of sin than does Protestantism. But code there is, to be taken seriously; and Catholic education would not be Catholic education unless it were very much in earnest in this sense. One who is not a Catholic need not accept it. One who is a sincere Catholic must. The evidence indicates, as we shall see, that Catholic elementary and secondary schools succeed in inculcating some parts of the code more effectively than they do others. But at all events they try and some of it sticks.

On the other hand—though there are considerable divergences in this matter between the performance of one teaching community and another—evidence appears to indicate that the teaching done in the first three years of the elementary school is not as flexible psychologically as is desirable. In part this may result from class size, though many observers do not think so. It seems rather that it follows from the relative absence of the "guidance mentality" from Catholic schools. Not all the claims made for applied psychology may be valid, but some of them unquestionably are. That the absence of such a "mentality" from segments of Catholic elementary education is so pronounced can only lead us to the conclusion that if we are not to witness abandonment of the earliest grades, which some dioceses have already inaugurated, improvement must be sought.

We arrive now at the exceedingly grave problem of what can be done in terms of religious instruction and training for young people who are not in Catholic schools. One reply is that all of them ought to be in such schools, and that it is the collective duty of Catholics to see that room is provided for them. This anwser has the merit of being logical. If the reason Catholic education came to be in the first place is considered sound, then the fact that more than half of all Catholic children never see the inside of St. Brigid's or St. Joseph's School is pretty hard to justify. The opposite thesis is that it really does not make much difference. Are Catholic-school graduates any better, religiously speaking, than Catholic public school graduates? This question obviously can be answered only after meticulous research has been done, and it has not yet been done satisfactorily.

A variant of this position is that provided by Mary Perkins Ryan,•

• Cf. her *Are Parochial Schools the Answer?* (New York: Holt, Rinehart and Winston, 1964).

whose intentions are admirable and who may be termed the poet
laureate of parish life. It is impossible to deal adequately with her
argument in capsule form, and it is an impressive argument. In
essence it says that Vatican Council II has proposed a great new
idea of what the life of the Catholic in the Church and in the world
should be, and that the big task is to acquaint people with this idea
and train them to realize it in everyday terms. The parish should
be a sort of *agape* scene and armory combined, from which the
lovers of man and the warriors for his soul would go out on their
mission to redeem mankind. This would mean that teaching sisters
and brothers, instead of being penned up in schools washing selected
souls clean and concentrating on lesson plans, would be out preach-
ing the glad tidings. But of course one inevitable question is, just
how good would the sister or the brother be at that kind of job?
Father C. Albert Koob, Executive Director of the National Catholic Education Association, has expressed his doubts.

*I'm not as sanguine as Mrs. Ryan about what these people could
do if they were released. I don't think you can take any segment of
the human race, let alone religious, and suddenly legislate that they
begin tomorrow to do a different job, to perform a new function.
This may shock some people, but the science teacher probably
couldn't teach religion adequately if you wanted him to. So you
save a Brother somewhere and make a catechist out of him, but if
he doesn't have adequate training for the work, you're no further
ahead.*•

A third suggestion embodies schoolman's realism, and I think it
is probably sound. Catholic schools are not going to close down.
There is no one in sight who seems likely to promulgate an order
that on January 1, 1969, these schools will be boarded up and Sister
Mary Immaculata will thereafter be found in a storefront in the
East Bronx. But we may rightly assume that, the educational mis-

• See "Catholic Education in 1980" (*National Catholic Guidance Conference
Journal*, X (1965), 1, 48–49.

sion of the Church being an immemorial one, some sisters will be doing something comparable. Or priests, brothers and lay folk. In order to see more clearly what they ought to be doing, we should certainly have to take into account the methodology and experience of out-of-school catechetical activities to date. The information amassed by the Notre Dame Study throws some light on this, but not much. One could also correlate what is available from all Catholic studies with the research undertaken by some Protestant Churches.* Even so we do not have a solid basis on which to evaluate the situation, let alone for making decisions as to what ought to be done.

In the United States, the Confraternity of Christian Doctrine has been considered the agency which would assume responsibility for the instruction of children educated outside the Catholic orbit. But until 1967, the Confraternity had only a small office financed entirely by the proceeds of a translation of the Bible. There was no organization of Confraternity directors, nor had experimentation with a course of study made much headway outside a very few dioceses. No funds were available for a director's use. It is to be hoped that the unity between directors which has now been created will be productive of excellent results. Meanwhile a good deal of attention has been given to the possibility that, under a recent Supreme Court decision, "objective" courses in religion can be offered in high schools as well as in colleges and universities. Pilot studies are in the realm of possibility. If they prove successful great changes may occur in the out-of-school religious instruction of young people. It will be much more difficult to provide adult education classes.

Certainly a marked change in attitude is taking place. For years we isolated Catholic-school children so that they would not be contaminated by other children or get into fights with them on the way home—which are two sides of the same coin. It must be admitted that as a result the Catholic school developed a character

* To date most prepared statements by Protestant groups are still "confidential."

quite its own, in many respects admirable and intriguing. Father Joseph Fichter's *Parochial School*• may be a portrait etched in sociological ink, but it is a very persuasive one even so. People have rightly loved such schools, though some citizens in contemporary suburbia may not. They had much of the charm of convents in a time less affected by *aggiornamento*. There was an air of piety about, but usually it was not too sticky. The rosary which dangled from Mother Superior's waist was a bit oversized but it jingled decorously, like a tiny carillon slightly out of tune. And of course all the saints who might be able to help with this, that, or the other mishap had their effigies in the parlor and along the corridor. Our common humanity was reduced to size in the convent's burial plot, where the little crosses marked the spots where the bodies of nuns who had asked precious little for themselves lay in confident expectation of the resurrection of the dead. American convent schools had, I think, no real counterparts in the rest of the world. They retained some of the simplicity of our frontier, which at its best loved people for what they were and not for what they were supposed to be.

Whatever nostalgia we may feel for the past is not reprensible, but we all know that we cannot have that past again. And the principal reason why we cannot is very simple. We are, as Americans, citizens of a world having totally different dimensions. When I was a boy, my father often took me with him when he had to inspect some bridge site over a creek or a small river, and we drove along in a buggy. He draped the reins around the dashboard; the horse jogged on; and we looked at the stars, when there were any, and talked. He had lived in that country all his life, knew every farm in it and practically everybody on any farm. We heard dogs bark in the distance, or listened to the hoot of an owl in a woods along the road. But—I can say this with candor and without cant— the presence of God was all about us. We never spoke of it with

• (Notre Dame, Ind.: University of Notre Dame Press, 1958).

any unction. And when we were tired of talking my father hummed old German tunes, which his father and grandfather had brought with them from the Old World. Most of them were more akin to the goliardic songs than to the Psalms. Yet sometimes we would hum a passage from the Latin Mass or the German *Singmesse*, and there would not seem to be any marked difference. In short, we were embedded in nature and in a great tradition, and nothing else really mattered.

Intellectually we were, of course, rather primitive. The preparatory school to which I went had a genuine awareness of currents of thought then significant in world terms. We got a rather restrained version of the Modernist controversy. This was because our teachers were Europeans. Later on I was to find that the formation I had received was far in advance of what was generally provided by Catholic schools in the United States, and so I had to endure throughout most of the rest of my life the delights and the terrors of anticipating Vatican Council II. Meanwhile our society was undergoing profound transformations in terms of thought. William James's *Varieties of Religious Experience*, a great book to which one now returns again and again, was then considered dangerously relativistic. We had very little use for the theological positions of our Protestant neighbors. It was of course, as one looks back, the turning from Hegelianism to Determinism, which initiated the abandonment of revealed religion on the part of John Dewey and other leading intellectuals, which plunged American Protestantism into a sea of doubt, just as the excessive literalism of older interpretations of the Torah tore much of the Jewish youth from its moorings. But though some of us, on our side of the tracks, staggered a bit, we were by and large loyal to the Catholic faith.

Today a young person finds himself in a totally different world. The walls of enclaves in which his parents lived—call them ghettos if you like—have been razed. We cannot say, of course, how, by reason of the impact of the sciences or the sudden discovery of the ecumenical landscape, these things will affect the education of the future. But dripping down to the bottom of intellectual awareness, change is already manifest in a certain aloofness of religion from the major concerns of the day. Pope Paul VI effectively advertised the Church's concern with the preservation of peace and the spread of social justice. But in the very nature of things he could not present a scholarly report on how peace is to be achieved and a just social order created. Like his great predecessor, John XXIII, he could only emphasize the responsibility of Catholics to work for the realization of these ends. If the impact of all these developments on young people actually in Catholic schools and colleges, however real, has been nebulously understood, how much more difficult it will be for those isolated from Catholic instruction to comprehend the strength and the weakness of the Church in terms of contemporary society.

Clearly, then, a change in the attitude of pastors and teachers must take place. They must see that while the parish may be unintelligible without a school, it makes no sense either if half of the congregation is hardly identified with the parish or the school. Children in public schools and their parents must be cordially invited to share in the common life, the school included. If we can find any number of college students and other volunteers to help with a neighborhood study program, surely we can do something equally effective in terms of religious education. As a matter of fact, the prospect which looms up is a very stirring and heartening one. The Catholic school will be thought of no longer as a closed corporation into which as many are squeezed as the place will hold, but indeed as the center from which the energies needed for the task Mary Perkins Ryan has outlined will be generated. But it will require imagination, candor, openness of mind and heart, dedication, and patience. It seems to me we can find these in the United States in the light kindled by Vatican Council II.

Evaluating Achievement

Catholic schools come in assorted shapes and sizes. Some are large; many are small. There are approximately 10,427 elementary schools and 2,460 secondary schools.[*] They were built for reasons which have already been explored—ethnic considerations, the "mission" work of religious communities, the zeal of pastors, and the action of bishops—to carry out as best they could the mandate that every child was to be in a Catholic school. A great many schools have stayed just where they were first put, which means that they are out of date and hampered in many ways. Others are large and well equipped but nevertheless still bulge at the seams. In some an almost perfect balance has been found between plant, staff, and students. These, the study staff believes, are very good indeed.

Traditionally, Catholic secondary schools have segregated the sexes, but there are a number in which coeducation is the order of the day. This is in violation of canon law, but the arguments successfully resorted to by the bishops who have authorized them stated nothing else was possible financially, or that young people would go to public schools otherwise, or even that the prevalent mores required coeducation. The coinstitutional high school likewise came into being, primarily because the rule of some religious communities obliges them to instruct one sex only. In such high schools boys are taught by brothers, while the girls are placed under the care of sisters. Some facilities, for instance gymnasiums, are normally used in common. All these various kinds of institutions are carefully classified and described in the Notre Dame Study, with such comment as objectivity permits.

But virtually all Catholic schools have one thing in common. They are not vocationally oriented. Exceptions can be found to this rule—one high school even has five "tracks"—but they merely set

[*] The figures are those reported for 1965–66 by the National Catholic Education Association.

the prevailing pattern in relief. This pattern is what we are accustomed to call academic, or to identify with the "liberal arts." Accordingly if one were to attempt to compare the Catholic schools with the public schools—which is what the Notre Dame Study scrupulously avoids doing*—the exercise would have to be restricted in the main to one kind of school.

That there came to be only one kind was probably inevitable. Virtually no religious communities have a tradition which identifies them with vocational education, an exception being the Salesians, who have a long history of teaching the arts, crafts, and so forth. Moreover, setting up vocational schools, or vocational courses in existing schools, is a more expensive operation than Catholic education has normally been able to afford. This may change to some extent owing to provisions in the recent educational legislation of the federal government. But I have not been able to find anyone familiar with trends in Catholic education who thinks that things are going to be very different in this respect from what they are now. Indeed many influential persons hope that they will not be different.

When, therefore, the directors of the Notre Dame Study undertook to gather evidence concerning how well the Catholic schools have been accomplishing what they set out to do, it was "academic" education they were looking at. Moreover, as we have seen, the system of admissions and dropouts favors children who are attuned to that kind of training. Occasionally school authorities, smarting a little under the charge that only "nice, bright" youngsters get into Catholic schools, have deliberately established quotas for differing IQ and social-status levels, but about all they seem to have got for their pains is an exchange of a somewhat salved conscience for an infinite variety of headaches. On the other hand, oddly enough, special programs for the talented boy or girl, involving honors courses and independent study, can seldom be found in Catholic

* Comparative study is still in its infancy, although more has been done than is generally realized. An analysis of unpublished dissertations is badly needed.

schools. Such programs create additional demands in personnel, time, and money. But they certainly add up to something to think about when one considers the future of Catholic secondary-school education in particular.

Another aspect of the situation in these schools which needs stressing is that follow-up of pupils entering college—which an ever increasing number do—has been virtually nonexistent. About all that most schools know about their graduates is that transcripts of their records were sent to at least one, or maybe a dozen, colleges. This probably was no great handicap so long as a school was virtually a "feeder" for certain designated Catholic colleges or universities. But it is no longer possible to place the majority of graduates in Catholic institutions of higher learning. As a matter of fact, the trend to state universities will increase markedly once enrollments go up as a result of opening still more Catholic secondary schools. Therefore neither those in charge of curriculum nor those who offer guidance can know how effective their work is, or how well designed, until follow-up becomes a standard procedure. It simply must be done, the study staff concluded.

This, then, was the situation as those in charge of the study began to probe into the results obtained by Catholic education. But of course it was also true that the inquiry really had no precedent. Fortunately it turned out that the schools sincerely wished to co-operate and that in many instances they went to great pains to do so. Nevertheless a number of the customary paraphernalia of investigation—tests, reports, and records—did not exist. They had to be created specially, or inprovised. Under the circumstances, it is quite extraordinary that the results were what they proved to be. The first inquiry dealt with a subject currently of vital interest to parents who want their children to go up the educational ladder as far and as rapidly as possible. How effectively do the Catholic schools teach academic subjects? Yet even if they did so better than anyone else, a further consideration would arise because of Catholic education's claim that it must exist as a separate enterprise since only in this way can a truly religious formation be provided for young Catholics. At the very first meeting of the Notre Dame Study's advisory committee, stress was placed on the fact that the public must be told whether this claim could be substantiated. The director promptly set to work trying to find out.

Doubtless the deduction most difficult to manage from the evidence about religious instruction is this: In what sense does teaching young people about religion contribute to forming rational, or socially desirable, attitudes? As the study began to probe attitudes, such a deduction was confronted with all sorts of demurrers. One may ask meekly, How is it possible to come upon an answer to such questions with any certainty that the answer will be valid? And of course someone may suggest boldly that the sociological profession, despite the fact that it has trained a variety of bright young men and women in techniques which the ignorant elder will sometimes liken to alchemy, cannot always respond in a way which inspires confidence.

There are two other dimensions of comment on fireside theories about American Catholic education. The first is, What do parents expect that the schools will do for their children; and the second is, What do the children themselves believe is happening to them? The study resolutely ran the whole gamut. As we shall see, neither the director, nor the committee of consultants, nor the large group of experts enlisted in the effort, thought they were omniscient. Catholic educational woods are full of those who think they could have managed to do almost anything better than people who have shared in carrying the burden. And good though modern investigative techniques are, they still do much better with quantitative data than with qualitative judgments.

What did Catholic parents think of the enterprise? And how do the youngsters feel about what was happening to them? In what follows we shall make no effort to reproduce the data provided by the study, except in so far as the conclusions suggest reflection. The first question asked what the students appeared to have learned in terms of the academic disciplines. A fairly large sampling of children in the thirteen dioceses co-operating in the depth studies was made—192 elementary schools and 7,300 students in the secondary schools. The director of the study realized of course that the method he had to use was of restricted value. He could not interview that many young people, nor were data available as to their performance after they had entered college. He therefore used standardized tests as measures of both ability and achievement, since it was obviously impossible to learn much of value unless these two were correlated. In so far as the elementary schools were concerned, it was possible to evaluate the results of tests in actual use; but the great variation found in the secondary schools compelled the study director to administer a common test battery; and this was done at the twelfth-grade level in forty-four schools in five dioceses only.

The barest summary of the results obtained from inspection of tests scores used in elementary schools will be attempted here. First what had been surmised earlier was confirmed. Since admissions policies are almost uniformly selective, "90% of the school grades had median IQs or above the fiftieth percentile (which is the national average), . . . and 84 per cent had achievement scores at or above the national norm." • Little comment is needed. However many things Catholic elementary schools may lack in terms both of teacher-qualification and equipment, the children in them learn pretty much (within the limits of the course of study) what their indicated learning potential says they should. Naturally this discovery does not prove either that the best-endowed American children are in Catholic elementary schools, or that all these schools have used or are using the best instructional methods. The results show that the average child in them is relatively well endowed mentally and satisfactorily taught in comparison with national norms. Nevertheless the picture

• Reginald A. Neuwien (ed.), *Catholic Schools in Action*, pp. 72–73.

which emerges is brighter, perhaps, than might have been expected; and it seems to indicate that the Catholic elementary school has a rather strong base from which to improve.

What the study itself does not show is the extent to which experiment and orientation are used in seeking improvement. Through observation and conversation, those who participated in the depth studies discovered much that was encouraging from this point of view, as well as not a little which demanded change. This information does not fit into the rigid reporting pattern of the study, but it suggests very fruitful fields of inquiry to be carried out, not for their own sakes, but for the purpose of making the scope of desire for improvement broader and more effective. Many schools need opportunities for self-study, undertaken with the help of competent persons who are sympathetic with their objectives. It is likely enough, therefore, that desirable progress in Catholic elementary education can be anticipated, provided that the underlying problems are satisfactorily met. These problems have already been pinpointed but may for convenience's sake be summarized here. Teacher-training must be fostered in the spirit of the Sister-Formation Movement, and something similar should be inaugurated for lay teachers. A better pupil-teacher ratio must be established. An effort must be made to develop or improve school libraries. Guidance programs are needed. Even so, the scholastic levels of these schools are at present good, and a variety of sources indicate that further progress has been made since the study was completed.

The tests administered to twelfth-graders, though admittedly the sample is smaller and is limited to a restricted number of dioceses, reveal an even greater impact of admissions policies based on pupil selection. The secondary schools are conducted under the auspices of religious communities, or of parishes, or of dioceses. The first group, which admits 38 per cent of the total enrollment is Catholic secondary schools, selects students on the basis of learning potential. It also charges tuition and other fees, which is of course an additional hurdle. Parish and diocesan high schools likewise can rarely admit all who apply, though their policies are usually less restrictive. But they profit from the "tie in" of pupils from the elementary schools, the prevailing academic level of which has already been described.

Since almost without exception Catholic secondary schools are "college oriented,"• and are seldom concerned with "terminal" or vocational training, the testing was accordingly directed to four content areas: language, social studies, mathematics, and science. Once again achievement scores were correlated with ratings for mental ability. The schools were then classified by type and area. The study concluded that "these groups of twelfth-grade students are meeting their indicated potential in a better than satisfactory manner." Some interesting results were obtained. The all-girl schools surpassed the all-boy and coeducational schools in the language arts; the all-boy schools led the field in the social studies; and the coeducational schools went ahead in mathematics and science. This, however, is apparently not due to marked differentials in teaching preparation.

One may therefore conclude that the academic achievements of Catholic secondary schools are satisfactory. This does not mean, once more, that all young people in them are superior, or that there are no differences between one school and another. Like all research of a comparable kind, the Notre Dame Study establishes medians. There are Catholic secondary schools of decidedly poor quality, many too small to provide diversified learning opportunity.

• Further information on this point is provided by pupil responses to the following statement: "The opportunity to go to college is extremely important to me." Of the eighth-graders who answered, 85.15 per cent agreed "strongly" or "somewhat." Only 10 per cent disagreed "strongly" or "somewhat." The rest were "uncertain." Of the twelfth-graders who responded, 73.89 per cent agreed "strongly" or "somewhat," while only 7.24 per cent "strongly disagreed." When one takes into account that these pupils were studying in a great variety of high schools in several dioceses, the general character of the schools can easily be surmised. (Neuwien, *Catholic Schools in Action*, p. 217.)

There are also very good schools. What needs to be stressed, however, is that only in very rare cases does a Catholic high school provide a layman with the scope, the challenge, and the means which he can find in certain first-rate public high schools. This situation must be corrected, despite difficulties such as inadequate financial support. The high school of the present time cannot rest on its laurels. It is constantly being shaped anew by devoted and dynamic men and women. Catholic education must have its share of them. Changes in the theory of learning based on experiment and practice are great, and others are in the offing.

The report of the Notre Dame Study provides no data about academic curriculum-building in the secondary schools, nor does it evaluate teaching. These are areas in which probing is still necessary, and there are indications that the directors will undertake additional inquiries in the future. But in general it may be said that Catholic secondary schools have pretty largely outgrown earlier courses of study which were, in effect, those of a European Gymnasium. They also have left behind, broadly speaking, the concerns of a once seemingly irresolvable debate between the "moralists" and the "intellectualists" (the first of whom place the major emphasis on saving souls, while the second advocate above all the training of the mind), and have set to work trying to implement the statement on "The Objectives of Catholic Secondary Education in the United States" which was issued by the National Catholic Educational Association in 1944. Though it may perhaps be viewed as an adaptation of Catholic schools of similar statements prepared by educators serving the public school system, it is far more than that. One has no hesitation in saying that it is the most valuable statement about educational objectives so far produced by Christian educators.•

It is through its inquiry into the effectiveness of religious teaching

• For a comprehensive, intelligent and aggressive analysis of this statement and of the existing situation see James Michael Lee, *Principles and Methods of Secondary Education* (New York: McGraw-Hill, 1963).

that the Notre Dame Study has doubtless made its most significant contribution to the discussion of Catholic education. The question to be faced was not whether a child learns more about the Catholic commitment than he could otherwise learn at home, with the help of good Sunday-school instruction. Nor could one expect to filter out the influence of the school from the total complex of forces, often intangible, bearing on a child's religious life—including native temperament, the home, the church, the "hero" or "heroine," companions, reading, music. For example, interesting attempts have been made, especially by Protestant investigators, to discover whether a relationship exists between religious teaching and reading habits. But for better or for worse no such influences or interrelationships were explored in our Study.

Very, very few tests of religious knowledge and awareness had been designed prior to 1961, and the best of these was woefully out of date. The decision was therefore reached to prepare one designed to find out what a child understood as well as what he had tucked away somewhere in his memory. What emerged initially was startling, at least to those of us who had never entertained a comparable idea. The first question was: How does one go about deciding how much a youngster should actually know, in terms of factual knowledge, and what should that knowledge convey? Obviously, it could be taken for granted that boys and girls who have spent eight years in a Catholic elementary school and four in a Catholic secondary school (eighth-graders and twelfth-graders were to be tested) would have committed to memory the standard Catholic responses to catechetical questions. All had been taught who made the world, who the Twelve Apostles were, and what happened on Pentecost. They would not hesitate to reel off the Ten Commandments and the seven capital sins. No doubt a child who had spent twelve years in Catholic schools might also know more than other children about esoteric matters of doctrine or history, but if that were all he had to show for his labors, one might well wonder whether they had really been worthwhile.

But if one wanted to try to probe more deeply one was face to face with the fact that the theologians, especially those who concerned themselves with education and pastoral care, had devised in sequence several different ways of presenting and interpreting religious knowledge. The older method, considered advanced in its days, believed that doctrine and moral teaching could be clearly defined and explained in short, crisp statements. There existed a "deposit of the faith"; and about all one needed to do was to hammer into a child's memory the various items in that "deposit." Thus one learned that if a person who had been divorced married somebody else he would thenceforward have to live outside the Church. As the phrase has it, he was excommunicated. The *Baltimore Catechism*, in its original or revised versions, was the standard textbook in which this "intellectual method" was expounded. It provided what for generations were considered satisfactory formulations. Many Catholic children committed all or most of this catechism to memory; and of course there is no doubt even now that memory work is an indispensable part of teaching religion, even as it is of teaching almost anything else.

Then, after World War I, when American Catholicism took its first great step toward close identification with American life, the teacher, without departing from the outline of religious knowledge which added up to the basic teachings of the Church, began his attempts to relate intellectual knowledge to individual and social conduct. That one-half of the "greatest Commandment" stated that a man must love his neighbor as he does himself remained a fact, but a new stress was placed on the meaning of this injunction in daily life. The most significant pastoral letter of the American hierarchy to date reflects the Catholic temper of the time (1919). There was now a "social gospel" which could be transformed into individual and corporate action. This seemed likewise to be in harmony with the "new" pedagogy, legacy of John Dewey and his followers, which held that a child learned best through doing. Thus Holy Communion ceased to be an awesome and exacting rite to which one went penitentially once or twice during the year, and became a daily or frequent participating in the commemoration of Christ's preparation for his Passion, believed to have assured the salvation of mankind.

A third change came about after World War II, when the influence of leading European theologians began to make itself felt. In their view the Church, aware that it could no longer depend on any alliance with secular power and, indeed, harassed by anti-religious revolutionary forces, was compelled to conceive of its mission to the human race in new and invigorating terms. What did it, what could it, offer other than the jubilant tidings of Pentecost, when the Apostolic Community realized that Christ was truly risen and that what had happened on the Cross was therefore not the end but the beginning of religious history? The total scriptural story was one of divine love seeking to kindle human affection. The Church was to become once again the "family of God," in which the vices and passions so rampant in recent history would be exorcised. This theology was by no means anti-intellectualist, nor did it turn its back on what was effective in the educational philosophy and psychology of the pragmatists. But the manner in which it restated the core of Christian knowledge and tradition gave its thought an "affective" character which doubtless brought it further away from the textbook and closer to what in the life of the Church may be termed "pastoral care." At any rate, this altered concept of the Church's mission, anticipating the Second Vatican Council, was reflected in the religious pedagogy, implied in A Catholic Catechism,* a product of years of German research and experimentation.

This catechism has not been widely adopted by our American schools, but the "catechetical" theology underlying it was more and more eloquently expounded in summer school and institutes, as well

* (New York: Herder and Herder, 1958).

as in religious communities. More and more literature was concerned with education in terms of this theology and the liturgical movement which was its counterpart. The influence of the *Katechetik* of Joseph Andreas Jungmann, a pioneer work which appeared in 1953, can hardly be overestimated when one thinks of the United States alone. Therefore good reason existed for assuming (as did those who set to work to design the test used in the Notre Dame Study), that the new approach had influenced the teaching of religion in Catholic schools, especially those in which instruction was given by religious, much more than would appear on the surface.

The question therefore became: How can one ask Catholic school children about their religion unless one knows what approaches to it have been suggested to them? It then became necessary to formulate sets of questions in language which those to be interrogated would understand. These questions and the methodology which dictated them are set forth fully in the report and the appendix to it. Here we shall content ourselves with noting that "refining the instrument," to borrow from the semantic storehouse of the sociologists, was an exacting undertaking. By the time the final version of the test was completed, more than a hundred experts had been consulted, and at least a modest amount of pretesting had been done. The list of items had been greatly reduced, a number of safeguards had been built into the instrument, and three categories of concern—doctrine, liturgy, and the law of the Church—had been stressed. In round numbers, 15,000 students attending selected elementary and secondary schools in thirteen dioceses would now proceed to demonstrate whether anything significant would be discovered.

One item (No. 28) dealt with worship. It read:

The best way to join the liturgy (Mass, sacraments, and so forth) is:

(a)   to attend Church services regularly

(b)   to read about the vestments, music and ceremonies
(c)   to follow the rites and rituals in approved books
(d)   to learn how to serve Mass or help in the sacristy
(e)   to take an active part in performing the liturgical acts•

Item (e) was the "advanced" answer and (c) the "moderate" one, (a) was adjudged "conventional," (d) "moralistic," and (b) "nominalistic." The reasoning which underlay these designations is obvious to everyone who has some knowledge of the "new" liturgy, but was probably generally less clear at the time the test was administered. Stress is laid on participation, so that mere reading about "vestments, music and ceremonies," though unobjectionable, comes last in the scale of values. The results obtained are quite startling. Only 1.44 per cent chose to make the (b) or "nominalistic" response, while 76.91 per cent opted for "contemporary" theology by choosing either (e) (advanced) or (c) (moderate). It may be added that 21.7 per cent selected the (a) answer, which the test designers consider "conventional," while 1.72 per cent chose (d), held to be "moralistic."

A much more difficult item (No. 47) presented the following problem.

The Bible teaching that God created man in his own image and likeness means:
(a)   man's spiritual powers of intellect and will are God-like
(b)   all men are equal in God's eyes
(c)   man's soul somehow looks like God
(d)   man's spirit has a capacity for the Divine
(e)   man reflects the qualities of God••

It may well be that in this instance the designer-theologian had not quite caught up with the English language. Just what was meant by "man's spirit has a capacity for the Divine?" At any rate, this [(d)]

• Reginald A. Neuwien (ed.), Catholic Schools in Action, p. 63.
•• Ibid., pp. 164–165.

was held by the authors of the test to be the "advanced position."
Answer (a) was deemed "moderate," (e) "conventional," (b)
"moralistic," and (c) "nominalistic." Of those answering, 4.48 per
cent seem to have been baffled by the question, because they did not
respond. At any rate, 33.33 per cent of those interrogated opted for
the "moralistic" response, which does them honor because (at least
in my opinion) (b) is the only statement which makes complete
sense. But, alas, 9.25 per cent favored the proposition that "man's
soul somehow looks like God." Admittedly the teaching is difficult,
but the theologian who phrased the "item" removed it far beyond
the boundaries of metaphysics. If (d) had read "man's spirit is able
to receive the grace of God," probably all but a few of the benighted
would have said "Yes." The "item" is adduced here because it indicates that the test given, prepared as it was in inevitable haste, needs
revision.

Concerning the results as a whole, it may be said that the responses were comparable regardless of whether the item dealt with
doctrine, worship, or moral teaching. Thus the basic assumptions of
the "new theology" (of course not as "new" as that currently being
formulated) were not considered merely in terms of one or another
aspect of Catholic life. It was to be anticipated, perhaps, that girls
in all-girl Catholic high schools would triumph over all other students in selecting "advanced" answers. They did. This may indicate,
though the basis on which a judgment can be formed is probably
too limited, that summer sessions, institutes, discussions, and ran-
dom or controlled reading have propelled sisters further in the
direction of changed attitudes than they have other instructors in
religion. It may well be that seminaries for the training of priests had
been relatively conservative during the period under consideration.

At any rate, however marked the differences between individual
schools (and dioceses) may be, and however difficult may be any
attempt to filter out the service of the school as distinguished from
that of the Church or the home, it would appear reasonable to as-

sume, on the basis of the evidence gathered, that the Catholic school has succeeded in its task of introducing young people not merely to some knowledge but also to some understanding of the basic tenets and presuppositions of the Catholic faith. One finding, however, must make everyone stop and think. The results of the test indicate that although high-school students did manifest some additional growth in perception, the differences between their response and that of eighth-graders (considered in terms of maturity and breadth of view) was not as great as had confidently been assumed.• May it be the secondary program in religious instruction in general has not adequately recognized potentialities for growth?

• See *What Is Happening to Catholic Education?*, edited by C. Albert Koob, O. Praem (Washington, D.C., 1966).

5

Attitudes
and
Social
Behavior

Catholic Teaching and Social Environment

We may now proceed to the next section of the Notre Dame Study, which was the outgrowth of an attempt to find out about "attitudes." Assuming that boys and girls do as well at school academically as could reasonably be expected, and rather better in acquiring a knowledge and understanding of their religion, what are the results in terms of individual and social morality, prejudice, and readiness to promote the general welfare? What do they think of their schools? Would they have preferred to go somewhere else? What are their impressions of their teachers? What do parents expect of the schools to which they send their children? Do they have ideas about how well these expectations are being met?

Attitudes are difficult to assess, especially when they are young people's. One may not look at things the same way on Tuesday as one did on Monday. A low grade given by a teacher, resulting in subsequent parental admonitions, may temporarily sour the child's opinion of his school. Or suppose we look at the matter another way. Since nearly all Catholic-school youngsters live at home, their ideas about other people or about the world at large will be shaped more by what they hear at the dinner table than by what they learn at school. Their parents are likely to share ethnic points of view. Or something may happen in a neighborhood which for days on end will induce negative states of emotion. Nor can one ignore the impact of radio and television, especially the latter, because they do much toward setting in motion currents of conversation in the home. For example, it is simply impossible to assess the total effect of the assassination of President Kennedy on the minds of young people, in terms of the impact of the television presentation of his death and funeral rites. We have no instrument sensitive enough to measure such upsurges of public emotion, and a sociologist who attempts to deal with them in retrospect is inevitably a bit like somebody who would try to reconstruct the mood prevailing at a picnic from the litter on the ground the next day.

I shall therefore cheerfully confess that I entertained for a long while some reservations about this part of the Notre Dame Study. But obviously there is so much interest in and concern with these results of Catholic schooling that attitude-inquiries were absolutely necessary if the whole effort was to prove convincing. A great deal of thought and professional skill went into devising the questionnaires; and in each case a sociological monograph was prepared of which the study report furnishes only a digest. Perhaps one or the other of these will eventually be published separately, for use by scholars. Here we shall take another step toward simplification. The results will not even be presented in capsule form. Emphasis will be placed on some insights into the prevailing climate of religious opinion, and into selected social attitudes of children who come from a variety of social backgrounds.

It is well known that Catholic schools produce most of the vocations to the religious life. On the basis of a careful inquiry, Father

Joseph Fichter, S.J., estimated that "The parochial school produces 70% of the vocations out of 50% of the children of elementary school age, while the Catholic high school produces 60% of the vocations out of 25% of the Catholic high school population."[•] Probing into attitudes toward the religious life, the study asked two questions:[••]

1) If one of my best friends said she wanted to become a sister, I would pray that she would succeed in that vocation.
2) It makes me happy to hear that one of my best friends is going to the seminary to become a priest.

These questions carefully skirted delving into the query as to whether the young person interviewed personally thought well of the religious life. The affirmative responses were slightly in favor of the boy who wished to become a priest. Nevertheless, relatively few wholly negative votes were cast. Probably—the question is one which would interest a humanist who has no knowledge of sociological technology—some girls did not want certain boys to ignore their lures in favor of celibacy, and some boys came near to suffocation when they thought of an idolized Patricia or Kathleen wearing a wimple. At any rate, 85.1 per cent agreed that they would respond with great or moderate enthusiasm to the news that a male friend had decided to enter the seminary, while 83.9 per cent welcomed a girl's decision to enter a convent. But, and the mathematical data will not be adduced here, the study indicates that female responses to both questions were more affirmative than the boys' answers, and that the child of parents who had received a considerable measure of Catholic education outdistanced others in the rate of saying "Yes" to both questions.

Another problem presented was:

• *Religion as an Occupation* (Notre Dame, Ind.: University of Notre Dame Press, 1961), pp. 41–42.
•• Reginald A. Neuwien (ed.), *Catholic Schools in Action*, pp. 185–187.

Even when there are serious differences in the family, I still believe that divorce with remarriage is always wrong.

If all Catholic-school youngsters were brainwashed, or if no one had acquainted them with the agonizing problems which divorce sometimes brings with it, or if there had been no discussion of exceptions such as those recognized by the Roman Rota, one would expect that every one of them would have answered in the affirmative. But the number who "strongly agreed" was 70 per cent of the total, while 10 per cent (the fractions are approximate) said that they "agreed somewhat." As usual the girls who opted for the absolute outnumbered the boys. Likewise children growing up in families in which both parents were Catholics favored the proposition more strongly than did other children. One can regard with a measure of satisfaction the vote in favor of stable homes. It is clear that both Catholic parents and children desire such homes. But if no Catholic children were aware of problems and of nuances, the critic might rightly conclude that the Catholic school is an institution established for assuring the most abject kind of rubber-stamping. Catholic education cannot be either Montanist or libertarian. And apparently it is not, however parrot-like it may sometimes be.

One of the inquiries which most concerned those in charge of the Notre Dame Study proposed three statements:*

1) Manual labor and unskilled jobs seem to fit the Negro's mental and physical ability better than more skilled or responsible work.
2) It would bother me to sit next to or near a person of another race in school.
3) There is something strange and different about Jews; it is hard to know what they are thinking or planning, or makes them tick.

* *Ibid.*, pp. 189 ff.

These statements contained loaded questions, but the students did not confront them in the sequence here given. They were judiciously separated and probably were not related in the respondent's mind.

Since the questions are obviously important in the light of contemporary American mores, we shall reprint in a somewhat different format the responses obtained:

Unskilled jobs fit the Negro		Dislike sitting near one of another race		Jews are strange people	
Strongly disagree	45.9%	Strongly disagree	61.0%	Strongly disagree	31.6%
Disagree somewhat	20.9%	Disagree somewhat	15.0%	Disagree somewhat	15.8%
Agree strongly	7.6%	Agree strongly	7.3%	Agree strongly	6.9%
Agree somewhat	14.9%	Agree somewhat	8.7%	Agree somewhat	13.0%
Uncertain	10.7%	Uncertain	8.0%	Uncertain	32.7%

When one considers that the sampling was done in a number of states (more than 14,000 pupils were involved), it is not too surprising that some bias or uncertainty about the Negro was expressed. However deplorable this undoubtedly is, the view that the Negro is primarily suited for unskilled labor may still be widely prevalent. Forty years ago the average white American probably felt this way, and it is not wholly startling that this bias should persist to some extent. Dislike of sitting near a person of another race is, however, unmitigated racial prejudice; and it was very embarrassing to discover that one Catholic-school child out of four either shared this dislike or was not sure whether he or she did or not—and this despite age-old Catholic teaching! The gap between religious knowledge—that is, realizing that Christ redeemed all men, and that therefore all are and must be brethren—and social attitudes is in this respect glaring. Although in one sense the views expressed concerning Jews were equally regrettable, at least there was nothing to indicate that Jews were looked upon as belonging to another race. It would seem rather that the statement uncovered an amazing amount of ignorance about a people who profess another religion.

The analysis provided by the Notre Dame Study was probably as thorough as the circumstances permitted. In general the examination of the responses in terms of sex, social status, and family religious background strongly suggests that group and ethnic prejudices sometimes cancel out the impact of teaching in the schools. Thus the percentage of students who "strongly disagreed" with the statement that the Negro's function is to do unskilled labor drops from the 58.2 per cent reported from all-girl high schools to the 33.5 per cent for boys in coeducational high schools. The statement concerning dislike of sitting near a person of another race was "strongly disapproved" of by 73.3 per cent of all-girl high school students, but by only 50.7 per cent of boys in coeducational high schools. But the statement about the Jews brought "strong disapproval" from only 42.8 per cent of all-girl high school students, while the disapproving responses of coeducational high school boys reached a nadir of 23.2 per cent.

Perhaps the most unanticipated and disheartening part of the analysis is that which indicates that only a very slight change in attitude occurs when the number of years of Catholic schooling increases. In the case of the Negro, as a matter of fact, children who have been beneficiaries of such schooling for twelve years assume Negro inferiority to a slightly greater degree than do children who have had only four years. The one marked trend to a diminution of either prejudice or lack of understanding occurs when inquiry is made into the amount of education the parents have received. The study reaffirms what has already been widely noted about American society as a whole, namely that good education is, when continued, a liberalizing force.

Some conclusions may be attempted. First, the fact that girls in all-girl schools are significantly less prone to making prejudicial assertions seems to indicate that these schools, particularly at the secondary level, do make a real effort to teach a Christian social ethic. Everything we have learned about the teaching of religion in these schools reinforces that indication. But when the schools come squarely up against strongly entrenched family bias rooted in occupational and ethnic concerns, they confront a formidable counterforce. Are parents likely to feel, when they think of "practical life," that the teacher, especially the teaching religious, lacks experience or lives in an ivory tower? As we shall see the Notre Dame Study skirted fringes of this problem through its inquiry into "parental expectations."

A broader question emerges and it is one which has always come to the fore when there has been discussion of Catholic education. Does this education isolate young Catholics from the total American community and so keep on immuring them in what has been called their "ghetto"? At this point I think one must carefully distinguish two trends which run through the vast amount of writing which has been done about enclaves in American society. Here of course the matter can be discussed only in the most tentative way. The first "ghetto" is manifestly religious in character. The second is ethnic. Probably only one who has lived in both for a good while can see where the two have coincided and where they have not. The great Catholic movements to the United States from Europe, whether planned or not, differed in important ways from the Anglo-Saxon quest for Tocqueville's new social and political order. They moved from an old world where the peasantry and (until a relatively recent date) urban workers were solidly identified with a traditional commitment to the Catholic life. The British Crown had tried in every possible way to tear the Irish loose from their religious and cultural moorings. In Germany the Reformation had erected a solid wall between Catholics and Lutherans, even though that wall zigzagged erratically in the geographical sense, because of the maxim that the ruler of each princedom was to decide what its religion would be. The Pole was only too aware of the pressure which had come from Prussia and Russia alike. As a result every effort was made by immigrant groups, and it was eminently natural that it should be made, to keep the religious commitment alive in this country as well.

This situation has led to a great deal of discussion of, as well as much adverse comment on, what is called "dominant Irish Catholicism" in the United States. This does not mean a Catholicism faithful to the mores of the Irish people, but rather one which came into being as a necessary consequence of the hostile, or at least unsympathetic, environment in the New World. It was characterized by a sentimental clericalism, which received its warmest praise in the movie *Going My Way*, and its mordant criticism is a sheaf of books and essays by now generally forgotten writers like Francis Sugrue and Father Francis Whelan. It seems to have propelled Paul Blanshard into his crusade against the Church, and (in quite a different mode) given F. Scott Fitzgerald something to write about. Yet these diatribes seem to be appropriate only for the eastern seaboard, especially New England, where, for the most part, the Irish ethnic minority coincided with the Catholic religious minority. It was a dual minority feeling which created the simple "obedience Catholicism," against which everyone is now in revolt. In an earlier time the simpler the "faith" became in the phrasing, the more satisfactorily orthodox it seemed. One might grumble about a bishop who ruled clergy and laity with an iron hand guided by a closed mind, but even critics as distinguished as Orestes Brownson had no mass appeal.

Irish Catholicism on the east coast of the Republic sometimes walked on sinister political streets. The fault lies only partly with it, but I shall not belabor the point. Often enough the clergy of those areas grossly misused their ties with the politicians and the police, and as a result sometimes came pretty close to the nadir of social ethics. But to hold that this is all there is to say about Irish Catholicism in this country is shockingly unfair. Though the eastern landscape may seem crowded with diverse mayors of Jersey City, Boston, and New York, the great public figures of the Middle West have been Senator Thomas Walsh, almost puritanically honest, and, later on, Senator Eugene McCarthy, a distinguished political scientist. This region also knew great prelates like Archbishop Ireland and Archbishop Keane, and Bishop Fitzgerald of Little Rock, Arkansas, the lone American dissenter at the First Vatican Council.

Nor, with due apologies to Monsignor John Tracy Ellis, were Irish Catholics without scholars. There were reputable historians like John Gilmary Shea and Patrick Healy (of the Catholic University of America), and their tradition has been carried by Father Thomas McAvoy, Matthew Fitzsimons, and others into our time. Monsignor John A. Ryan was a good economist, as well as a moral theologian. Wherever Irish Catholicism in the United States emancipated itself from Eastern Seaboard complexes, it showed itself capable of scholarship, though this did not often enough include the natural sciences. But here the fault lay just as much with the dominant Protestant majority as it did with the struggling masses of Irish Catholics. A handful of great humanists, like Harvard's Grandgent and Babbitt, Columbia's Fletcher, and Yale's Karl Young, were deeply aware of the riches of the Catholic tradition. But of most of the faculties at this time, it could be said that "their neckbands were their horizons." Ludwig Lewisohn's *Upstream* continues to have documentary value as an angry tirade by a young Jewish scholar about the discriminatory practices of which he was a victim. Many a young Catholic scholar could have given a similar account of his experience. Today that is all over and done with. But when one evaluates American-Irish Catholicism, one should not ignore this background.

Let us now consider two instances in which ethnic and religious "ghettos" did not coincide. The first example is that of the Maryland Catholics for whom no ethnic enclave existed. When *Commonweal* was founded in 1924, it was largely supported by what were then called the Calvert Associates. Not all were descended from the founders of the Maryland colony, but they symbolized a Catholicism which was in every respect socially acceptable. Father John LaFarge entered and survived Harvard College with no affront to his dignity. Father T. Lawrason Riggs, whose legacy to Yale is the beautiful St. Thomas More Chapel, was a man of Old Eli to the very core of his being. Whether these men were conscious even of membership in a Catholic enclave is questionable. Nobody, not even the most rabid critics of the Catholic Church, could entertain a doubt that they were the descendants of good families, and one bowed discreetly when they entered the room. The major purpose of the early *Commonweal* was not to break down ethnic barriers but to make it possible for Catholics to enter into a vigorous participation in American cultural life.

The second example is that of the Italian immigration. The men and women who came from Sicily and the Italian mainland were emotionally, intellectually, and socially distinct as soon as they got off the ships. But the identification of the Italian with any sort of religious ghetto was tenuous, indeed. He had his brand of Catholicism, of course, but his problem was assuredly not one of being immured in a *religious* ghetto. One of the major tasks assigned to the Irish clergy on the Atlantic seacoast was to find a way of salvaging the identification of the Italian minority with the Church. Somehow the Italian came through. Isolation in a religious ghetto was not a difficulty for the German minority either, except to a certain extent in terms of the German group itself as a whole. Intellectual and journalistic leadership was often assumed by the Liberals of 1848; and the German immigrant group was not homogenous in a religious sense. There were, for example, large numbers of Lutherans and Mennonites. The Italian, for his part, had to rise above dominant clichés concerning his ethnic singularity.

At any rate, I would draw the conclusion, admittedly based on experience and not on rigorous attitude-studies, that in the story of American Catholicism ethnic solidarity has played a much greater role, in so far as intergroup relations are concerned, than has religious commitment. This commitment dictated fidelity in church attendance, the quest for sacramental grace, respect for the clergy, and acceptance of the Catholic school. Ethnic solidarity, however, has often served to identify Catholicism with moral attitudes relatively alien to the social teaching of the Church. Now that the lines of ethnic cleavage are dissolving, one of the principal questions to be put to Catholic education during the second half of the twentieth century is this: Can the policy of isolating young people who attend the schools it operates provide for these young people an opportunity to gain sufficient personal insight into the mores of other religious, social, and ethnic groups to eliminate prejudice?

There was one qualifying fact established by the Notre Dame Study which seems of special interest here. I shall quote the language of the report:

The more the respondents attend Mass, the less prejudice do they express. If they are not regular in their attendance 31 per cent reject Negro inferiority; if they are regular in Mass attendance the percentage rises to 44 per cent. If they attend more often than they are obliged to, it rises again to 49 per cent. Those who accept Negro inferiority drop from 21 per cent of the irregular attenders to 9 per cent of the regular attenders, to 6 per cent for frequent attenders.[*]

In other words, "the life of prayer" seems to make a difference. Perhaps if Protestants and Jews were to analyze the attitudes of their young people similar responses would be obtained. But these are the blessed, in terms of the scriptural beatitudes. They are the source of the Church's inner life. Into them, no matter if their daily lives be spent in the office or the workshop, has been breathed the true spirit of Christianity, for the healing of themselves and the world. Perhaps it is for their sake that Catholic education exists. Paradoxically, this is what Catholic education must never say about itself—for, in finding this life, it would lose it.

* *Ibid.*, p. 198.

Influence on Sexual Mores

The Notre Dame findings on social behavior do not seem to be particularly significant in terms of Catholic-school influence except when they indicate deviation from accepted national or ethnic norms. Attitudes in the realm of sexual behavior now seem to be far more permissive among Catholics in the United States than used to be the case. This does not mean, as has been indicated earlier, that young people are more wicked, or that their morals have improved. But it seems very probable that traditional ethnic standards for youth behavior are being superseded by new nationally accepted patterns. In this highly important area of growth and development children tend to wish to be like other children. Undoubtedly the daughters in some ethnic groups used to be quite restricted in terms of dating and courting. Perhaps a few still are, but very probably these ties are losing their strength.

The study posed several sets of questions.* The first had to do with mixed marriage. Children in both elementary and secondary schools were asked (the language of the item has been revamped):

Will the person you love and marry have to be a Catholic?
Will he or she most likely be a Catholic?
Do you intend to marry?
Though you would like to marry a Catholic, would you marry a
   non-Catholic?
Does religion make any difference when you think of marriage?

A digest of answers reveals:

23 per cent responded affirmatively to the first question.
25 per cent responded affirmatively to the second question.
12 per cent responded negatively to the third question.

* Ibid., pp. 207 ff.

36 per cent responded affirmatively to the fourth question.
44 per cent responded affirmatively to the fifth question.

The analysis of the data showed about the same deviations that were noted in connection with queries about prejudice. That is, the all-girl schools reported the highest rate of commitment against mixed marriage (as seen by combining the responses to the first and second questions), while all-boy-school boys reported the lowest rate (63 per cent against 45 per cent). Boys and girls in coeducational schools took about the same view of the situation (55 per cent and 56 per cent respectively, thus indicating incidentally that in-school sex attraction was not especially evident). But some rather interesting data emerged. High school students proved more committed to marrying a Catholic than elementary school pupils. Young people with parents further up the social ladder were somewhat more tolerant of mixed marriage than were those with parents further down the scale, and those whose religious life was most intense seldom reported that they were indifferent to the religion of their partner in marriage. In short, the influence of the Catholic school in maintaining religious group solidarity is marked, but by no means as great as might perhaps have been anticipated.

A number of interesting questions present themselves, but the data supplied do not suffice to indicate that answers to them can be found with any ease. To what extent do young people belonging to certain ethnic groups desire to marry outside these groups? If an appreciable number do so desire, may not a non-Catholic spouse appear to be a way of satisfying that desire? Does the marriage picture of older sisters and brothers, or indeed of the parental home itself, affect the outlook of children in Catholic schools? Does the old assumption that opposites attract play a role here? Finally one may note that although for the most part the study's data-collecting was done prior to the Second Vatican Council, which clearly laid less stress on the ban against mixed marriage than had been traditional, a rather marked change in the general American Catholic outlook may well have been taking place.

In order to find out at least a little about what kind of mate young people considered desirable, a question was asked which may be presented as follows:

> Should he be a "good provider" or she "a good household manager?"
> Should the partner be one with a pleasing personality?
> A morally good person?
> One who loves children?
> A deeply spiritual person?

The answers are summarized in the study as follows:

	Very important	Fairly important	Slightly important	Not important
A good provider or manager	62.5%	29.1%	3.8%	1.70%
Pleasing personality	73.5%	23.1%	1.5%	.30%
Morally good person	82.3%	13.7%	1.2%	.45%
Lover of children	79.5%	15.3%	1.8%	.76%
Deeply spiritual	36.5%	42.9%	9.1%	3.90%

As usual, girls, at the high school level particularly, rated each of the qualities higher than did the corresponding group of boys. Thus 42 per cent of the girls wanted a husband who was deeply spiritual, while only 27 per cent of the boys wanted deeply spiritual wives. The category "not important" may perhaps be dismissed because in all groups there are some perennial dissenters. Unfortunately the questionnaire did not include a query as to whether the spouse should be handsome or beautiful. It would have been interesting to analyze the opinions of this age group. In general nothing very startling was uncovered. The comment made in the study may be cited:

It is apparent that while morality in a spouse is considered highly desirable by all groups, spirituality is relatively less so. The essential family values of love of children and pleasant personality are high-lighted, while the skills of bringing in a good income or being an efficient manager of a household are considered relatively less important. It is to be noted that in this type of question one alternative received fewer "very important" designations than others. That fact does not necessarily imply rejection of the value of that alternative, but only rates it less in comparison with other alternatives. In this case, we would not be justified in concluding that deep spirituality is not valued by the respondents, particularly since 43 per cent of the respondents designated deep spirituality "fairly important." On another question students were asked if they thought money and the things money can buy are likely to be harmful to one's religious and spiritual life, and a measure of their evaluation of the spiritual against the material can be gleaned from the fact that two-thirds of them agreed, either strongly or somewhat, that such a danger really exists.*

A third question was concerned with the now widely discussed practice of "going steady" and an inquiry was made at the eighth-grade level of the elementary school and the twelfth-grade level of the high school. Since the eighth grade is from this point of view relatively inconsequential, we shall report here only on the data for the high school. Of the girls, 32 per cent said that they "went steady" with one boy, while 35 per cent of the boys said they sought the company of one girl exclusively. The analysis of these data produced some interesting cross-cultural results:

Percentages going steady decrease as fathers' total years of schooling increase. Thus when the fathers had only 1–7 years of schooling 26 per cent of the children report going steady; if the fathers had 17 years or more the percentage drops to 17 per cent. When the years of the Catholic education of the fathers are considered, the trend is the same, declining from 23 per cent of those whose fathers had no

* Ibid., pp. 212–213.

Catholic schooling to 14 per cent of those whose fathers had 17 years or more years.

Similarly, mothers' total schooling correlates negatively with children's steady dating, percentages dropping from 28 per cent to 16 per cent as mothers' years of schooling increase. Catholic education of mothers likewise discloses a negative relationship, percentages falling from 22 per cent to 16 per cent. Clearly the fact of either parent's having been educated under Catholic auspices tends to keep the rate of going steady moderately lower among their offspring. Children of parents who have had some college education go steady in lesser proportions than do the children of parents who have none. And the impact of college education tends to reduce steady dating slightly more if the background is that of Catholic institutions.

Steady dating is related negatively to associating chiefly with friends in Catholic schools: 21 per cent of the respondents go steady in such a case, but of the students who say most of their friends do not attend Catholic schools, 26 per cent report going steady. If half their friends attend Catholic schools, 22 per cent go steady.

Young people who go steady and who are thinking seriously of marrying soon would not be expected to plan more Catholic (or any) education, and it is therefore an expected finding that those who plan more Catholic education go steady 17 per cent less than do those who are not planning to continue their Catholic schooling (14 per cent compared to 31 per cent). If they are uncertain about future educational plans their rate of going steady reaches an intermediate position at 26 per cent.*

The student-attitude questionnaire also examined opinion on the popular theme of "necking and petting." Nothing terribly interesting was uncovered. In all-girl high schools, 67 per cent of the girls "strongly disapproved" of a statement that these practices are not objectionable because they are "just a part of growing up" while

* Ibid., pp. 214–215.

only 4 per cent of boys in all-boy high schools did. The boys doubtless were professing their "manliness." In coeducational high schools
30 per cent of the boys "strongly objected," as did 55 per cent of
the girls. We still know too little about coeducation in general to
justify any definitive pronouncements on the subject. But one might
propose for investigation, on the basis of the data given, whether
the conventional Catholic commitment to separate schools for boys
and girls is as justified in American society as has been assumed.

The question previously posed—whether ethnic patterns of sex
behavior are being superseded by new nationally accepted patterns—
is also not cleared up by this part of the Notre Dame inquiry. One
is inclined to think that concerns which are definitely religious play
a part, though it is impossible to adduce reliable evidence about
them. For instance, in view of the fact that so many vocations to
the religious life are developed in Catholic schools, it is probable
enough that many young people, naturally idealistic, consider at
some length whether they should not choose this calling. In all
forms of corporate Christianity, the ministry best expresses self-
abnegation for the sake of others. Young Protestants who accept
this framework are apt to be "cleaner" in terms of moral behavior than are those who do not. But the great difference between them
and young Catholics is that the "counsels of perfection" by which religious orders and the priesthood are governed include celibacy. It
would therefore seem entirely plausible to say that if the idea of a
religious vocation is entertained by a boy or girl, it can strongly
affect his or her attitudes. Thus one may perhaps conclude that in
Catholic education partially surviving ethnic attitudes toward sex
may coincide with religiously motivated orientations.

A final problem raised by the study is of genuine significance and
interest. It read as follows: "Sometimes I am uncertain as to what
the Catholic Church teaches about what is right and wrong in behavior." The answers uncovered a great deal of bewilderment.
Granted that the word "sometimes" provides an escape-hatch in

both directions, nevertheless it is most interesting to discover that
62 per cent of all high school students answered in the affirmative,
while the negative vote was 33.3 per cent (the uncertain youngsters
constitute the difference). The study analyst practically ran out of
breath at this point, but obviously from an educational point of
view this is the most significant color in the whole spectrum.

We should keep in mind that the question was asked before the
impact of the Second Vatican Council could be felt in the schools.
Nevertheless, young people must already have sensed marked differences of opinion among their teachers on a variety of issues. Both
conservatives and liberals of the older generation, in the school and
the home, were likely to suggest an identification of their views with
the teachings of the Church. For many years the ultra-conservative
Catholic citizen framed Pope Pius IX's Syllabus and hung it in his
living room, together with utterances by admired members of the
hierarchy. Liberals had their own arsenal of official dicta. While
there was never any doubt about the Ten Commandments and the
major laws of the Church, one can be fairly certain that the students
at St. Richard's High School listened on many an occasion to cham-
pions of quite antagonistic views, each sure that the Church—the
consensus fidelium—was on their side. Often the contest was uneven. While the "liberals" may sometimes have too rashly identified
themselves with wisdom and social morality, it was the "conservative" who hankered after censorship and often enough resorted to
it. Today there is a different story to tell. We have all apparently
become so ecumenical that religious discussion, even inter-religious
discussion, is in some danger of becoming an endless repetition of
Glory, Glory, Hallelujah. Perhaps we should remind ourselves occasionally of the past in order to be prepared for what the future
may again become. For instance, Father Roberto Tucci, S.J., the
present editor of *Civiltà Cattolica*, Rome's Jesuit periodical, is a
very intelligent and persuasive "liberal." One hopes that his pre-
decessors are enjoying the Beatific Vision and are therefore aloof

from the old, unhappy concerns of mortal man. For if perchance they alighted on earth and read a couple of the current issues, they would certainly be knocking on the doors of whatever Sacred Congregations were functioning. And we all know that their semblances still exist in the United States.

When, therefore, one finds that 33.3 per cent of the young people —mostly girls—who commented on the problem presented to them encountered no difficulties, one is led to entertain certain doubts about the heterogeneity of the feminine mind. Perhaps a greater measure of agreement existed in their schools than could have been found elsewhere. Certainly in general, at least prior to the final session of the Council, many opinions about social and economic problems had tough sledding in Catholic circles. *Mater et Magistra* and *Pacem in terris*, the great encyclicals of Pope John XXIII, induced shock in various segments of the American Catholic population, as have some of the encyclicals of Paul VI. That the young ladies in selected schools were immune to the excitement is one of the marvels of the time.

Pupil and Parental Opinions

While they were studying thirteen dioceses in depth, the directors asked slightly fewer than 15,000 elementary-and secondary-school youngsters what they believed was happening to them in schools at the eighth- and twelfth-grade levels. They were instructed to fill out a "Pupil Opinionnaire." The drift of the inquiry was to obtain answers to two basic questions: what were their Catholic schools hoping and trying to do; and how well were they succeeding? Those who designed the "instrument" had some fairly clear notions as to what they expected to find, and by and large they were not mistaken. For instance, they believed that most youngsters would think that the school's principal task was to provide religious and moral education. This proved to be correct.

Here no more will be attempted than to explore the survey and the findings in a quite summary fashion. Three sets of questions were asked about educational objectives:

1. Suppose someone were to ask you: Why are you going to a Catholic school?" Think for a moment and then rank in the order of importance your reasons, not those of your parents or teachers. Mark the most important reason (1), the next important (2), and so on. Assign all five ranks.
   (a) To obtain a superior training in school subjects
   (b) To develop a strong moral character based on religious principles
   (c) To form a group of true friends
   (d) To prepare myself for being a good citizen
   (e) To become a patriotic American citizen

2. Rank in the order of importance . . . the advantages you hope to receive from your Catholic schooling. Assign all five ranks.
   (a) Group of loyal friends and companions
   (b) A practical knowledge and appreciation of my duties as a Catholic
   (c) A clear understanding of the various subjects I have studied
   (d) A deep devotion to my country and a knowledge of my American heritage
   (e) The knowledge and ability to make a good living

3. Different people strive for different things. Here are some of the things that you have probably thought about. Among the things you strive for during your school days, just how important are each of these? Rank from 1 to 5.
   (a) Living up to my religious ideals
   (b) Becoming a better American citizen
   (c) Preparing myself to make a living

(d) Learning as much as possible in school

(e) Being accepted and liked by other students

Probing into the pupil's opinion as to how well the school was helping him to attain these objectives, the questionnaire likewise posed three principal queries:

1. In addition to "regular school subjects," Catholic schools also give special instruction in the teachings and practices of the Catholic religion. As you look back over your years in a Catholic school, *how would you describe the religious instruction you have received?* Choose one.

(a) Superior

(b) Very good, but could be better

(c) Average

(d) Below average

(e) Poor

2. You are often asked by friends or relatives how you are doing in school. Suppose, instead, they asked you how well your teachers are doing in helping you to learn. Considering your present class as a whole, *how well do you think the religious (priests, brothers, sisters) who have taught your class have succeeded in teaching you the regular school subjects?*

(a) Exceptionally well

(b) Very well, but could be better

(c) Moderately well

(d) Only fairly well

(e) Poorly

3. In addition to religious teachers, most Catholic schools now have lay teachers as members of the Faculty. Considering your present class as a whole, *how well do you think the lay teachers have succeeded in teaching the regular school subjects?* •

• *Ibid.*, pp. 228–242.

Other questions were asked, the most important having to do with whether, if the pupil were free to choose, he or she would elect to attend a Catholic school; and with parental influences and attitudes. The pupils were also asked to rate themselves academically, thus permitting the designer of the test to correlate the pupil's opinion with his school status. Of course a great many other questions could have been asked, as the study directors were well aware. We have no student opinions on library resources, recreational programs, and similar matters. Yet some indication as to overall school atmosphere does appear.

What did students think of the objectives of the schools they were attending, as correlated with their views of desirable personal goals? First place was assigned to religion and morality by 60.5 per cent. Students who assigned second place to religion and morality brought the total to more than 75 per cent. As a result no other objectives or goals had a chance to win out in this popularity contest. Preparation for making a living and academic prowess received almost equal endorsement. Citizenship captured only 6 per cent of the first-place votes. If one looks at the last-place choices, much the same pattern emerges, though there are some differentiations. Six per cent of those interviewed ranked religion and morals last, while "making friends" was named most frequently in this category.

How successful did young people think their schools were in helping them to reach these goals? In so far as religion and morals are concerned, the response reveals nothing very unlike the results of other inquiries. Girls are more enthusiastic than are boys, but even their opinion of accomplishment becomes less favorable as they move through high school. The boys, however, refuse, as the study report indicates, to take a rosy view of what is happening unless they are very good students. No significant difference in the trend of opinion is revealed when academic intellectual objectives are appraised.

Where teachers are concerned the level of dissatisfaction is not very high, though again it is higher during the high-school years. According to the study report, lay teachers on the whole fare less well than do religious, but the difference is not as great as might have been supposed. What is of considerable interest is the fact that girls in all-girl high schools hold both groups of teachers in much greater esteem than do students in any other schools, including girls in coeducational high schools. This is, as the study analyst indicates, a result which does perhaps indicate that the sexually segregated high school may have a certain advantage in terms of relationships between students and teachers. Once again, pupils who rated themselves high academically tended also to be most appreciative of the instruction given.

But what is missing from all this, and would be most useful, is information concerning the attitudes of young people who have either been transferred from Catholic schools or public schools, or who have been dropped. This might above all provide a basis of sorts from which to approach the problem of guidance in Catholic schools. That counseling has improved considerably of late is widely reported to be a fact, though there can be little doubt that a great deal remains to be done. A skillful sampling of the opinions of young people whose experience in Catholic schools has been truncated or unsatisfactory might well provide some insight into ways in which improvement could be effected.

The Notre Dame Study also asked parents a variety of questions about what they expected of the schools, and what they thought had been done to meet these expectations. Only a scholarly monograph can provide an adequate analysis of the responses and one may hope that such a volume can be published eventually. The terse comment which follows offers little more than a hint as to what has been going on in parents' minds. What was the method used? First, group interviews with parents were conducted. Second, to quote the language of the report, a larger group of parents of first, eighth and twelfth grade students were mailed an open-ended,

non-directional questionnaire asking their reasons for choosing a
Catholic school for their children."• The number of documents
returned was 24,502. The design and the analysis were largely the
work of a sociologist, Donald M. Barrett, so that both data and
deductions are more technically sociological in character than are
those in any other part of the report. It is therefore now possible
to correlate attitudes toward Catholic schools with parental social
status, education, and religion. For instance, the responses showed
that 14 per cent of the families reporting represented mixed marriages, whereas the nationwide percentage is held to be more than
20 per cent. Ethnic backgrounds are likewise shown to have a significant bearing on whether parents desire Catholic education for
their children.

Parental expectations were summarized under six group headings:
religious virtues, personal virtues, social virtues, academic goals,
school-operation goals, and practical goals. Those interrogated were
not, however, aware of these groupings. In so far as religious expectations were concerned, nearly all Catholic parents agreed that
teaching children to know about God, Christ, and the Church was
important, and the majority expressed the conviction that the
schools were doing this well. They were less inclined to think that
"only religious teachers (sisters, priests)" should constitute the
staff. Nevertheless 40.3 per cent said this was "most" or "very"
important. A measure of reluctance to have their children live in a
strictly Catholic social milieu is reflected in the fact that 24.3 per
cent said giving "children Catholic friends and a good example" had
little or no importance, although a somewhat larger number indicated that they thought the schools met with success. The least
enthusiasm was shown for fostering "vocations to be priests, sisters
or brothers," but very few (2 per cent) expressed a negative verdict.
It should be added that although real differences of opinion on these
matters exist between Catholic and non-Catholic parents, they do

• *Ibid.*, pp. 255–256.

not appear to be as great as might have been thought, thus pointing to a substantial amount of parental harmony.

In the social virtues category, considerably less of a commitment was manifested. Only two of the six goals that parents were asked to comment on obtained a majority vote as being "most important" —that of making children good citizens of the United States, and that of training them "in respect for persons and property" (the second ranked higher than the first, indicating perhaps that some parents think in concrete rather than abstract terms). The goal described as teaching "children to help others in foreign countries" kindled little rapture in parental breasts. Almost three times as many Catholic parents attributed to this some, little, or no importance as attributed "most" importance. In estimating the success of the school in meeting this goal a large number of parents—nearly 20 per cent of Catholics and almost 30 per cent of the non-Catholics— professed ignorance of what the schools were trying to teach in this respect, indicating clearly that there was little talk about the matter at the fireside. Interestingly enough the question whether the schools should "teach children to get along with others such as Jews" was answered "most" affirmatively by a majority of non-Catholic parents (50.4 per cent) while 46.8 per cent of Catholic parents did so, but the small "no importance" vote was equal (0.9 per cent). The number of the ultra-prejudiced would therefore appear to be small. Here again a comparatively large number of parents were unaware of what the schools were teaching about the matter, if anything. Oddly enough, when seen in the light of much recent Catholic self-criticism, a considerably larger percentage of Catholic than of non-Catholic parents (49.6 per cent and 41.2 per cent respectively) attached most importance to the role of the schools in producing "leaders for our nation and communities," and also expressed more doubts about the success of the schools in this respect, which a relatively large number felt was only moderate (36.1 per cent and 31.4 per cent respectively).

In terms of "practical expectations" the six hypothetical goals suggested were these:

1. Train children for good jobs when they grow up
2. Not be expensive for Catholic parents
3. Get help from parents when needed
4. Get more money from the federal government
5. Have space for all Catholic children
6. Help parents control dating of children

In no case did a majority of parents assign "most importance" to one of these goals. The greatest acclaim was given to having "space for all Catholic children," and the least support was secured for the idea that the schools might help "parents control dating of children." Nevertheless 56.7 per cent thought that the schools had been of at least some help in dealing with the last-mentioned thorny problem. There was strong sentiment, of course, for securing more money from the federal government, but it was expressed more moderately than one might have supposed. It must be borne in mind, however, that the questionnaire antedated the Education Act of 1965. The parents were also quite realistic about the role of the school in training children for good jobs when they grew up.

What a child learns in school is naturally of signal interest to parents, and these Catholic parents do not differ notably from parents generally in their ideas of what is most or very important. Thus priority was attached to reading and writing "clearly and well" (94.4 per cent) and to being "proficient in arithmetic and science" (86.7 per cent). Reading and writing were taught excellently or very well in the opinion of 71.1 per cent of the parents, while 53.8 per cent had similar opinions concerning mathematics and science. In view of the waves of criticism to which all schools in the United States were subjected at the time, these evaluations should be encouraging to the schools. "History and today's social problems" seemed highly or very important to 87.3 per cent of the parents, and 49.2 per cent were satisfied with the school's achievement in these areas. "Music and the arts," however, seemed important to only 46.1 per cent of the parents, and a mere 29.8 per cent thought that the schools accomplished anything notable in this field considering the traditional view that teaching sisters retain some of the old-time finishing-school attitude toward piano-playing, painting, and so forth, the verdict is somewhat surprising.

The questionnaire listed as "personal virtue expectations" two that would have delighted the soul of Thomas Carlyle: training in "self-discipline and hard work," and training children to be "honest, truthful and moral." The third would have brought a nod of approval from John Henry Cardinal Newman: "teaching children to think for themselves." There was virtual unanimity of approval of these goals, though "discipline and hard work" lagged a little behind the others. Some parents doubtless had seen prototypes of Shakespeare's young scholar, "creeping like a snail unwillingly to school." There was a general feeling that Catholic schools helped develop a sense of honesty, truth, and morality, though a small number of dissenters seemed to indicate that a few Huckleberry Finns were still about. A favorable vote was also cast for the schools in terms of self-discipline and hard work (61.8 per cent). But although 95.9 per cent of Catholic parents assigned high importance to teaching children to think for themselves, only 50.3 per cent found that the schools were signally or very successful in doing so. In this respect they differed hardly at all from non-Catholic parents who responded (50 per cent).

The segment of the inquiry labeled "School Operation Expectations" elicited the most diversity of critical opinion, as was anticipated in view of the problem areas alluded to. Indeed the tables in the Notre Dame report which summarize responses in this category are very revealing indexes of what are generally held to be the major weaknesses of Catholic schools. Questions were asked concerning the importance of providing well-qualified teachers, both religious and lay. While 63 per cent of the parents interviewed indicated that they thought a high degree of success was being achieved in so far as teaching sisters, brothers, and priests were concerned, only 45 per cent felt the same way about lay teachers. The negative votes are even more revealing: 4.7 per cent took the view that little or no progress had been made toward finding able teaching religious, but 13.7 per cent felt that way about lay teachers. On the widely discussed question of class size—that is, large classes in single rooms—77 per cent of the respondents felt this was an important matter, but only 23 per cent felt that the schools were succeeding in this respect. Should physical fitness programs for boys and girls be offered? Although 76 per cent of the parents were strongly in favor, only 24 per cent believed that the schools were significantly successful in this respect. Even more indicative of weakness, it would seem, was the verdict on whether adequate assistance was being given to gifted and slow-learning pupils; 87 per cent thought this highly important, but only 29 per cent were well satisfied with what their schools were doing, and 20 per cent felt that this was an area of activity badly in need of improvement. On the other hand, 86.4 per cent felt that the schools should prepare children for college, and 61.6 per cent felt they were very successful in doing so.

The Notre Dame Study indicated that younger parents who have received comparatively more "total and Catholic education" and whose social status is relatively higher tended to be more critical of school performance than other parents. Almost every spot check made under other auspices and so far reported affirms this view. The group to which such parents belong senses the competitive value of education in the society which we now all share. Whereas the majority of fathers and mothers of the "pre-education-explosion" days held simpler views of intellectual training and even tended to believe that above all a deeply inculcated respect for religious faith and good morals was necessary, those of the new generation have added insistence upon adequate academic standards. As the report indicates, they retain a strong commitment to the Church, and for that reason prefer Catholic education for their children. But they will no longer support it strongly if they feel that their children will be, intellectually speaking, at a disadvantage.

6
The Financing of Catholic Schools

Basic Problems

Any serious observer of Catholic education will conclude sooner or later that many, probably most, of its *special* problems have something to do with money. One must add at once that these problems are not of the same dimension as the crucial difficulties faced by American education in general. These latter difficulties are first administrative and then personal, in the sense that the school, college, or university depends on how well it establishes the right relationship between the generations, that is, between the teacher-scholar and the student. As a necessary prelude to the discussion of finance, I shall present some rather tentative views on these two difficulties.

It is becoming harder and harder to find and retain school superintendents, college presidents, and chief executives of universities. A recent survey (1966) found 174 posts as college and university presidents had not been filled, although in some cases the search had gone on for more than a year. Why? Without passing judgment, we may use the widely advertised situations arising in St. John's University, Brooklyn, and the City University of New York as examples. The first had grown very rapidly, under the pressure of a metropolitan college-bound population of quite unprecedented size. It had developed two campuses, each at some distance from the other. As a result, it could not easily do several things which are requisite if peace and harmony are to be achieved in the academic kingdom. Recruiting and giving status to the large number of instructors who were to be employed was not an easy task. It also became much more difficult to give advanced specialized studies the separate identity and prestige which they needed in order to achieve their purpose. And finally, it grew harder and harder to put into words a philosophy of education and a definition of faculty autonomy which would be widely found convincing.

In the case of the City University, there already existed a core of four long-established colleges of high academic quality and good *esprit de corps* resulting in large part from a tradition of democratic orientation. Each of the four had, through a consensus of the view of the faculty and the administration developed its own special character. Hunter College, for example, was not like Brooklyn College, although both were institutions of quality of which their faculty and their students could legitimately be proud. Each of the four had a very sizable enrollment, not only of regularly matriculated students but of those, young and old, who attended special evening courses. With this structure there were gradually associated newly created two-year colleges, designed to provide either terminal instruction or preparation for admission with advanced standing to the four-year institutions. Even more important was the fact that, owing initially to an unprecedented demand for teachers in the schools of the city and its suburbs, a five-year program leading to the master's degree rapidly became a routine part of the enterprise. This was not easily managed.

Rather suddenly, two broad additional changes were decided

upon. The undergraduate student enrollment was increased by lowering the admissions requirements, taxing the physical plant to the limit of its capacity. The second change was the establishment of a graduate school, and creating a university in the accepted sense of the term, as a separate academic entity, served at least initially by a staff which had been siphoned off from the colleges. It is no wonder that in the final state of the development, nerves should have been frayed. Living through the complete transformation of an educational system is not too difficult provided that enough time is allowed. But if change comes rushing in like a wind from Lake Michigan, it will bowl people over. And so it did, at least temporarily, in New York.

These two situations may be fairly remote from the experience of smaller colleges and universities, but in varying ways these also have to wrestle with serious problems of growth. The City University in New York has financial problems, of course. But it resources are limited in a way which the small institution can hardly understand, for the question always asked by the City University (or its counterparts elsewhere) is *how much support can we obtain for the added obligations we are expected to assume?* The resources needed for what has *not* been added are available. The average small college is in a totally different position, particularly if it is conducted under denominational, and therefore private, auspices. It does not actually have money enough to safeguard its ongoing operations. There is usually no endowment to speak of, and such hat-passing as it can manage postpones rather than disposes of problems of solvency. Tuition is one golden egg, other charges another; and if the college can husband these frugally by limiting the number of course offerings, by adding an hour or two to teaching schedules, and by placing just a few more students in each class, it can cut its cost per student down to a point at which it need not be too fearful of being raided by more affluent institutions. It has also been able to borrow money cheaply from the government in order to erect additional buildings to take care of additional students. The salaries paid to certain professors may even be competitive, provided they are not particularly research-minded and do not object strenuously to their teaching loads. The basic requirements of university life cannot of course be met. The "best scholars" will not be found on such campuses, and if either the economy or the college-population curve were to drift downward, skimping and perhaps catastrophe would be at hand.

Nevertheless, it is probably correct to say that, provided the student body is not as exacting as perhaps it should be in terms of intellectual stimulation to cope with the "knowledge explosion," the small college may establish a better intergeneration relationship than do the larger institutions. This the University of California may have proved, though the forces at work in Berkeley are too complex to be brought under a single formula. If the function of the scholar is conceived of as being as free as possible from association with students so that he may devote virtually the whole of his time to research, it is clear that young and old will have relatively little opportunity to meet. As a matter of fact, in many an instance where the contemporary university has fully imposed its will on the college, the "teacher" in the traditional sense of the term has become hard to find.

Catholic higher education is now deeply involved in a state of transition. On the one hand, the best of the universities it sponsors must of necessity strive to acquire the status of their illustrious secular contemporaries. For these possess the keys to research methodology and success; and unless a Catholic university can find out how to get those keys for itself there is hardly a chance in the world that it can attract students wishing to become full-fledged scholars —unless it pretends to be able to do what it cannot do. It is caught in a frightening dilemma; either it must profess to be something it has not a chance of being, or it must succeed in its quest of financial support, for faculty, and for the most gifted students. The average small college, however, does not face that kind of challenge. It may contentedly say that it is serving the "average" young man or woman as well as anyone, doing the job from an intellectual point of view while broadening his outlook and preparing him for citizenship. Provided it is actually doing this, and provided that it does not claim to be doing more, it owes no one an apology. But these are big "ifs"; they cannot be disposed of by saying that the religious purpose of the Catholic is so august that little else matters. Taking up again in terms of finance a point discussed previously, the often repeated statement that a multiplication of colleges means undue dispersal of resources is open to serious question. As a matter of fact in this respect Catholics have not differed from Protestants. Indiana, for example, is dotted with colleges operated by denominations and some of them are very good. The only non-state university in the area except Notre Dame is Valparaiso, a Lutheran establishment of high quality. Nor does the argument that Protestants are necessarily more diverse in terms of commitment seem too effective. Catholic religious communities differ, too.

The threat to the financial stability of all such colleges is of recent origin; it arose when the state universities began to create affiliated colleges both to solve the problem of congestion in the central establishment, and to make education more economical for students who could live at home. To point this out does not mean that the affiliated colleges should not have been established. Separation of Church and State being the doctrine so rigidly adhered to in the United States, no other solution was possible. It may be that New York State, which has recently established a commission to deal with the matter, will take steps to effect a measure of equal treatment for public and private colleges, but no solution of the problem can be expected for some time even there. "Dispersal of resources," is, however, no different when it takes place under public auspices than when the auspices are private.

Concerning elementary and secondary education, the Notre Dame Study was not able to concern itself specifically with the problem of school finance, but it could not avoid encountering aspects of that problem. As a result the discussion which follows is not without some empirical foundation. Although discussion of parochial schools usually gets round to wondering how much state or federal aid can be obtained for their support, no one seems to have very solid information about what their financial situation actually is. The average teacher, religious or lay, is likely to feel the pinch—the lay teacher looking at his check or the religious in quest of a new wimple, a raincoat, or a shawl. People are apt to be impressed by the fact that a religious community can buy a piece of property, perhaps a country mansion which a wealthy owner can no longer afford to keep going, and transform it into a well-shaded college for young women, but few know much of the begging and self-sacrifice which keep such places going with the help of tax-exemption. Nor is much publicity given to the ventures which fail.

Some summers ago, I happened to be close to the communion rail in Notre Dame's Sacred Heart Church. Doubtless I should not have succumbed to such a distraction, but I noticed that the shoes of practically every sister who knelt at the rail were half-soled. This quite modest and unplanned inquiry into Catholic educational finance may serve to introduce what is meant to be a meditation rather than an exposition. Right now anybody who wishes to find out how the money needed to keep Catholic education going is obtained, or how it is expended, will find getting answers to his questions extremely difficult. This is not due to ill will, inefficiency, or any kind of dishonesty, but is the outgrowth of tradition and diversity. Some current financial reporting by Catholic institutions, for example the University of Notre Dame, is frank, complete, and as little open to question as are the audits of the Chase Manhattan Bank. Undoubtedly there will be more such examples as soon as lay boards of trustees increase in number and acquire influence. The annual reports made by many pastors to their congregations, however honest, are not really very useful to the student of parochial school finance.

When one inquires about the sources of financial support, it is rather surprising to discover that in spite of the almost chaotic variety which has existed in the Catholic-school system, until very recently the pattern was relatively uniform. This is not a statement made on the basis of rigid statistical analysis, but rather on what principals of schools think that the sources of support are. The directors of the study assumed that the schools would have to depend on sums collected for tuition and other fees, on support given by the parishes with which the schools were associated, on grants-in-aid from diocesan authorities, or on such forms of assistance as gifts and collections.

The answers received from school principals, though admittedly subject to more rigorous checking, would seem relatively correct. We may quote from the findings of the study:

The parish, interparish and diocesan schools get their major support from funds provided by the parish itself. Private schools, on the other hand, benefit primarily from direct tuition payments. Very little assistance is obtained from the diocesan authorities. Only a very small number of these schools received significant income from money-raising activities, gifts, and so forth. Since there exists a stereotypic assumption that Catholic schools profit from bingo games and the like, this information was somewhat surprising.

The principals of secondary schools report that direct tuition charges are a more important source of revenue for all types—parish schools, interparish schools, and diocesan high schools. But parish support nevertheless remains the principal revenue provider for parish and interparish schools. In the case of diocesan high schools, it takes second place. Privately operated schools at this level list tuition charges and miscellaneous receipts as the main sources of income. All secondary schools, too, do not count heavily on "miscellaneous receipts."•

Catholic schools would, of course, have to close their doors tomorrow were it not for low salaries. The Notre Dame Study makes this

• Reginald A. Neuwien (ed.), *Catholic Schools in Action*, p. 64.

evident on the basis of responses obtained both from teachers and from principals. While the percentage of response was not one hundred, it was so close to it that the amount of co-operation may safely be termed very satisfactory. Any short summary of the results, like the one here offered, cannot indicate all deviations from median figures, but the tables in the study report do. They also show clearly the relationship between salary and teaching experience. It must suffice to indicate here that in the elementary schools salaries paid to laywomen ranged during the period studied from $2,500 to $3,000 plus. The number of laymen teaching in these schools is relatively small, and the average pay was $500 higher, the median being in the range between $3,000 to $3,499. The range for laywomen and laymen teaching in the secondary schools was the same, but the median salaries were higher—for laywomen $4,000 to $4,499; and for laymen, $4,500 to $4,999. The rates, therefore, compare unfavorably with those prevailing in the public schools, though improvement has taken place since 1963.

It was the rapid increase in the number of lay teachers which created a very serious financial problem. The expansion of the Catholic secondary-school network during the period from 1950 to 1963 brought with it a relative decline in the percentage of teaching religious. The total number of secondary-school teachers was 27,770 in 1952. Of these only 4,623 were laymen and laywomen. When 1961 came round, the total number of teachers was 46,623 (an increase of 67.9 per cent!) and the number of lay teachers had grown to 12,470 (an increase of 169 per cent!). No firm over-all figures are available for the 1962–63 period, but the study data indicates that the ratio of lay to religious teachers had become 1 to 2.64.

The growth of the elementary-school system likewise brought about a startling change. There were 66,525 teachers in 1950, whereas in 1961 there were 110,911 (an increase of 66.7 per cent), and the number of lay teachers grew spectacularly to 32,723 (an increase of 589 per cent!). The ratio now was 1 lay teacher to 2.38 religious, and this became 1 to 2.24 in the subsequent two-year period. Catholics, therefore, might wonder whether, short of some miraculous windfall in terms of federal aid, the limits of manageable expansion had not been reached.

Forty years ago, prior to the great increase in the number of educational institutions, it was usually taken for granted that lay men and women willing to dedicate themselves to teaching under Catholic auspices stood ready above all to share in the mission of the Church. The idea that they were working to "make money" was by and large wholly alien to them. They were paid enough, in terms of cash, sustenance, and lodging, to enable them to live at about the same standard as that enjoyed by the religious themselves; and the fact that some of them managed to accumulate tidy sums which they then bequeathed to the institutions they served is proof, if that were needed, of how fully they identified themselves with the communities they aided. Teaching being what it then was, no need for scholarly activity or further advanced education, for sabbatical leaves and personal libraries, was often felt. Many such lay persons earned the respect and affection of generations of young people, but one must immediately add that virtually none of them would have felt at home at a meeting of a learned society. Today that society is the hub round which education moves, and it even plays a part on the stage of secondary education.

Understandably, the religious community sees the lay teacher as the basic problem of Catholic school finance. It has been suggested by a number of commentators that another major difficulty is lack of training on the part of administrators in business administration. It is true that if a more significant measure of uniformity could be introduced, substantial savings could be effected. We have only to imagine the potential benefits of central purchasing agencies. But it might be kept in mind that religious have often found ways of coaxing lower prices out of suppliers, even though such practices are now anachronistic. In general, although progress in assuming provision for sound business management has been slower and more spotty than is desirable, the situation is considerably better than it was ten years ago. A number of relatively well-trained persons have entered school administration, and the literature on the subject is more extensive than is generally believed.*

One major problem arises out of the fact that dioceses generally have not been able to achieve centralization of financial management. This runs counter to the feeling for "diversity" which, as we have seen, is a major characteristic of Catholic education. But the inability to disentangle the financial affairs of a large number of small schools from those of the parish proper is another source of great difficulty. In many such cases the pastor would be hard pressed to determine how to allocate costs. Utilities, custodial service, and even the school library may be centralized, for use by the parish as a whole. Moreover, not a few pastors are on record as not wanting diocesan school superintendents "breathing down their necks." Sometimes, too, a pastor may not be the easiest person in the world to get along with; but when one considers what might be called his "job description," this somewhat lamentable attitude can be understood.

Religious communities likewise are not pieces on the same chessboard, but fortunately more information is available. Since every community is, ideally speaking, a concrete, institutionalized expression of the mission of Christ and his Church, it possesses property and collects money only for the purpose of serving that mission. When this is really so (for it has not always been, and is not always, the case), motivations are created which are radically different from those which govern public or business enterprise. Neither the individual religious nor his community will have acquired anything specifically like private property. Let us compare this situation with that of a city government or an industry. The first may be thoroughly honest, and wholly dedicated to the good of the citizenry, but still be subject to power factors which, from its point

* In addition to many unpublished dissertations, see Leo V. Ryan, C.S.V., *A National Study of Business Management in Catholic Central High Schools* (St. Louis University, 1958).

of view, are of a predatory kind. Unionized municipal workers sometimes provide an example. They may or may not be justified in striking for higher wages or improved working conditions. But the result
of their action, if successful, seldom leads a city government to impose a proportionately higher charge for the service they render.
Rather it will resort to increased taxation of the citizen, regardless
of whether or not he uses that service. And conversely, a business
enterprise may reduce labor costs—which means the amount of
money paid for work—by resorting to mechanization or automation.
The religious community is a totally different kind of economic unit.
Traditionally speaking, it is wedded to the idea of making as little
money as possible; and at least in our society it always has a chronic
shortage of workers. It cannot supply the teachers, nurses, catechists
needed. It is unable, however, to say that since the demand for its
services is so great, it will charge accordingly for them. The religious
community never goes on strike.

Of course, human nature being what it is, communities have
sometimes grown rich—richer than they should have for the good of
the mission of the Church. It was once possible for monarchs to
overendow communities, just as it was a simple matter for others to
despoil them. It may be that in the United States as well some communities have upon occasion become obsessed with possessions.
Hybris is not absent from the house of the Lord. But all the criticism
which now comes from within and without the convent or the monastic house, to the effect that the communities have become too de-
pendent on their benefactors, and too remote from those who in one
sense or other are needy, will never erase from my mind the story
of personal renunciation and sacrifice which I have come to know
—within my own family and outside of it.

The teaching communities have now to deal with two economic
facts which are quite novel and which will further strain both their
resources and their powers of adaptation. The first is the academic
training of their own members. The second is making financial
provision for lay teachers in the schools they operate. In so far as the

first is concerned, we may define it as the heavy tribute exacted by the extraordinary advances made by scholarship in our time. The university demands its pound of flesh. The second results from the decision that "every Catholic child in a Catholic school" was a target which could be aimed at with some prospect of success. A great many schools came into existence in rather pell-mell fashion, and it was taken for granted that they must be maintained. Manifestly the two facts just cited contradict each other. One cannot send religious to the college or the university to seek the benefits of higher education and at the same time have them in classrooms.

One of the major issues is rate of return to the communities for the service of teachers they supply. On the basis of a sample questionnaire, Sister Cecelia Maureen Kehoe, F.C.S.P., estimated that the cost to a community in terms of educating, maintaining, and taking care of the old age of a sister could be met only if each active member of the community had an annual income of $2,015.* But as a matter of cold fact the stipend paid to a sister (teaching in an elementary school) in 1963 averaged $853 (over three hundred dollars more than had been paid during the previous year). Another study, by Sister Maria Concepta, C.S.C., analyzed income and costs for the teaching members of her community, the Congregation of the Holy Cross, based on statistics pertaining to the period between 1955 and 1963.** She reached the conclusion that the cash stipends paid to sisters teaching in parochial schools remained almost constant. The average sum reported in 1956 was $187; $207 in 1963. This actually meant that although 67 per cent of the active teaching sisters of her community were assigned to parochial schools, the return accruing to the community for their services was only 16 per cent of its total income!

Another significant fact established by Sister Maria Concepta is

* *Economic Contribution of Religious Communities to Parochial Education through the Parochial School Teaching Sister* (Gonzaga University, 1963; unpublished M.A. thesis).
** *The Making of a Sister-Teacher* (Notre Dame, Ind.: Fides Press, 1965).

that the cost of the five-year formation program is $13,710 per sister. This seems at first glance a rather high figure, but it includes a percentage of the costs of maintaining the community as a whole based on the number of sisters "in formation" compared with the total number. Assuming a life teaching span of forty years, and positing in terms of Sister Maria Concepta's statistics an average annual cost per teaching sister of approximately $1,700, the amortization of the training costs would not quite bring the average annual burden on the community for each member up to the figure of $2,015 arrived at by Sister Cecilia Maureen. The difference is due to calculations for rent of the convent facilities, and so forth, incurred by schools when the sister is on mission.

The data are corroborated by those recently supplied by Father Ernest Bartell, C.S.C., on the basis of a study recently conducted by him under the auspices of the Department of Economics of Princeton University:

He said that his analysis shows the average cash cost to a parish in San Francisco to be $1,375 per year and $1,390 in Youngstown, Ohio. These figures include convent repairs, furniture and other perquisites, he said.

Father Bartell held that the capital cost of construction of convents should not be counted, but that imputed rent can be properly added on. When this is done, he said, the cost figure rises to about $2,300.

"The total cost to the entire Catholic community is of course higher," he said. "It must include a return sufficient to pay back the investment in the Sisters' education as well as sufficient annual savings for retirement." He said this would raise the average annual cost to $3,656.*

Since it is not evident from the comment just cited what portion of parish costs is allocated to secondary schools and what portion to

* N.C.W.C. News Service (February 18, 1966). Father Bartell's dissertation will be published by the Notre Dame Press at a date not yet determined.

elementary schools, we may assume relative congruence of the data, Sister Maria Concepta reports markedly higher income for secondary-school teaching. At any rate we may assume that the average cost to the parish is not more than $2,300, and to the community not more than $3,656. Since the conclusion drawn from virtually complete national data by the Notre Dame Study is that the average salary earned by laymen teaching in Catholic schools is $3,450 a year, (if one uses Father Bartell's figures) this may seem to mean that, in terms of the entire Catholic community, teaching religious cost little less than teaching laymen as paid at present. But in terms of the parish, again using Father Bartell's figures, the difference is approximately one third. The conclusion one must therefore draw is that even if these data were found to prevail nationally, and if salaries paid to laymen were not to rise, a school taught in its entirety by laymen would necessitate an increase in parish income of a very substantial sum.

But of course like all statistical averages, these data establish medians only. There are Catholic schools, and the number is increasing (though almost exclusively on the secondary-school level), in which salaries paid to lay teachers are comparable to those paid in the public schools, while those paid to members of the religious community are much below the norm, even that established by Sister Cecilia Maureen. Somewhere in this vast and fluid picture there are doubtless schools and school systems which could serve as paradigms for the future. But it will require a good deal more research than has been carried on so far to find out.

These inquiries have led to speculation which is at least worth considering briefly. As we have seen, Sister Maria Concepta suggested that the total cost of training a teaching religious was $13,710. Assuming that the lay teacher joins the school faculty with equivalent training, he or she will have left all training costs behind. What would then happen if the teacher trained accordingly took over all teaching duties in the Catholic school at current salary levels? We have seen that even so there would be a difference in terms of cost to the parish. *But* if the trained teaching religious left the Catholic-school system and took a job teaching in the public school, the income to the community would be considerably more than doubled. Father Bartell concluded, on the basis of salary schedules in effect at the time his study was undertaken, that he or she would earn between $6,000 and $8,000 annually. This is just another way of saying that the contribution made by religious to the Catholic schools is very significant. But it could lead to the conclusion that their communities would add to their affluence if their members, minus regulation garb of course, found positions in the public schools. Since the majority of Catholic problem children are in these schools, would not the religious have their greatest influence in them? There is more support for this view than observers of Catholic education sometimes realize. But it seems obvious that taking such a step would lead ultimately, and indeed perhaps soon, to the dissolution of the communities involved. It would be just one more way of "de-institutionalizing" the Church.

Proceeding to another and different aspect of the problem, discussion has turned for a long time around the issue as to whether Catholics, obliged to contribute to the support of the public schools, are being "taxed doubly" for the education of their children. To their credit, Catholics generally have not demurred at the tax bill for education any more than they have lagged in their support of publicly operated hospitals. There are exceptions. It is said, for example, that public schools in this or that state suffer by reason of silent Catholic opposition. The Notre Dame Study was unable to concern itself with these allegations. At any rate, there is no good reason why Catholics should emancipate themselves from any part of the tax burden, however strongly they may feel that more state aid should be provided for the schools their children attend.

But is their burden really so great, after all? A number of studies have been undertaken in this area, none of them seemingly based on the requisite research methodology. In one instance it was found that in a given community approximately 1,000 children were enrolled in Catholic schools while virtually the equivalent number attended public schools. For purposes of discussion we shall assume that the cost data provided were correct—that the cost per child in the public school was $450, while the cost per child in the Catholic schools was $160. We shall likewise assume that all parents having children in the Catholic schools paid tuition in some amount (though this may not have been the case), and that parishioners without children met only their share of the costs borne by the parish as a whole. We shall also not take into account, though the factor is important, the state subsidy which may have lessened the burden on the local taxpayer. The conclusion must therefore be that if the Catholic schools were to close their doors, the price tag on each pupil's education would rise to $450. One half of the increased tax burden would be $225, to be borne by all Catholic taxpayers in the community. Their Protestant and Jewish neighbors, some of whom may have been very critical of what was going on in St. Margaret's School, would find to their chagrin that the cost of living in Town X had suddenly gone up. Catholics would also discover the same dire fact. The difference between $160 and $225 happens to be more than the tuition charged in any school in the community surveyed.

A number of other studies similar in character have been undertaken, but unfortunately none has come to my attention which was conducted with sufficient rigor to be more convincing than the one described.* Even so, it appears reasonable to say that Catholic elementary and secondary education make it possible for taxpayers outside the household of the Catholic faith to pocket considerable amounts of hard cash. But Catholics might also reckon with the fact that increasing their contributions to parish schools would leave

* E.g., A Study of Per Pupil Expenditures in a Mid-Western Diocesan High School, unpublished ms., based on an inquiry directed by Xavier J. Harris, O.F.M. (Notre Dame, 1963). This arrives at similar conclusions. A number of other writers have commented on the topic, but the data they adduce are rather meager.

them better off than they would be if those schools ceased to exist. The inquiry is worth pursuing.

Sources of Assistance

Financing American education is now an exercise so tremendous in scope that it is all but impossible to see it in perspective. Suppose we assume on a purely theoretical basis a national population "stabilized" at 200,000,000. (Unless all the demographers are wrong, the figure will be considerably higher in a relatively short time.) Suppose further that we project an average active life span of 56 years, taking into account further advances in medical and nutritional care. The total number of years available to a population of the size indicated would therefore be 11,200,000,000 years. If the average number of school years were eight, and this it approximately is at the present time, one seventh of the total years—or, 1,600,000,000—would be spent on education. But if we raise the average number to sixteen years, which we are now bent on doing, 3,200,000,000 years will be spent in school. Assuming an average annual cost per child of $500 for schooling alone (the assumption doubtless is too conservative), the sum expended would be $1,650,000,000,000. This is a colossal pile of money. Let us finally imagine that each of these school years would cost only one dollar spent for educational materials purchased outside of the classroom—encyclopedias, books, magazines, films—and the amount will make all purveyors of such materials think they have found the rainbow's end. Indeed, many of them know they have. Today educational publishing is big business. Education as such is far and away the most gigantic of American enterprises, and ten years from now it could be again as big as it is now.

It is in this kind of financial world that Catholic education must be conducted. We may maintain without being the least unreasonable that in terms of the public treasury all schools of equal merit should be treated equally. Just why one should insist that the pupils in Central High have a status utterly different from those in St. Malachy's High is not a question of educational aims, methods, and philosophies. The admissions officer at Queens College, New York, a state institution, can approve for matriculation only such young people as possess stipulated qualifications; and she does approve graduates from Catholic and other private high schools, without ever raising a single question as to why they did not attend public schools. Just because Mary O'Brien has taken courses in religion and belonged to a sodality is no reason she should be set wholly apart from another Mary O'Brien who goes to the public school and is sternly prohibited from listening to a reading from Scripture. The courts have during recent years made a great many salutary deductions from their discovery that racial discrimination plays a role in American education. Perhaps in the long run they may decide that whoever educates a child well is entitled to equal treatment. I am not sanguine about the matter, since Catholics have created and continue to create a great deal of sentiment in favor of the dictum that, whenever they have a chance, they do not wish to enjoy a position of equality but rather to throw their weight around.

Federal aid to education, while not a new phenomenon, as witness the Morrill Act which established a network of land-grant colleges, assumed vast proportions during and after the Second World War. If we review briefly what the government wanted from education during the total mobilization of national resources which the great conflict demanded, a number of far-reaching changes in its relationship with the universities, colleges, and schools of the country can be noted.

To begin with, the government used educational facilities, both public and private, on a wholly unprecedented scale. Most of the research which resulted in the use of atomic fission, synthetic rubber, and armament chemicals was done in university laboratories usually with government assistance. But though this far outdistanced the past in terms of dimension and originality it was not basically new in the sense that the federal government was directly involved. Doubtless more novel was the widespread use of institutions of higher learning for training purposes. Sometimes facilities were simply commandeered. The Armed Forces set up units on campuses which depended to a great extent on the resources and curricula of the institutions involved. These varied considerably in character.

In addition, very heavy demands were made for university and college personnel. Though the natural and the social sciences were most directly affected, historians and linguists were not overlooked. Such needs as those for intelligence services and language study could be met only by siphoning off the cream of the crop of American humanistic scholarship. That these sacrifices could be made was due of course to the dwindling of student enrollments during wartime.

Through the G. I. Bill, the government utilized higher education as a demobilization resource. The various implications of this action could not be dealt with adequately in a short or cursory study. But I believe we might emphasize here the vast size and complexity of this undertaking. Even colleges for women temporarily made male veterans at home; and nevertheless the demand for class space was so great that special institutions were established.

A highly important corollary fact is that no distinction was made in connection with these endeavors between higher education under public, private, and religious auspices. No one, it would appear, raised a constitutional question; and if he had he would probably have been hailed before the House Un-American Activities Committee or something of the sort. To have hamstrung the government by limiting its use of personnel and facilities to public or non-religious institutions would manifestly have been folly.

Although the conflict ended with victory for the United States, the shadow of a possible new and even more severe struggle fell over the land. It revealed itself first as a contest between ourselves and the Russians for superiority in the area of nuclear weapons, and then as a no-doubt-too-luridly-visualized competition in the over-all fields of technology and science. From this point of view, the Russian success with the first sputnik triggered a demand for greatly intensified scientific training and research. Every schoolboy was now called upon to serve the country by gobbling down the calculus.

The result was a continuing demand for the use of the resources of educational institutions. The Atomic Energy Commission, the National Science Foundation, the Armed Forces and the Department of Health, Education and Welfare have all carried on or developed forms of co-operation in the national interest which had for the most part originated during the war. It was often contended that the reasons for so doing were more compelling than those advanced during the war itself. The sums made available by Congress for purposes described as necessary either by government agencies or by educators have been very considerable.*

While government requirements for university personnel may not be as great now as they were during the war, there are unmet demands in a number of areas—e.g., for competent persons to serve in international organizations. Qualified persons are also needed to accept appointment under the Fulbright Act and comparable legislation. These are grants, of course, made to individuals and not to institutions, but they require the co-operation of institutions and so involve intimate reciprocal relationships between the federal government and educational establishments.

Congress and the government of the United States have also devised ways and means for assisting higher education with funds which impose no new taxes. Perhaps the most impressive of these from the financial point of view has been the deeding over to education of surplus properties.

* They are conveniently summarized in The Federal Government and Education, a report prepared for the House Committee on Education and Labor (1963).

The point is that no distinction was made in any of these actions between public and private institutions. And indeed, if the critical situation in which the nation found itself during the cold war was hardly less grave than that which it confronted during the period of armed conflict, it would have been preposterous to declare that only the public sector or the so-called secular sector of education could be of assistance during the emergency. This fact was recognized by all the major organizations of persons concerned with higher education, with one possible exception. There developed a pattern of complete and cordial association between administrators regardless of their affiliations. Though the National Educational Association opposed the grant of federal aid to the lower schools, its division for higher education did not do so for its domain of interest. In so far as the law is concerned, the burden of comment by the major legal authorities is that in a number of ways the courts have upheld the manner in which federal aid to higher education has so far been administered.

Meanwhile the Supreme Court, pursuing its difficult and tortuous way in interpreting the First Amendment, recognized the validity of still other ways of extending public assistance to schools conducted under religious auspices. These take the form of public services. Here the basic decision is probably that of *Everson vs. Board of Education*, in which the Court held that parents might be reimbursed out of public funds for expenses incurred in sending their children to parochial schools by bus. The key sentence reads in part: ". . . we must be careful . . . to be sure that we do not inadvertently prohibit New Jersey from extending its general state law benefits to all its citizens without regard to their religious belief." Certainly no one could expect, said the Court, churches and schools to establish their own fire departments and police forces. In conclusion, therefore, it may be said that two areas in which federal or state aid to religious education is permissible were staked out. The first is that in which support is given to the national defense or, as is sometimes said, the national interest. The second is that in which public services are utilized.

But everything thus chronicled did not suffice to prevent a mighty controversy when the federal government proposed in 1961 "a four-year program of federal grants to states." This appeared primarily as Title IV of the text of the act under discussion in 1963. Before presenting the legislation to Congress, the then-Secretary of the Department of Health, Education and Welfare requested legal counsel to prepare a memorandum on the constitutional questions involved. In order to understand fully what then ensued, it is necessary to compare this memorandum and the rejoinder to it presented by the National Catholic Educational Association. These in turn need to be read in the light of the purposes for which the funds requested were to be expended—namely, a program of salary increases for teachers, the construction of school facilities, and "special projects or programs directed toward improving educational quality and opportunity, particularly for educationally deprived children in slum or other economically depressed areas."

These were certainly all worthy purposes. The most novel of them was, of course, the proposed schedule of salary increases. I do not know what really happened, but it looks as if some of the more powerful teacher organizations, at least in so far as the majority of their members were then concerned, concluded that if the butter were passed round among the private schools, too, it would not really cover the bread. Perhaps if they acted with greater restraint, matters would have proceeded somewhat more amicably. At any rate, the battle was now on. The powerful appropriations committees of the Congress are chronically reluctant to approve increases in the budget, and formidable opposition to any measure designed to do so usually means the end of the affair.

The major argument advanced in the HEW memorandum is plausible enough. In greatly condensed form it added up to this: To date, all assistance provided for education by the federal government has been based on the assumption that a distinction can be made between education which serves the national interest and education which supports the objectives of religious indoctrination. When the Atomic Energy Commission supports research in atomic chemistry at Notre Dame, or when the National Science Foundation gives Boston College a grant for work in mathematics, it is quite obvious that teaching the Baltimore Catechism is not involved. But is the case the same at the elementary- and secondary-school levels? Many spokesmen for Catholic education, ignoring Cardinal Newman, were wont to argue that religion must "permeate" every subject in the course of study. But if the "permeation" is successful, there is not much reason to suppose that one can easily distinguish between what the Catholic elementary or secondary school does for the secular national interest and what it does for religion. This is a good example of the curse which dogs all public relations. If one was urging Catholic parents to send their children to a Catholic school, the "permeation" argument was effective, but when there was a question of federal aid, the rules and precedents were all on the side of a strict line of demarcation between the sacred and the secular.

No doubt, it was largely a matter of semantics. An intelligent nun who has studied mathematics at the University of Chicago will teach the subject quite as effectively as a lay teacher who has graduated from the same institution, even though she may pause occasionally to say that everything the class is doing is for the glory of God.

At this point we may profitably consider what the Supreme Court has said about the relationship between public education and religion. I shall not go into detail, though the decisions in question have a bearing on the matter under discussion. On June 17, 1963, the Court held that religious exercises and Bible-reading were not permissible in public schools.

The emphasis here was on institutional recognition of religion in events (assemblies, etc.) attended by the student body as a whole.

After the decision was rendered, it seemed that, legally speaking, the president of a publicly maintained college could read from *Lady Chatterley's Lover* but not from the Psalmist. It was the most severe restriction on religion imposed in the nation's history, and seemed clearly to mark the end of an era. Later, however, the Court ruled that if religion were dealt with as an academic subject, "objective" courses in it could be offered in public educational establishments. Just what the word "objective" could be taken to mean, other than that evangelizing and proselytizing were prohibited, gave rise to a good deal of speculation and experimentation. But very considerable interest was shown on major university campuses; and staffs were assembled on an "ecumenical" basis. Indeed it seems as if comparable instruction may be possible in the secondary schools and perhaps even in the elementary-school classroom. A new profession, that of instructor of religion, has seemingly been created in secular education; and not a few Catholics are preparing for it. We have no way of knowing what the long-range significance of this development will be. Obviously, however, it is no longer possible, in the light of Vatican Council deliberations, to state categorically that *denominational* religious instruction is necessarily to be preferred to *interdenominational* instruction. All this makes it still more difficult than it has been in the past to decide whether, except in the forms already sanctioned by legal tradition and public opinion, government can countenance religious education as an enterprise of a private character.

Before attempting to pronounce on this dilemma, we may pose some questions of importance: Do we need additional federal assistance to education; what would be the probable outcome of a Supreme Court review of the permissibility of granting such aid to religiously supervised institutions; and what is to be said about individual states as recipients and dispensers of federal moneys? It may be taken for granted that American education needs a great deal of financial support, and that the federal government can be expected to provide it. No other agency can stage so successful an assault on the citizen's pocketbook, although the states and municipalities are not indifferent campaigners. The public has come to take heavy federal spending for granted, both because of the impact of that spending on the total economy and because the processes of review and opposition are necessarily more indirect. For example, the citizens of a county can vote down a bond issue, but they have no voice when a federal levy is proposed. The fact is that pressure on Congress from the states is devoted far more to getting some of the "gravy" than to keeping appropriations down.

In his pleas for amending Title IV of the act so as to include benefits for Catholic education, Monsignor Frederick Hochwalt stated frankly in behalf of the National Catholic Education Association:

I wish I could assure you that we will not be negative. I am afraid we will be. . . . Not with the intention of blocking something for public education but of sharing at the same time, because it has been our legal experience that unless you meet with the same treatment, equal treatment at concurrently the same time, you will wind up at the Federal level, as I said earlier, where we have wound up at the State level. And we have never gained back the ground at the State level for not having been considered at the very beginning.

This stated the position taken by Catholic education very clearly. It is obvious that Monsignor Hochwalt, wordly-wise in spite of his high calling, was persuaded that once the law was enacted it would prove to be a little elephant with mighty powers of expansion. Certainly that has generally been the case with other forms of federal aid to education.

It was very persuasively argued, for example, by Dr. John T. Caldwell, then president of the Association of State Universities and Land-Grant Colleges, that since we Americans have arrived at an impasse concerning the permissibility of federal aid to religious institutions, a judicial review should now be permitted:

Obviously many educators and other citizens have been reluctant to approve or positively oppose recommending measures to the Congress which in their judgment would further erode the principles of separation of Church and State and which would establish new precedents in that direction which might become applicable to broader programs of Federal Aid to elementary and secondary schools. I would hope that the inclusion of a court test device in the Federal legislation granting aid to all types of education would find the objectors ready to support or at least not oppose such legislation.

This suggestion was based on the fact that since 1923 no taxpayer's suit could be brought in connection with an appropriation by Congress. Therefore all such suits brought before the Court had to do with the teaching of religion in the public schools. Dr. Caldwell did not, of course, wish to alter this tradition. His proposal was developed to give the commissioner of education the right to reject an "application for a benefit" on the ground that it would necessitate a violation of the First Amendment, and then to accord the applicant the privilege to "litigate the constitutional question in court."

Such a suggestion had little chance of gaining support from spokesmen for religious education, primarily for the reason that the general position adopted in recent years by the Court was considered, rightly or wrongly, to have been based on a resolve to build the "wall of separation" between Church and State so high that neither could any longer see each other. Many therefore feared that even if the commissioner were to deny an application in the area of education's contribution to the national defense there might be danger that the Court would rule in his favor. Dr. Caldwell, assuredly no "anti-religious secularist," held it "already established that State tax support for sectarian elementary and secondary education is not permitted under our Constitution and that the proscription applies also to the Federal authority." As we have seen, the Court had authorized support in so far as public services are concerned. And, as a matter of fact, there is considerable diversity in the practice of the states. The gambling instinct is not highly developed in spokesmen for religiously oriented educational institutions.

There was another approach to a possible compromise. This would take the form of tax allowances to parents who pay tuition in private schools. One of the most eloquent spokesmen for this solution has been Senator Abraham Ribicoff, who had the misfortune to be Secretary of Health, Education and Welfare during the battle-scarred year of 1961. Though his proposal has not been immune to attack, it has been warmly endorsed by many of the ablest students of American education. Senator Ribicoff's proposal was to "allow a deduction of up to $100 a year for certain expenses incurred in providing an elementary and secondary education for a child in a private school," and to "allow a deduction for certain expenses in obtaining or providing a higher education" in any college or university. Assuming that the deduction is for tuition costs actually paid, and that they could be approved as made from net income, the total assistance given to education under private or religious auspices would be considerable. Unfortunately, no information is available as to cost studies made in Jewish or Protestant schools, but I think we may assume that they would show results roughly comparable to those secured from the limited sampling of Catholic schools to which reference has been made.

The "private sector" in American educational financing is of course no negligible one, although it is at present quite impossible to determine the sums involved. In the religious segment of this "sector" Protestants and Jews have a very reputable share, but the Catholic-school system plays the dominant role in terms of numbers. The Notre Dame Study of Catholic Education has, I think, shown that supporting and even expanding the system is entirely feasible provided that an adequate supply of qualified teachers can be found and appropriately compensated. This is a very formidable "if" for reasons which have to some extent have been discussed, but the crucial fact seems to be that the religious schools must be placed in a position to compete with the public school system for teachers. This means that salary scales for lay teachers must be virtually the same.

But the overriding issue is how to finance the nation's education. One simple way of taking a look at it may be to compare what happens in the vast area controlled by the Armed Forces and what the current situation is in many huge urban communities. The educational program of the military is comprehensive and of course utilitarian. Needs for officers are met not only by the various academies but also by a far-flung ROTC program in universities and colleges. In terms of their rank-and-file employees, the services begin with the principle that modern warfare and preparation for waging it require the equivalent of a high-school education. The principal emphases are on technology and communication, the latter requiring an adequate command of the English language. Here, then, is a vast training program geared to meet the needs of the national defense.

Nevertheless, it is inadequate for two major reasons. First, the specializations which technological development require grow ever more numerous. Second, industry in general needs the same skills as do the Armed Forces, so that persons laboriously recruited and trained are steadily siphoned off from the military manpower pools. In general, therefore, programs of federal aid to education, whether in the form of assistance to higher education, or of aid to teacher-training institutions, or of grants for education in such subjects as mathematics and foreign languages, have tended to be somewhat akin to national defense needs. In other words, the underlying philosophy, to quote from a statement by the American Council on Education, is to view education as a "national resource." The logic here would seem to be ironclad. Nobody can doubt that the efficiency of the Armed Forces depends on the training of the personnel they recruit, and it would seem impossible to question the fact that if the Armed Forces cannot meet this challenge unaided, the federal government must help them do so by farming out support for education through other instrumentalities. Surely few would argue that this is the kind of job which should be done by local communities.

Let us now look at the other side of the picture. One of the truly poignant statements made during the 1963 hearings before the Committee on Education and Labor of the House of Representatives is buried in fine print at the close of the enormous volume containing the testimony. The author is Wilmer V. Bell, Director of Adult Education, Baltimore Public Schools. I shall quote three passages, with the prefatory remark that Baltimore is surely not more retarded from the educational point of view than are other large cities:

Maryland has approximately 229,000 unskilled and semiskilled workers, of which about 60,000 are currently unemployed. It has 72,448 welfare recipients, many of whom are functionally illiterate. . . .

In Baltimore, the educational level is lower—a median for the adult population of 8.9 years of school completed for the city versus 10.4 for the State. This means that more than half of the adult residents of Baltimore never finished junior high school. Moreover . . . 3 per cent (16,603) adults 25 years of age and over have never been to school. . . .

Baltimore has had an adult education program for 120 years, but the resources made available by the city do not currently match the growing intensity of need. Consequently, less than 20,000 are now enrolled in adult education classes, even though the recently imposed fee is only $4 or less per semester. Even this modest fee, imposed in 1961 by reason of municipal financial strictures, caused drastic reductions in enrollment. . . .

While these statistics will doubtless not startle anyone, being reminded of them at a time when we are trying to help improve education in the world at large will give some indication of the baffling problems we face at home. "More than half of the adult residents of Baltimore never finished junior high school"—if the nation could not exist half slave and half free, it can obviously not flourish if its citizens are similarly divided in terms of education.

But where is the money to come from to provide the education that is needed? So far, the heaviest burden has been placed on the local communities and the states, and this will probably continue to be the case for as long as anyone can foresee. The federal government has acted in three ways, all of them traditional. First, it has permitted tax deductions for educational purposes, which has enabled foundations to come into being; these in turn have greatly benefited education in all its forms. Second, it has itself acted as a quasi-foundation, making grants through the National Science Foundation and other agencies for purposes deemed to be in the national interest. Third, it has transferred to the states some of the tax moneys it has itself collected. None of these has been a perfect instrumentality, but without them our problems would be far more serious.

Personally, I believe—and it is the only conclusion which I shall permit myself to formulate at this time—that, although its authors did not resolve the thorny problem of how to deal with religiously oriented schools, both elementary and secondary, the National Education Improvement Act of 1963 on the whole presented a more adequate philosophy of federal aid to education than anything else the country had been asked to consider up to that time. Critics have found a variety of faults with it, sometimes probably with reason. Of course, the act did not answer the major query: how shall we add to the citizens' tax burden without drastically curtailing the amount of free choice in the crucial area of education? No answer is available at present, though the amount of study and thought expended on obtaining a response is considerable. But it was at least made plain that neither the Congress nor the people wishes to restrict the area of free choice. There are some who would like a single, nationwide, educational system, but at present they are relatively few in number. In addition, it is doubtful that, education today is administered with the needed concern for stringent economy. This is true of all sectors, private, state, and federal. Educational administration has certainly improved but there is need for greater professionalism. Finally, when we confront conditions such as those described by Mr. Bell, we know that in an important respect we have failed. It would be interesting to discover the reasons for that failure, but that is not the point. The point is, what do we do?

New Responses

To a limited extent an answer to the questions just asked was provided by the Elementary and Secondary Education Act of 1965. President Johnson and his major advisers were convinced that the nation faced an emergency different from and yet in a sense comparable with those created by two great wars. They publicized a situation which was recognized to some extent but for the most part had been ignored: the plight of millions of American citizens who for one reason or other were doomed to a ghetto-like life characterized by isolation, poverty, disease, and ignorance. How could we, the most affluent of peoples, turn our backs on these unfortunates even while we were safeguarding freedom and aiding "economic and social development" in other parts of the world? Some have held that the directives of the act are too vaguely phrased and too optimistic. Perhaps they are right. But the illiteracy of very many older Americans and the drop-out patterns of young ones are surely starkly real.

The legislation does not make the burden of local and state taxation any easier to bear. It is designed to provide support by the federal government for special educational services to young people needing remedial assistance and guidance, and for improvements in plants and facilities which schools would otherwise find beyond their means. Nor has the traditional pattern of state and local control of education been changed, though the legislation establishes "regional centers" which in time could lead to a greater standardization of the educational process. At any rate, it is the public authority acting at state and local levels which decides how the money made available by Washington is to be allocated and spent. What is new is that private schools, whether denominational or not, can share both in the job to be done and in the funds made available.

Therefore, the Education Act can be looked upon as an extension into the lower schools of patterns of federal aid which have long since become commonplace in higher education. Nevertheless, the terrain mapped out is novel in several respects. The emergency is obviously of a different character and the assistance provided affects much more directly the total ongoing operations of the schools. Some groups raised the issue of separation of Church and State but Congress was more influenced by the fact that the National Council of Churches and Jewish day-school supporters endorsed the proposed legislation. The general concern for the segregated and the disadvantaged was an even more effective factor. It seemed eminently fitting that all schools play their parts in the unfolding drama of a nation at war with its own weakness.

The challenge to Catholics was and still is great. Despite heroic precursors like Father LaFarge and Dorothy Day, speaking and acting years prior to *Mater et Magistra* and *Pacem in terris*, the average urban parish had shown little sense of responsibility for the plight of Negroes, Puerto Ricans, and poor whites. Nor were Catholic schoolmen quite ready for the fact that federal aid, talked about pessimistically for so long, was now a reality to an extent previously hardly imaginable.

The Elementary and Secondary Education Act of 1965 is a complicated document and its administration is so diffuse that no very clear picture of what is happening has as yet emerged. In some communities the program was speedily put into practice, so that the reports of authorities in charge list public, Catholic, and other denominational schools side by side. There are also communities in which little has been done, and some in which the separation of Church and State issue has been raised. It would of course be idle to predict the extent to which the courts may concern themselves with that issue, but logic certainly supports the contention that if the emergency is as great as the authors of the act assumed—and of this there can be little doubt—not to use the strength which Catholic education has to offer would be as self-defeating as not to set up military training units in Catholic universities during the war. Second, as has been indicated, a phalanx of Protestant and Jewish educators has on this issue joined forces with Catholic schoolmen. The schools for which these educators spoke—Lutheran, Episcopalian, Seventh-Day Adventist, Mennonite and Jewish—are impressive in terms of both numbers and quality. Third (and perhaps specially important), a sufficient number of projects and grants-in-aid for religiously oriented educational institutions are now on the books to make it, speaking pragmatically, very difficult to bring the endeavor to a halt on constitutional grounds.

Although no satisfactory data were available at the time of writing, it would appear that Catholic education has participated widely and with a measure of effectiveness in the program, in spite of bias encountered in some communities. To what extent has this benefited them financially? No firm and fast conclusion can be reached. Perhaps some improvement in the quality of teaching has become possible, but the major contribution has been in terms of the enrichment of the course of study. Considerable sums of money have been expended to provide teaching materials in the form of reference works, films, film strips, projection machines, closed television, etc. Much of this would in all probability greatly benefit the schools, provided teachers really understood what could be done with these new possibilities. There is insufficient evidence to prove that they actually do know.

By far the greatest benefit to Catholic schools is sociological in character. Implementing the programs financed under the legislation of 1965 has broken down barriers between differing school systems. A wide variety of schools have been impressed into the service of the disadvantaged, and all have loyally tried to be effective. The "wall" between the public and the parochial school has been lowered at least a notch. Individuals participating in diverse denominational efforts have also begun to realize that they share common interests, by no means merely financial. It seems very probable that they will continue to co-operate in research, in the endeavor to improve religious instruction, and in service to the American community as a whole. Were no other benefits to accrue to Catholic education from the 1965 Education Act, these alone would justify grateful recognition.

What can one say about the financial future of Catholic education? The picture which is emerging from a cluster of studies of the poverty program is not very encouraging. It may be that we have been witnessing still another refutation of the fallacy to which public opinion in this country has often been addicted, namely that education is a total-spectrum antibiotic which can cure all intellectual diseases and fill every spiritual vacuum. In any case, there is little sign of pay dirt having been reached in terms of the solution of the problems of the "inner city" or of the backward rural areas. Whether this rather gloomy picture will suggest a different approach to the situation or whether the support so far given to the schools under the Education Act of 1965 will be continued are questions which cannot be answered at the present time.

But it is improbable that any future federal legislation will draw a clear line of demarcation between public and private education. Indeed, it is likely that in the several states greater heed will be taken of financial assistance to Catholic schools under the rubric of "services," the constitutionality of which has been affirmed. Free text books could become the norm in so far as Catholic education in a number of states is concerned, and it may well be that this benefit will become nationwide. On the other hand, the status of a decision by the courts of Maryland, based on an interpretation of the First Amendment, barring state aid to colleges with an overt religious orientation, remained unclear in 1967. Since federal legislation making funds available on a matching basis gives privately conducted institutions the same right to request such funds as public colleges and universities, there is a serious question whether the established practice may be prohibited. If it were, Catholic higher education at least would be gravely affected in a number of ways.

Quite as serious a threat is created by increased inflation. Partly— but by no means exclusively—as a result of the war in Vietnam, the basic value of the dollar was by the middle of 1967 ominously less than it had been for some time. This is obviously not the place to discuss monetary or economic theory, but it is certainly clear enough that privately financed education cannot easily cope with a significant inflationary challenge. The teachers' strikes which have erupted in some parts of the Catholic educational empire already demonstrate the difficulty. If funds are poured out lavishly from the public treasury to cope with the cost of living, the sources from which Catholic support for education derives must somehow meet the challenge.

It is, however, far from evident that these sources have been explored with the requisite thoroughness. We shall revert for the moment to what was said earlier. Closing Catholic schools and transferring responsibility for the education of the children now or potentially in them will not make life economically easier for Catholic citizens. If this fact could be brought home not merely to parents who now pay tuition fees but to every Catholic parishioner, possibly a mood would be created to consider giving to Catholic education the same sums as would be collected in terms of taxation were all the schools to become public establishments.

But this would require effective salesmanship and in turn would necessitate a clear presentation of how all the funds of a diocese are collected and expended. The need for such reporting becomes more evident with each passing day. One can no longer expect the Catholic citizen, accustomed to scrutinize the public budgets as well as the reports of corporations in which he has made investments, to have a clear understanding of his duty in so far as his Church is concerned if no data are furnished to hm. That this requires good accounting procedure as well as salesmanship is evident. We can no longer ask for money successfully unless those from whom it is requested know what happens to it.

7

The New Direction of Catholic Education

Some Realistic Appraisals

What road will Catholic education in the United States take? What is it likely to come up against on that road? Will it be well and wisely guided? These are the crucial questions, though one might well add another: Will the religious instruction and formation provided by the schools provide depth and intensity of insight? We cannot, of course, answer any of them. Even if dependable research findings were adequately available, they would provide little more than clues to what the future holds in store. The major considerations are: what are the probable dimensions of the student body at the four levels—the elementary school, the secondary school, the college, and the graduate and professional schools; what financial provisions are likely to be made to provide for the adequate, or more than adequate, education of those who enroll; and what can and will be done to provide effective over-all administration?

In so far as the last consideration is concerned, it is doubtless correct to say that in general the office of the diocesan school superintendent has now acquired greater stature than it had some time ago, when it was little more than an appendage to the chancery office. Even so the Code of Canon Law was not written to make unique provisions for the system of Catholic education in the United States, so different in many respects from what can be found elsewhere in the world. The law is concerned primarily with the organization and functioning of parishes and dioceses, so that the bishop and his pastors have carefully defined interrelationships. School superintendents therefore could work successfully only when they could obtain not only hierarchical support but also the good will and cooperation of pastors. In many instances this has been most difficult. But at least it is now known that top administration is important, and the efforts of superintendents to confer together in order to exchange views and consolidate their work are meeting with increasing success. What is unquestionably also needed is a university center where the study of and research in administration can be effectively conducted. It will take time to bring about the improvement needed, but we may hope not too much time.

Concerning the school population to be served, it would seem that the evidence available and the forecasts based on that evidence indicate that recent unprecedented population increases are not likely to recur. That is, while the number of married couples will be larger, the birth rate is declining and presumably will continue to do so. Elementary school enrollments may well tend to "stabilize" some years hence. One may also venture the opinion that although the secondary school population will increase not only for demographic reasons but also because of the results of "Upward Bound" and similar programs, the problem of making provision for expanded numbers should be manageable from the point of view of the Catholic school, if its present character as an "academic" institution is maintained. Matriculation in the four-year college will be more eagerly sought for some time to come, but probably will taper off. The most notable expansion may well take place in the junior college and its companion piece, the technical institute. Since, as has been indicated, very few such institutions are conducted under private auspices, the problem is largely one with which public education must cope. A variety of predictions about graduate and professional schools are available. An arbitrary selection from among these forecasts rising enrollments, with emphasis on the professional schools, though no further mushrooming is anticipated. A great deal depends on whether graduate study fellowships remain obtainable in large numbers. The recent decision by the Ford Foundation to make substantial sums available for the purpose seems to augur well for the future, but only in so far as the more affluent universities are concerned.

Qualitatively speaking, the principal question is whether the training of teachers for all educational levels can continue to improve as it has during the past two decades. We cannot assume that an automatic escalator is in action. As a matter of unpleasant fact, taking care of the "baby bulge" made it necessary to recruit teachers for public and private schools alike, who in more stable times might have been considered marginal. Meanwhile it is true that teacher-training colleges generally have improved, in terms both of method and content courses, and that admission standards have been raised. Institutes for "retraining" teachers in such fields as the "new mathematics" or language instruction have also served a useful purpose, as has a notable improvement in the quality of audio-visual materials. But if we are candid we shall admit that all these were merely steps toward scholastic progress. The numbers problem has not been solved anywhere along the line. Perhaps the elementary and secondary schools have been most hard pressed in confronting that problem, but one has only to read the papers in order to see that the college and the graduate school have also had their troubles. The graduate school has faced problems largely created by the siphoning off of scholars to serve enterprises deemed to be in the national interest. Everyone is aware that the economy is called upon to dig down deep in support of such ventures as putting a man on the moon. But the scooping up of trained scientists and social scientists is doubtless a still more important item in the debit columns of the ledger. Nevertheless, in some respects present-day American education may well have more "quality" than in any previous time.

Let us now take a look at some of the implications for the Catholic educational "system." First, the elementary school. Granted a relatively stable number of vocations to the religious life and some increase in the amount of financial support, it would not seem unreasonable to expect that some manifest faults could be corrected and some well-recognized needs met. The largesse currently provided by the federal government should make possible a measure of modernization, particularly in the area of teaching materials. In addition, it is at least conceivable that even a not-too-impressive increase in the amount contributed by Catholics to the support of their schools would enable them to reduce inordinately heavy teaching loads, provide some salary increases, establish guidance facilities, and set up in-service training for lay teachers. We might even expect that the precarious assumption that the principalship is strictly an extra-curricular activity could be relegated to the past. To be sure, some opinions are currently voiced that teaching religious might best serve the Lord by catechizing the ungodly. If such a policy is followed, it would drain off important resources of both personnel and dedication. At the moment this seems relatively improbable. Does it appear equally unlikely that the financial support given to Catholic schools will increase?

What do we see in actual practice? Notable is a trend, first seriously inaugurated by the archdiocese of Cincinnati, to lop off the earlier grades of the elementary school. Also, we read reports that schools are being closed in a number of smaller towns and cities, presumably because keeping them going is too difficult. Do these things portend a serious effort to curtail, if not indeed to abandon, the elementary school? A realistic answer is difficult to come by. If paying for and maintaining a school were only a local problem, it would soon become apparent (as has already been suggested) that closing parochial schools would benefit no one, Catholic parents included. But as a matter of fact the public schools derive more and more of their support from state budgets. This is an equalization measure, but it tends to make it seem as if the local problem were being eased. Something similar could be done in the Catholic sector if diocesan, or perhaps multi-diocesan, support within a given state could be made available. At the present time the simple truth is that the parish is by all odds the most efficient collector of Catholic revenue. Some experimentation with diocesan collecting for education has, it is true, been in progress, but it is far too early to judge the results. The present situation is clearly indicated by the fact that when the state of Louisiana levied a one per cent tax increase for the support of public education, the resulting rises in teachers' salaries drained some Catholic schools of their lay staffs. The loss was not one of numbers, merely, but of quality.

Therefore, we have now come to the point where not only laymen but priests, religious, and even bishops are asking whether it may not be wise and necessary to think of a drastic curtailment of the parochial school effort.* Of course, there are many parishes whose revenues can support a school plant in which the twelve grades are closely associated, and it will doubtless take a long time before these abandon the ship. Other parochial schools, one can be pretty sure, will not be closed by the religious communities which operate them. But it certainly looks as if the percentage of Catholic children now in Catholic parochial schools—52 per cent at the time the Notre Dame report was being written—will decrease, perhaps more rapidly than many of us have thought.

* Enrollment statistics released for the beginning of the school year 1966–1967 indicate a sharp drop in the number of those admitted to the elementary schools.

It is difficult to discuss an issue like this without pro- or anti-sentimentalism. There is no use crying over heroic effort which has no chance to succeed. But would the Catholic community gain or lose? Perhaps we are currently so interested in the growth of higher, and what is now generally called "continuing," education that we tend to think that the equivalent of the "little red schoolhouse" can be taken for granted, even as are the perambulator and the diaper service. How far from the truth that is! For instance, however desirable it is that more young people from socially disadvantaged groups should enter college, it remains far more important that good elementary schooling be provided for all children in these groups. And how much time must be wasted later on in life by those who find that their first eight school years were practically meaningless!

We shall now concern ourselves with the major purpose of the Catholic school, which is primarily to develop religious knowledge and practice. In a time when religious and ethical assumptions are subject to change, and are being challenged as never before in the United States, what of lasting value can be accomplished by the elementary school? Indeed, may not the simple loyalties which are encouraged in grade-school pupils later come to seem either chains of habit or impediments to sophistication? I have dealt with this problem in another context and will repeat what was said there:

As one who has no special competence in the teaching of religion but who has had occasion over not a few decades to evaluate some of its fruits, I may, perhaps, be allowed to make a few comments on one or the other of its aspects. There can be no doubt that in this area children profit by some of the oldest uses of project methods. The boy acolyte comes breathtakingly close to the Mass; the little girl who strews flowers on Holy Thursday identifies herself with service to her Lord; children bless themselves with holy water, St. Francis gave them the Christmas crib, they live in a world of bowed heads, folding hands, genuflections, burning candles. The way to the reality of First Holy Communion thus passes through a field of symbols every flower in which is precious. No one who has walked there can forget—not Renan or James Joyce or Mary McCarthy.

But the time comes when questions are asked. These will at first be the interrogation points of innocent rebellion. But later on they will harden into negations. The world of concrete symbol will change into one of intellectual abstractions and emotional fixations. In this last there will loom up large as the moon the question as to the relationship between freedom and obedience. This is the most fateful of the warning signals that maturity is impending. One can only be candid and admit the more of ripeness there is, the greater the danger to the religious spirit. There could be no point in denying that Newman wrote the GRAMMAR OF ASSENT, and that indeed it was imperative he do so. In the face of a perennial peril he offered, anxiously and painstakingly, a path to salvation. That path is not paved with the symbols we have noted with grateful reverence. It is hewn through the rock of intellectualized doubt with the pickaxe of analysis.

It is, in my judgment, during the years identified with the high school that everything will depend, at least for the most gifted and restless, upon how ably and deftly the young person is led from the land of obedience to the symbol to the other domain of freedom to question and to weigh answers. Of course one can go on for a long time saying and doing things without any longer believing in them. But normally the boy or girl of nineteen will have chosen, often quite unconsciously, to be or not to be in the spiritual sense. How grave the responsibility therefore is! How easily an unwise curb or an injudicious answer can bring a soul to a road which may for some distance seem parallel but which in actuality is veering off. One can only hope that those whom education so heavily burdens will have the strength and wisdom required. Even when the best is done there *will be strange, inexplicable failures. When it is not done, God help us!* •

A different sort of question is asked by Andrew M. Greeley and Peter H. Rossi. Their valuable study is based on the results of a very elaborate questionnaire designed to secure from a sample of respondents information about whether religious commitment and practice over a long period of time are really affected by attendance in Catholic schools. The authors conclude that, although "further research is necessary before it can be said with any confidence whether one level of education is more influential than another, a hypothesis for further research . . . in so far as religious values are concerned, is: that neither grammar school nor high school is as important as attending both grammar school and high school in a value-oriented system."•• This may not help much at the moment, but at least it indicates what one would have to look for if one wished to base a decision about the elementary school on a careful inquiry into the facts.

It seems tenable that the development of the high school system would come closest to assuring that *all* Catholic parents who desired to do so could provide Catholic education for their children. This view seems soundly based if one considers either statistical evidence or trends which now seem clearly indicated. As we have seen, the percentage of Catholic children who can be admitted to elementary schools will drop and not rise, at least if all the grades are taken into account. The majority of college- and university-bound young Catholics will not have the slightest chance to obtain higher education under Catholic auspices. Hypothetically, therefore, the high school does hold out a promise of service to the whole

• *Education and Moral Wisdom* (New York: Harper and Row, 1960), pp. 75–76.
•• Andrew M. Greeley and Peter H. Rossi, *The Education of Catholic Americans* (Chicago: Aldine Press), p. 164.

Catholic group attending that school, except for certain kinds of vocational education.

Three trends may be signalled which support this opinion. The first is naturally the fact that enrollments at the high-school level still lag behind enrollments in the elementary school. To this one must add the fact that there are only four years of high school and eight of elementary school. The second trend, already referred to, is toward the "upgrading" of teaching religious. More education naturally paves the way to the high-school classroom. But, and this is probably more important, it should, as a result of greater participation by religious, be possible to employ a substantial number of lay teachers on a basis of relative* parity with public schools in so far as salaries are concerned. The third trend is doubtless the most significant. Each new day brings with it the creation of clerical-lay boards concerned with the secondary schools. In many instances these boards include in their membership citizens of substance and influence, both Catholic and non-Catholic. It is already apparent that wherever Catholic school superintendents are willing to work enthusiastically with such boards they can add greatly to the resources of the schools in terms of finance and good will. Admittedly we do not have at present an over-all report on the manner in which such boards function. But on the basis of the samples which we have considered, it seems reasonable to assume that there is solid ground for hoping for success in the future.

Whether it is desirable to concentrate on the high school, in order to provide a measure of Catholic education for all children whose parents wish them to have it, is a query which must be submitted to those in charge of Catholic education as a whole. As has been said, its adoption would not automatically mean the demise of the parochial school, but that school would henceforth be in

* The word "relative" is used here because there seems to be little prospect of paying salaries of the kind now demanded for high-level administrative personnel in the public school system.

some measure peripheral. Many—and not merely those who resist the influence of the Council—believe that such a radical change would be a serious mistake. Their argument is necessarily more intuitive than "scientific," but the Notre Dame report does indicate how successful the Catholic elementary school has been in general when it comes to the teaching of religious "values."

The question naturally remains, how effective is religious teaching in the secondary school at the present time? We have already considered some of the evidence gathered during the course of the Notre Dame Study. While these data do not suggest either rejoicing or despair, they clearly indicate that the life of the teacher of religion is not an easy one. A study prepared for the 1966 workshop on the Christian formation of Jesuit high-school students of the Jesuit Educational Association by Father Joseph H. Fichter, S.J., based on "attitudes, impressions and experiences of 7,307 American boys,"• digests the answers to what we have called a "pupil opinionnaire." It is all the more interesting and valuable because of the long association of the Jesuits with secondary school education, and because of the superior quality of both their student bodies and teaching staffs, which consist of Jesuit priests, scholastics, and laymen. Moreover, the present study is one in a series dating back to 1962, and thus reflects a continuing concern by this group of Catholic educators with the quality of their achievement. In terms of expressed interest, classes in religion declined steadily during the four years spent in high school; the popularity of teachers of religion was similarly affected. On the other hand, the majority of the boys studied had given some consideration as to whether they should decide to follow a religious vocation, even though in the end only a relatively few actually decided to do so.

The Jesuit sociologist realistically accepts two premises. First, the character-building efficacy of the home is greater than that of the

• *Send Us a Boy* . . . . . *Get Back A Man* (Cambridge, Mass., 1966), Mimeographed.

school. Father Fichter cites one of his colleagues to the effect that a boy experiences two great influences—the home and the school—of which the first is by far the more important. And he adds, "In dealing with a boy with a good home background, our work is made relatively easy; with a poor one it is made extremely difficult, if not impossible." The second premise is that adolescence is a time for rebellion, and that boys are naturally more likely to kick against the traces than are girls. We have, so far as I know, virtually no information about the boys who drop out of these schools after entering them, for academic or disciplinary reasons. They may represent the outer fringe of rebellion, and it would be of general interest if more could be learned about them.

Among the more puzzling aspects of the over-all high school situation is failure to inculcate personal honesty. Father Fichter's study makes clear that cheating during tests, exams, and similar ordeals remains a problem for Jesuit educators. As in almost all institutions which have reported on the problem, the amount of cheating increases as the student nears graduation and the process of seeking admission to college. There are no easy solutions for those who attempt to bring Catholic educational practice into conformity with the ethical teaching of the Church. Confusion in the home regarding moral values, as well as the pressures encouraging cheating, make clear how difficult secondary education will continue to be, especially if the elementary school is curtailed.

New Problems for Catholic Colleges

The college is now probably the most widely and intensively discussed of all the divisions of American education. What is even more important, much of what is being said is interesting and helpful, exception having been made for some comment on the teacher-training colleges, which often suffer because their critics are still belaboring conditions which have long since been corrected. The reason for all this attention is the startling growth which has taken place within a comparatively few years. Even the Depression, when jobs were scarce and leisure ample, did not witness a marked increase in the percentages of young people going to colleges, except in those cities which offered free tuition in municipally operated institutions. When the Second World War was declared, about 14 per cent of young people in the appropriate age groups were on college campuses. Demobilization, followed by the "baby boom," which, in terms of children already born, will not taper off until approximately 1980, completely altered the situation. The official estimate is that nearly 16,000,000 young Americans will be of college age in 1975, and that half of them will be seeking admission. In other words, the percentage will have more than tripled during the thirty-five years after 1940. It is an extraordinary phenomenon, which to some extent has a counterpart in a few other countries.

Here our purpose is to place the Catholic college in perspective; comment on the educational situation as a whole is only for the purpose of establishing a relationship. The GI Bill created an appetite not only for college, but for college at a price everybody could afford to pay. Vastly increased public support was called for and is being given in ever expanding measure. Thus the steady development of municipal colleges, offering either a four- (or even five-) year program or a two-year (community college) curriculum, has been vigorous, indeed, and has been followed by a very great increase in the number of branches of the state universities erected in cities other than those where these universities themselves are at home. At some of these colleges no tuition charge is made. In others the fees are moderate. Two results may be noted. The taxpaying parent is likely to feel that since he helps to pay the "bill," his children also have a right to a college education. The community college is a convenient device for meeting this demand because its admission requirements are lower, although it can reward achievement by transferring the best of its graduates to four-year institutions. On the other hand a marked change has taken place in the traditional campus environment. Although something like a college "climate" develops in the municipal institution, strong ties to the home and the neighborhood persist. They are generally not deeply affected by developments which involve the faculty and the administration of the college. Indeed, many will not have the foggiest notion about how the college is organized and operated. A large number will also have part-time employment, which further restricts their collegiate concern to the classroom and the course work done in connection with it. The quality of the academic performance tends to be high; faculty morale is assured by a frequently affluent salary and fringe-benefit scale; and "democracy" protects faculty status and incumbency. Some Catholic and other private colleges are "competitive" with the public-supported municipal institutions, notably in New York, Chicago, and Detroit. But it seemingly makes very little difference from a religious point of view whether a youngster attends, for example, New York University rather than St. John's University.

The expansion of colleges in the state universities themselves has been rapid and great. Robert Hassenger has observed that in the fall of 1965 the University of Minnesota enrolled 9,614 Freshmen, while the eight "Ivy League" colleges mustered 9,420. No data concerning the total enrollment in all the private colleges of Minnesota, many of which are of very good quality, were available to me at the time this comment was being written, but the likelihood is that the state university surpassed their sum-total. Looking at such trends, a number of veteran observers of American education predict that unless the private colleges can to some extent match the growth of the state-supported colleges their share in forming the outlook of youth will soon be that of a minority stockholder. But how is such growth to be managed? What the student pays in terms of tuition and other charges at the "quality" institutions is less than what it costs to educate him, the difference being made up through interest on endowment funds and through other contributions. Nevertheless the check signed by the parent is a substantial one. In some states scholarship money made available through public bounty is payable to private and public colleges alike. There is also the tuition tax plan sponsored by Dr. Oliver C. Carmichael, which may some day be enacted into law. But as matters stand now any phenomenal relative growth in the number and size of private colleges seems improbable, unless they greatly dilute quality.

It would be erroneous to try to separate Catholic colleges from other private colleges when there is discussion of this kind of development. Of course there are differences of motivation to be considered. The attractiveness of the best institutions in both groups derives from prestige and the loyalty of alumni, but colleges conducted under Catholic, Jewish, or Protestant auspices frequently profit also by religious or group solidarity. If institutions like Brandeis, Vanderbilt, Georgetown, and Notre Dame have both prestige and a religious orientation which commands respect, they can grow slightly without running the risk of impoverishing themselves through expansion. The University of Pittsburgh, which recently faced a giant deficit, has set an example in which there is implicit a warning to all private universities which are not amply endowed. The smaller college may, however, be in a relatively advantageous position to expand proportionately, though not ambitiously. Many parents hesitate to send their daughters in particular into the vast mass movement which takes place annually to the public campuses. If they can be sure of the "quality" of the college and of its basic "decency," they will most likely continue to patronize it, at least as long as our society remains comparatively affluent. Henceforth, however, that college must at least try hard to be a reputable academic institution, and not expect that its religious orientation alone will keep it afloat. This is true of course for all denominational or "religiously committed" colleges, and not for Catholic institutions only.

How are these trends reflected in the Catholic college in particular? We estimate that in 1965 approximately 400,000 Catholic students were enrolled in Catholic colleges, while somewhat more than twice that many were attending secular institutions. The 400,000 figure may increase slightly during the years which lie ahead, but the other side of the ledger will show far greater gains. Greeley and Rossi concluded from their study of Catholic youth that Catholics will probably for some time equal if not outdistance other groups in the quest for higher education; and the Notre Dame report corroborates this by pointing to the academic character of Catholic secondary education. Can we determine what this means? The prevailing opinion—at least I think that it is—appears to be that the traditional Catholic state of mind which led to the choice of a Catholic college *primarily* to safeguard the faith can be expected to survive no more than twenty years longer. A very considerable majority of Catholic young people will have attended secular institutions without much more visible impairment of their faith than would have occurred on a Catholic campus. In general, the secular colleges, particularly those associated with state universities, will respect the student's religious commitment or at least ignore it; and the large number of Catholics in attendance will make it seem desirable to college administrators to assist in making provision for religious education and guidance. Indeed, since the recent Supreme Court decision acknowledging the constitutionality of "objective" courses in religion, a profusion of such courses has begun to appear on public campuses. Many of these will be taught by Catholic scholars, a goodly number of whom are now being trained in the divinity schools of the University of Chicago, Yale, and Harvard. This is added reason why the Catholic college may well have no more than twenty years in which to demonstrate that it exists in order to provide first-rate education within the context of a Catholic community.

The first-rate college, besides providing opportunities to acquire needed skills, should observe four "ground rules":

It exists in order to inculcate awareness in depth of problems and situations of concern to modern man, and in order to foster inquiry into whether solutions of such problems can be suggested. In doing so it will fully take into account the history of man and of the ideas by which he has lived.

It is staffed by men and women able to stimulate student thinking to a degree of intelligent intensity which all but a very few could not generate if left to their own devices.

It is concerned not merely with the intelligence but also with fostering a profound regard for the effective and aesthetic life of man.

As a Catholic college, it strives to foster social responsibility in the spirit of the Second Vatican Council.

It is equipped with aids which are now indispensable if these objectives are to be reached. It has libraries, laboratories, opportunities for research, as well as a "climate of opinion" in which the worth and freedom of every individual are recognized.

To be sure, one might list other requisite characteristics. For instance, one could say that the faculty must be relatively harmonious and in the scholarly sense homogeneous, that the presidents and deans must have some visibility on and off the campus, and that the student body must possess the ability to participate with meaningful success in the educational dialogue. Is a "residential atmosphere" desirable? This is a debatable question. The campus on which the student is in residence has advantages, but there are "day colleges" which manage to create a genuinely educational climate.

And so one may legitimately and unabashedly say to Catholic colleges that unless they feel certain of their ability to observe the ground rules they would be well advised to get out of the game. There are relatively painless ways to get out . . . at least at present. One way is to exit through amalgamation; another is through transforming the college into a secondary school. But granted that anything like a rash of raw new institutions can be avoided, enough is now known on the basis of sound research done on a variety of campuses or through pertinent committees of the American Council on Education and the American Association of Colleges to enable college administrators to find out what the ground rules involve.*

It has often been said that only the student actually knows what a college is like, and that it is quite impossible to find out what that knowledge is. Social psychologists have, however, gone to great pains of late to see what they can discover, and their efforts have been supplemented by fairly courageous "self-studies." The inquiry into its innermost secrets conducted by Mundelein College, Chicago, under the leadership of Sister Mary Ann Ida and Dr. N. J. Hruby is now well known and is being duplicated in part at other institutions. Dr. Hruby did not, to be sure, limit his research to the student body, but nevertheless went to great pains to discover as much as possible what it thought or felt about its "environment" at Mundelein. The development of "instruments" designed to find out whether an institution provides the kind of common life which will engender the good qualities associated with education at the college has been impressive. Thus a given institution may be a very pleasant place in which to live but provide very little genuine intellectual stimulation. Another may offer academic instruction of high quality but fail to provide anything which resembles a rewarding student group life. What we know so far about Catholic colleges in these terms appears to indicate that in general they keep closer to

* See, for example, *The Reforming of General Education*, by Daniel Bell (New York: Columbia University Press, 1966), a careful study of Columbia College, admittedly concerned with an academic background with which a small Catholic college will not be familiar, but richly suggestive of ideas concerning the basic methods and aims of collegiate instruction at the present time. The literature is, however, very rich, even if it ranges from quite superficial and impressionistic accounts of conversations with students to sociological inquiries which are so specialized as to be of little use to any save experts. But anyone can secure guidance by consulting the American Association of Colleges.

the normal pattern of the secondary school than they do to that of the more "satisfying" collegiate institution in the United States at the present time. This "satisfaction" often fills the European observer with admiration mingled with awe. He has seldom known anything like it. The European student passes from the confinement of the lycée or Gymnasium to the university, unfettered by anything except political movements and fraternities.•

It is probable that the "satisfying climate" alluded to results from leisure and affluence, and of course there are people who think we Americans have too much of both and therefore permit our young people to live in an unreal academic world until they are suddenly propelled into the grim here and now. A case can be made for this point of view, and not infrequently a student outlines it for himself. That he never comes to grips with anything outside the make-believe "dream universe" of the campus, that he enjoys liberties which will be unimaginable later on, strikes him with full force somewhere along the academic path. Educators sometimes forget that a "spiritual crisis" is likely to involve a boy or girl during adolescence, just as love may suddenly seem the only important thing in the world. In our time, the "crisis" will probably occur in terms of action. Young people who live with big "brush wars" and underdeveloped countries on one side of them, and the poverty, violence and racism of urban America on the other, may easily come to feel that sitting in classrooms talking with their instructors and fellow students, miles away from the scene of action, is simply being on a kind of vacation. The older Catholic college did not permit its students to wander far from the contemplation of eternity. Through daily Mass and the annual retreat, the spotlight was thrown on the eternal destiny of

• See the long awaited report of the study of *Church-Sponsored Higher Education in the United States*, by Manning W. Patillo, Jr. and Donald M. MacKenzie, published (1966) by the American Council on Education, and *The Shape of Catholic Higher Education*, edited by Robert Hassenger (Chicago, University of Chicago Press, 1967). The latter has chapters summarizing the institutional research done to date.

life with God, and the vocation to the religious life was thought of as the highest and noblest of all callings. Today, although the Council schema on "The Church in the Modern World" does not reduce the hope of eternal union with God, it adds a new *thisworldly* dimension to man's search for salvation. The climate of the Catholic college is changing and will change further; the moment has come for it to develop its own climate of freedom.*

* At this point a gloss would seem to be in order. The word "freedom" is one of the slippery items in the language. Some years ago Mortimer Adler constructed a gigantic intellectual filtering plant through which he let flow the more or less living waters of the philosophies concerned with the word. Here the purpose is far more modest. In the great classical tradition the word is legal and juridical. It has meant that the individual human person could profess to have rights which the state was bound to respect. When the state agreed to do so, a civil liberty was born. Thus freedom of conscience was recognized, probably because Church and State had so often joined forces to propel that conscience into a desired mold. Caesar and his "church" did so in ancient Rome, making war on Christian and Jew. Later on institutionalized Christendom and a variety of states imitated Caesar to the best of their ability. Anyone who wishes to study the origins of the belief that "this will never do" should read the pertinent documentation concerning the English seventeenth century. Thoughtful Oxford and Cambridge men, looking back over the butcheries of the Tudor and post-Tudor times, decided that something better, or at least more interesting, would have to be devised. John Locke has run away with the laurels, but this is due to the fact that it is easier to read an author than to study a trend. Proceeding from Thomas More to Abraham Cowley is at least as rewarding.

The Constitution of the United States, heir to British experience but sired by men who did not take that of France lightly either, not only protects the right of the citizen to join and support a religion of his choice (the caveat against the Mormons was rather special, since people did not foresee that having wives in series was really not very different from having them at one time), but also establishes the now traditional deduction that a man's religion shall be outside the pale of government interference, even by the tax collector. We now acknowledge a number of other rights, but doubtless that which transcends all others is that which assures the citizen of a fair trial when he is alleged to have broken a law. This we might almost facetiously, were the matter not genuinely earnest, term the "last right," for then the citizen is pitted against society. No doubt it permits of explication through analogy. Thus integration can be said to be a continuing effort to accord the Negro the right to a fair trial.

During generations he has been tried and found wanting in so far as the use

The principal difference between the college and the graduate school—which is the heart of the university proper—is to be found in the fact that instruction and inquiry are much more rigorously concentrated on a given segment of knowledge. Training and guiding students in the writing of a dissertation, which should be a detailed statement about something one has studied in depth and with some originality, is the central concern of the graduate school.

---

of public and private facilities is concerned, by reason of his color, history, and race. He had long since been accorded freedom of conscience, speech, and assembly, but only if he exercised that right separately from his white neighbors. Negroes in Selma, Alabama, could meet privately in their churches or elsewhere and say whatever they pleased. But they could not appeal to or denounce others in their company. It was a great deal like being a prisoner at the bar who could appeal to a jury only through an attorney who had committed a similar offense. Unfortunately, integration does not mean that the Negro's white neighbors are legally deprived of their freedom to hate, deride, and shun. Negro children in a predominantly white school are often treated abominably, but most of their complaints are without legal redress. White folk have a constitutional right to assemble and demand, if they so desire, that the Chief Justice of the United States be impeached because he has advocated the doctrine that racial discrimination is illegal. In other words, the right to a fair trial does not mean that all citizens must accept the verdict.

The freedom of the Negro, or of any other citizen for that matter, does not imply that he is henceforth to be treated with courtesy, made to feel at home in a neighborhood, listened to with respect, or be invited to attend social functions at which his kind are not wanted. He is at liberty to feel angry and embittered, but the more vocally he exercises this liberty the more likely he is to come square up against the dichotomy suggested long since by Sidney Hook— that between heresy and conspiracy. In the light of the American tradition, and of course of the Christian tradition as well, discrimination against the Negro as we have known it is heresy. One may deplore or indeed attack it on the basis of a dozen orthodoxies. But if the Negro were to decide that the heretic has no rights, or that something like an inquisitional tribunal (very democratically organized, with guns, Molotov cocktails, and knives) should be set up, he would automatically become a conspirator against the very tradition which has assured him of freedom of conscience and a fair trial.

I wish to draw one rather simple academic conclusion from what has been said. Implicit in the constitutional grant of freedom of conscience is the right to institutionalize it. Any number of people who feel the same way about things, who for example are bound together in respect for a traditional creed, are as-

The course of study as such is designed to provide a comprehensive and probing consideration of the background of knowledge against which the dissertation must be written. This task will be taken seriously by some graduate schools, lightly by others. Implied is the truism that those who teach must themselves be research-minded; they may, therefore, tend to act as if teaching (except in the sense of guiding) were a chore interfering with the business at hand. And indeed, if the heart of the matter is the dissertation, are not the hours spent in the classroom of peripheral significance? Many an American or European graduate student has been led to accept such a professorial point of view with anguish, annoyance, or relief. At present it would seem that more and more graduate training is being done through participation in research.

The real problem, though, is of a different kind. How is a graduate student, normally likely to dedicate much of his career to college-teaching, to acquire some teaching competence? Several universities, notably Harvard, have exercised leadership in trying to associate teacher-training with graduate study. In some departments of Harvard a fellow may be supported through a five-year period, two years of which are devoted to "supervised" teaching. The program has interested some of the best of Harvard's applicants for fellowships,

---

sured of the right to build a church, a school, or a university. They are not assured of anything else. They may for example find that their neighbors are just as ready to repudiate Catholics in some sections of the country as they are to throw rocks at Negroes (or whites) in another. Some people in the United States hate Catholics so much that they would rather die than contribute a nickel to the support of anything in which Catholics are interested. There are others who feel the same way about Jews or Protestants.

Let us admit that they have a right to do so. But it makes no more sense to grant a right to the Negro, without doing something to clothe that naked right in decent apparel, than it does to acknowledge the civil liberties of Catholics while doing everything in one's power to circumscribe them. The United States has a good many choices to make in this hour. One it does not propose is to limit the defense of the country to this group or that. It would be rather odd if we died together under some rain from the skies before we began to realize the simple fact that sharing death is so much easier than sharing life.

and one may say that the training devised for them is of unusual merit. Other institutions attempt to "structure" the period of graduate study in such a way that recipients of grants can add a year or two of experience as teaching assistants. The faculty of the beleaguered University of California has recently resurrected an idea which I believe originated with Harvard's great humanist Howard Mumford Jones, and hopes to offer a degree preparation for which will demand less of a concentration on the dissertation field, so that the candidate can emerge less "research minded" and more attuned to teaching. I am afraid that I remain skeptical about the practical results likely to follow this effort. The prestige now attached to the straightforward doctorate of ancient Germanic vintage is too great. Nevertheless, many gifted young instructors, graduates of distinguished universities, are quite terrified by their initial classroom experience, and some of them even decide to abandon teaching.

These are other problems which every university, Catholic or not, must face. Can a university deserve the name if in addition to its undergraduate division it operates professional schools only, and not a graduate school in the strict sense? I would say yes, provided that what is meant is not a school so far removed from the undergraduate establishment as to make no impact on it. When they are first rate, the influence of professional schools on undergraduate instruction can be very great and academically significant. An excellent law school, for example, may actually do as much to inculcate social ethics in the general student body as a department of theology. This is a point which existing Catholic universities might well consider. Many of them originated as congeries of professional schools, following in this respect, despite European influence, the pattern of the land-grant college. Perhaps they could serve their student bodies best if they set about making their professional schools truly distinguished, so that when one thought of their law schools or their schools of business administration one would know that they were on a level with similar schools at Yale or Pennsylvania.

At any rate, the question is now sometimes asked whether the very idea of a Catholic university is at all tenable. Rosemary Lauer, in the heat of debate about a special situation, made the somewhat unphilosophical generalization that a juxtaposition of "Catholic" with "university" was a contradiction of terms. There are, of course, others who make the same statement because they hold that the "Truth" which Christian theology attempts to expound is at best a mirage, and perhaps a dangerous and deleterious one. We shall try to discuss the question *contra* and *pro*, with as much candor as possible.

The Role of the Catholic University

I shall try to present the case *against* the need for a Catholic university—or at least for many Catholic universities—objectively, though with little attention to minor caveats against including religion in education. To begin with, there is no reason to suppose that a contribution to knowledge in any field will be more significant because the investigator has studied or taught in a Catholic university. That would seem to be rather obvious in so far as the natural sciences and the social sciences in particular are concerned, but it may also be true in humanistic studies. Of course, a student will profit greatly through association with a truly creative scholar if such a scholar is present on a Catholic university campus. Normally, however, such scholars will be attracted to secular campuses not so much because of salary differentials, as is often mistakenly thought, but because the most gifted students seek to attend institutions which have prestige, impressive concentration of faculty, and other resources in quantity. At any rate, there is no discernible reason why a dissertation which probes into a chemical compound or analyzes voting habits in a particular city will be any better for being the product of a Catholic university. The only thing that counts is whether or not it is the outcome of sound, honest, and—if possible

—imaginative effort. Surely a world as greatly in disarray as ours provides the Church with challenges more significant than maintaining separate institutions in order to sponsor dissertations of this character.

Considered as citizens, Catholics may rightly be expected to carry their fair share of the nation's intellectual burden. It would appear that they have not been doing so, or at least this is the opinion of some of the ablest Catholic scholars themselves. Can it be that their own universities have been too isolated from the mainstream of American higher education? They may be and sometimes are pleasant places, well suited for undergraduate study. But why should they attempt to siphon off a few of the very scarce scholarly fraternity for service in their graduate schools, thus in turn isolating them? It is primarily for this reason that the Germans and the Austrians, by and large, have not favored the establishment of Catholic universities as distinguished from the secondary schools (Gymnasiums). German Catholics in particular, so often the victims of discriminatory practices in the past, or suffering by reason of a lack of interest in higher education on the part of some of their bishops, are now trying hard to achieve parity in so far as appointments to the eminent universities of their country are concerned. They will tell you that skimming off any considerable number of their colleagues in order to staff a Catholic university would be highly regrettable, if not indeed deplorable. Cannot a similar case be made for the United States? Might it not be easier to "get a dialogue going" (a horrible phrase but now everywhere in use) against the background of Harvard, Stanford, or Wisconsin rather than that of St John's University?

The Catholic university maintains that the principal reason for its existence is that philosophy and theology can be taught in it with due regard for what is alive in the tradition of the Church. At any rate this is what was thought not so long ago. The orthodoxy of the teaching theologian was to be assured by exacting an oath of allegiance to the *magisterium*; and it was the Thomistic philosophy which would establish the mode of reason which the theologian could profitably use. But, in the light of the realities all about us, what is the "perennial philosophy" now? The seminary mind used to feel it could wait until the "errors" latent in a given trend of thought had been revealed. After all, many thinkers in Communist-dominated countries have now become skeptical about almost everything in the repertory of Karl Marx. In their view, his theory of the class struggle led only to another such struggle, and his vision of the ultimate state turns out to be an infantile mirage. Why should not the "perennial philosopher" sit back comfortably and say, "I told you so?" It is a pleasant pastime, but unfortunately not very many people want to take it up. They do not simply agree that Marx is passé and that we need only study the *Summa*. Unfortunately, they have got used to wanting much the same things Marx wanted, and are apt to try to reach comparable ends with different means.

Or let us consider Newman's *Idea of a University*. This developed with great subtlety and imaginative power a case for a Catholic institution of higher learning in which the study of science and literature would spin freely round a center of theological studies. But his university turns out on inspection to have been a projection of a Catholic Oxford, with Catholic theologians doing pretty much what the Oxford Movement had done within the framework of Anglicanism. It was certainly not a medieval university in any sense. Professor James J. John has recently clarified the medieval situation:

> It is also common knowledge that there was a hierarchy among the faculties, with Theology at the head and ruling as queen, followed by law and medicine, and then arts in the rear and serving as ANCILLA or handmaiden. These commonplaces no doubt describe the medieval ideal, but the actual medieval university often fell short, especially in the number of faculties. And strange as it may

seem in a Catholic institution the faculty most often absent was that of theology. . . . Formal theological training on the university level was long reserved exclusively to the Universities of Paris, Oxford and Cambridge.•

The reason, one surmises, was that it was easier for the Church to keep an eye on a few theological faculties, which in turn found it simpler to exercise an influence on the always changing, scintillating, discoursing philosophers if they did not spread themselves too thin or get too deeply involved in the fracas. In the United States until quite recently we have had a somewhat comparable situation. Just one Catholic institution of the highest quality was dedicated to the study of systematic theology—Woodstock College —though there were several good schools of pastoral theology. And in so far as philosophy is concerned, as long as it was possible to "guide" the teaching of the subject by agreeing that it was to be Thomist, with the modifications based on monastic or university traditions previously indicated, many or most of the perils of the medieval time could be avoided.

But the Second Vatican Council has recognized that it is precisely this kind of control which the modern university man, or woman for that matter, finds unacceptable. Who but the scholar humbly rooted in faith can determine what inferences may be drawn tentatively in philosophical terms from the truth that is in revelation? Nobody, or at least hardly anybody, wants any more inquisitions, religious or secular. Human society is almost fanatically eager to think what it pleases, do what it pleases, read and believe what it pleases. Only, paradoxically, *it wants to believe something.* And so if one asks a Catholic university, moving around a core of theological and philosophical discussion that is itself in a state of flux, what it has to offer to meet this desire for belief, what response can it make?

• *Conditions and Purposes of the Modern University—The Christian Dimension* (Washington, D. C.: Aldine Press, 1966), p. 9.

We do not question the need for centers of theological and philosophical training. They should be of high quality. Above all they should be holy places. But why should it be taken for granted that a university, the contemporary university, should house them, except perhaps in the sense that it has, like Munich or Tübingen, a faculty of theology coequal with other faculties? Was it perhaps providential that the Jesuits in France and Germany were ostracized and frequently restrained from having a corporate domicile, so that they developed a "new theology" by reason of a sense of immersion in and responsibility for the society in which they lived as scattered and secret shepherds? Does not a university make proud claims to knowledge which faith must shun? Not even St. Paul could probe into the mystery of divine Providence. All he could say, magnificently, was:

How inexhaustible God's resources, wisdom and knowledge are!
How unfathomable his decisions are, and how untraceable his ways!
Who has ever known the Lord's thoughts, or advised him?
Or who has advanced anything to him, for which he will have to be repaid?
For from him everything comes; through him everything exists; and in him everything ends! Glory to Him forever! Amen.*

Nevertheless it is true that the believing Christian, contemplating the glory and the evil of these days, will not fail to sense with awe that Providence has not ceased in its love for man. And if this be true, is not our principal task to make this evident with insight and humility, patience and affection?

Is it not true that the Catholic university is destined to be a kind of enclave for a few, while the great mass of Catholics in quest of higher education will be found elsewhere? To be sure, the statistical estimate which forecasts that in the not-too-far-distant future 70 per cent of all young Catholics seeking higher education will ma-

* Goodspeed Version.

triculate in non-Catholic institutions is probably subject to some corrective analysis. Many widely patronized forms of collegiate experience in particular lie pretty much outside the Catholic bailiwick —junior colleges, municipal continuing-education programs, technical institutes, and so forth. Even so! If, for example, the state of Illinois puts into effect its almost grandiose plan for creating populous centers of learning, at the college as well as the graduate-school level, the question will immediately arise: Why should I, a parent named John Jones, pay five times as much in tuition costs to send my daughter Ellen to a Catholic college, even though I know that this college is in several important respects a good college? Since I am aware that many of my Catholic friends and neighbors are sending their children to public colleges, can I not assume that the Church, alert to its mission, will provide adequate centers in which religious life can be fostered and strengthened? Is it not already doing so to the best of its ability? Since priests, religious, and well-trained laymen are in short supply, why coop them up to take care of an "elite" while the spiritual needs of very large numbers are so great?

If this argument has any validity with regard to undergraduate education, how much more compelling it must be at the level of the graduate school! It is true that monetary problems of students may play a lesser role, since a Catholic institution with the requisite quality can secure some of the fellowships now available. In so far as higher technological education in particular is concerned, the state universities will inevitably attract the largest number. Religion there is *Privatsache*; in this sense the university is part of what Harvey Cox has called the "secular city," if it is not actually the core. Someday, of course, the worm may turn. Young people may find out that being a skilled craftsman can be a more lucrative and satisfactory calling than teaching English to Freshmen on a sprawling undergraduate campus, provided that reputable opportunities for humanistic education continue to exist. But as of the moment we must assume that the shadow of the multiiversity will continue to lengthen and that unless the Church extends a hand, the curtain will drop on repeated scenes of religious innocuousness and irrelevance.

Is not a new dimension of the Church as a teaching and mind-forming society therefore required? We must surely begin to puzzle out the inner and outer boundaries. Call to mind the Puritan William Prynne's seventeenth-century comment on the celebration of Christmas. He found that the connection between Yuletide revels and the Roman Saturnalia were so close—both of them being spent in "revelling, epicurism, wantonness, idleness, dancing, drinking, stage plays, and such other Christmas disorder"—that all pious Christians should abominate them. There have been times when the prevailing Christian attitude toward scholarly inquiry not directed to the study of the sacred texts was likewise that it could only be dangerous folly. It was in conformity with a long Augustinian tradition that Thomas à. Kempis wrote: "Never read thou the word in order to appear more learned or wiser. Study the mortification of thy vices; for this will profit thee more than the knowledge of knotty questions." In all truth, it is the folly of the Christian scholar that he must always be ready to say that this counsel is wise. If the pursuit of learning were to mean that we no longer "studied the mortification of our vices," or that in disentangling knotty questions we forgot the Maker of all things, then that pursuit would have to be avoided by individuals committed to the exemplification of Christ in a society which to so great an extent knows him not.

Yet it is precisely the fact that he is not known which, paradoxically, is the reason why the pursuit of knowledge has become the most important Christian missionary activity of our time. In a sense it has been so in all times. Nevertheless if we Christians of the present ask ourselves candidly where our brothers are, we must of necessity answer: they are dwelling within the knowledge of things, in the belief that the kind of knowledge which is science can change and improve all there is, even the psyche and the unborn baby in the test tube. They are living also in a new realm of the spirit, which is that of a humanity freed from physical labor, bondage to ignorance, and to a great extent physical pain. In a sense theirs is a utopian spirit, but never before has Utopia contained so hard a core of realism. The limits of our knowledge are now imposed by the cosmos, not by the human mind.

We cannot do much more than our share in the service of this utopia. But there is something else. The heart of man does not know less of anxiety, even of agony. The "death wish" which Camus found embedded in every human heart is complemented by the death knell which the bomb can sound. How different this is from the "reverent dread" about which Julian of Norwich wrote, saying that this is "the fair courtesy that is in Heaven afore God's face!" Knowing that the infinitude of God is today opposed, as never before, to the quasi-infinitude of the human mind, shall we who are Christ's followers love the men of our time enough to immerse ourselves in the mental and spiritual world which has created them and which in turn they also create? And if we answer affirmatively, do we not belong, as did St. Francis Xavier, in the wide world?

We have now made the argument against the Catholic university. What is the case for it? I should like to write off at the outset any notion that a return to the nineteenth-century conception of such a university is conceivable at the present time. It cannot be a mouthpiece for the *magisterium*, however deeply and sincerely it may respect that *magisterium*. But at the same time neither it nor any contemporary university can be *universitas*—that is, an organization of faculties which purports to provide a synthesis of, or at least a panoramic look (*Ueberblick*) at, everything which is known. It can only be a grouping of specializations. It is now just as difficult for higher education with an overt religious commitment to fathom the mysteries of God's world, the heights and depths of creation, as it would be to map out the "unsearchable ways" of God himself. One can arrive at generalizations about the methods of inquiry used by the natural scientist, but is it really possible to find out much that is basically significant when he himself reports that he has started out with a surmisal, an insight, or an intuition, all of which are beyond definition? Nor are the social sciences easier to integrate in terms of theory. They have attempted to emulate the procedures of the natural scientist; but apart from the previously stated fact that even these are only to a certain extent determinable, it has grown more evident that human conduct is not measurable in qualitative terms unless it is pressed into a mold which makes any other than quantitative responses impossible.

But if these things are true, theology cannot now be the "queen of the sciences" in any meaningful sense. To be sure, one might argue that since it is concerned with God, who is the fullness of being, theology takes precedence over sciences which are necessarily concerned with the contingent. But is even this way of looking at the matter any longer very relevant? If, as the Second Vatican Council has affirmed, the Church as the family of mankind is concerned primarily with salvation and salvation history, then theology is properly the study of some basically significant ways in which God is believed or known to have dealt with man, to have provided a path down which man can come to him, and to have given tangible human expression of his affection. But the perceptive scientist will also be aware of some of God's ways. The conclusion accordingly is that though a Catholic university must be concerned with theological studies—and with philosophical reflection which in some degree buttresses those studies, it will no longer maintain that this is the only reason why it exists. This change of emphasis is radical, but unavoidable.

Those who make up the core of its faculty and its student body may rather say: "We are men and women who have resolved to lead the life of the mind in a way which only a genuine university, combining rigor with courtesy, can provide in every dimension of scholarly venture and worth. At the same time we have accepted with all our hearts Pascal's wager that God is and has spoken. We have done this for a variety of reasons, so that in our diversity we offer, as does life itself, testimony which is one through many."

In listing these reasons, it would be found that some have been deeply moved by the testimony of the ratio, the data-analyzing activity of the intelligence. They are Thomists in one of the many senses which that term now implies, perhaps exploring the validity of a synthesis of the *Summa* and the *Grammar of Assent*. Others have been deeply moved by the testimony of the men and women who are called "mystics," whether of our own time or another, placing Rabindranath Tagore beside Hugh of St. Victor. Still others may have gone down a road similar to that once traveled by Simone Weil and come to the conclusion that "perfection" is "real"—in Augustinian terms, that only the desire for perfection can truly satisfy a human being, and that perfection is in God only. Many will have been bowled over by the person of the Lord Jesus, and have come to agree with Friedrich von Hügel:

For a Person came, and lived and loved, and did and taught, and died and rose again, and lives on by His Power and His Spirit for ever within us and amongst us, so unspeakably rich and yet so simple, so sublime and yet so homely, so divinely above us precisely in being so divinely near,—that His character and teaching require, for an ever fuller and yet never complete understanding, the varying study, and different experiments and applications, embodiments and unrollings of all the races and civilizations, of all the individual and corporate, the simultaneous and successive experiences of the human race to the end of time.*

Some, like Lecomte du Noüy, will have felt in their bones the weakness of the reed on which Positivism invited them to lean. They

* *Readings from Friedrich von Hügel*, Selected by Algar Thorold (London, 1928), p. 41.

may recall some phenomenon such as that reported by the German philosopher Peter Wust at the close of the first of the two great holocausts. God was never so dead as he was in the early years of the twentieth century! Wust wrote:

On December 31, 1913, the eminent Berlin jurist, Joseph Kohler, wrote the preface to a book. At the end of this preface he triumphantly spoke of the victory won by the modern mind. With particular pride he pointed out that war, like private revenge, has been, so to speak, left behind, thanks to the great strides made by modern reason which, as Comte had already said, must finally succeed in abolishing all irrational outbursts of violence. The fury of war, in Kohler's opinion, had been banished to the Far East, where it was lingering out its last days. Perhaps the Berlin savant wrote those proud words on the last night of the year, oblivious of the fact that with the stroke of twelve at his back the hands of the great clock of world history had swung forward to the fateful year 1914.*

Many—during recent years, very many—have held that a man thinks best about being man when he stops short and asks the mysterious questions, the ones which perhaps cannot be answered. Aristotle's "rational animal" definition is all right as far as it goes, but it excludes too much. Might not the phrase be more satisfactory if it read, "rational-irrational animal"? Then, however, one would have to reason about irrationality, and that is impossible. Is it not far better to say with the Existentialists that one can experience it, and see whether the experience can be shared with others, even God? The anxiety embedded in being human prevents such a thinker from exaggerating the value of humanism. In the case of Kierkegaard the major form of exaggeration was Hegel's. For Dostoevski it was the union of amoral intellect and power. And so on. At any rate the Existentialists are legion and their voices are strong in the concert of Christian and Catholic thought.

* "Crisis in the West," *Essays in Order*, ed. Christopher Dawson and T. F. Burns. 3 vols. (New York: Macmillan, 1931), I, ii, 129.

Some will cling to what was essential in Romanticism and drink their fill of the beauty of the Catholic cultural tradition. Perhaps this will not happen often to what is now the younger generation. They may not much care whether "The Middle Ages sleep in alabaster, a beautiful long sleep," to quote Wilfred Childe, or even whether the monks once saved the culture of the West. Nevertheless one should not disparage those who respond aesthetically to such a view of cultural history; as a matter of fact, they have effective and persuasive spokesmen.

Then there are those assailed by the doubt which rings itself around their throats like a hangman's cord never drawn tight, often losing the engagement temporarily but nevertheless returning to the struggle. Perhaps they are simply drawing on the memory of a mother who was "like a white candle in a holy place," which pursues them as Monica pursued Augustine's dreams and waking hours. The image we are suggesting is not that of a manufactured phrase ("we must seek truth," or "values are essential"), but rather that of a person—in some sense a saint—through whom the practice of the Christian faith was made so impressive and persuasive, though to the rebellious sometimes so exasperating, that it would be utterly impossible to blot the image out. We shall hope that among those who accept the wager for the sake of their university, there will be not a few such men and women. For they bring to the enterprise the realism of an experience which will build into it a constant struggle for spiritual adventure.

Thus the reason for the Catholic university's being is not a formula, not a philosophical theory or a theological textbook, not a simply defined task such as teaching values because they are not taught elsewhere. The Catholic university is the consequence of a congruence. It is a corporate resolve to achieve the interpenetration of religious and scientific experience. It is like a great farm on which wheat and corn, and woodland and beasts, draw diversified sustenance from the soil. Of course we know that in order to keep the enterprise going we shall need help. There will be places which some can fill whose participation in, and understanding of, the corporate expression of the Christian faith will be conventional, rooted primarily in custom or heritage. No one will toss them aside contemptuously.

In order to meet all the exacting demands of the disciplines we foster we must associate with ourselves men and women not of our faith, not of our group. This is sometimes wrongly held to imply a watering down of the idea of a Catholic university. Precisely the opposite is true. To be sure, if it did not have a constituent body of scholars such as I have described, if the great majority of those teaching were secularists, a given Catholic university should in all candor select another label, even as some universities founded by Protestants have done. But only a leaven of scholars who have different traditions, ranging from Lutheranism to Zen Buddhism, can provide the breadth of association with the whole human family which is the proper mode of the life of the Church. Indeed it is not too much to say that a Catholic university without such a leaven would be stale bread.

At any rate, we who form a Catholic university strive to deepen our realization of what our acceptance of Pascal's wager means. We are a company of gamblers who believe they have a sure thing. Of course, we need freedom. This requirement is often pointed out by friend and enemy alike, but the matter is not simple. Note that if men do not accept the wager, they must live accordingly, and that is deterministic enough. To be sure, they are free to select almost any way of doing so, but this does not in the end lead to much greater freedom of choice than we have. Whether they elect to follow Nietzsche, Santayana, or Marx or any of a wide number of other choices, it is, however, vital that Catholic Christians have comradeship with them, in order to comprehend the great diversity of our experiences, origins, disciplines, and aspirations, and for the sake of the university itself. To a Catholic, it makes all the differ-

ence which side of the wager a man is on, but, above everything, all
are members of the human family, guided by conscience and the
laws of evidence.

The Catholic university of the present, however, has possibilities
of freedom which until recently were not accorded it. The ecclesiastical censor who stopped intellectual traffic when that seemed to
him the right thing to do is out of date. During an earlier time he
could put Antonio Fogazzaro's *Il Santo* on the Index of Forbidden
Books; and inside the beleaguered Catholic fortress it required considerable courage even to ask why. Today the traffic in images and
ideas is so dense that regulating it through censorship would be like
trying to stop the leaves from falling off the trees during Novem-
ber. That in itself is sufficient reason why men need the wonderful
courtesy of a genuine university bent on living up to its name. In
it people can differ and debate without losing their tempers and
phoning for the police.

It is therefore the function of the Catholic university to replace
censorship with criticism. For all who are its members the Church is
holy, apostolic. By analogy, Catholic scholarship has the task of dis-
cerning what in the continuing life of the mind reflects the tradition
and the insight of the Church. No illustration is more indicative of
this need than the life story of Teilhard de Chardin. That the censor
kept on peeping over his shoulder while he was writing, making
publication difficult if not impossible, demurring and yet paradoxically being loving and gentle, is one part of the record. The other
part is now much, much more important: If the brilliant Jesuit,
looking so far back into the past and so far forward into the future,
had had the benefit of truly intelligent criticism from within the
university, his books might not reveal some of the weaknesses which
are now evident. They would have retained their originality and
drive, but they would have profited by awareness of the obstacles in
the way. It is now too late, tragically too late, for that; and modern
Catholicism has too often been too late. Sharp dissent there must

be, even repudiation, in religion as in every other field of study and inquiry. It is the duty of a distinguished modern Catholic university to provide them. For the sake of its own well-being, it must also retain a keen penitential conscience. One thinks again of Pascal:

All that is in the world is the lust of the flesh, or the lust of the eyes, or the pride of life: LIBIDO SENTIENDI, LIBIDO SCIENDI, LIBIDO DOMINANDI. *Wreatched is the cursed land which these three rivers of life inflame rather than water. Happy they who on those rivers, are not overwhelmed nor carried away, but are immovably fixed, not standing but seated on a low and secure base, whence they do not rise before the light, but having rested in peace stretch out their hands to Him, who must lift them up, and make them stand upright and firm in the porches of the New Jerusalem.*

Therefore we who in diverse ways have been prepared for the task of building a Catholic university must draw every consequence from our action. We are no longer locked in a house with drawn blinds, behind which—if we push them back a bit—we can smile a little at the assumed folly of others. We are out in the street, with the traffic and the dust, the neon signs, the poking elbows, the spittle dripping off the curb, the girls wearing dresses that cost $9.95, and the prostitutes who get their mink stoles second-hand. There is no significant book in the bookstalls we do not read and think about; there is no tune we do not try to hum; there is no job that promises to amount to anything we will not roll up our sleeves for. Anybody who wishes to stop at our university house will be welcome; we will listen to everyone who wants to talk. And in these days when the university must do many things which are in the public interest we will pitch in though the work may be distracting and sometimes disappointing.

In short, the men who direct the Catholic universities of the future, or teach in them, will take freedom of inquiry and expression for granted, because only the unfettered mind can be unimpeachable. But on another plane they will understand that of necessity a part of their institutional liberty must now be auctioned off. A university can no longer be what in a Platonic or Newmanist sense it should be. It is inevitably part of the contemporary scene, and quite as necessarily in the public domain. If its faculty are research-minded—and how could they be anything else?—it will respond to a recognized public need for studies which may yield some benefit for mankind or again may not. Who can tell in advance? Or who looking back can decide whether the research undertaken to create the atomic bomb opened a door to disaster? Alas, a modern university is like so much else in the modern world. It does not know what it is doing. And so for this reason one must frankly admit that the farther the Catholic university moves into the public domain the less individualized its character will be, and perhaps even the less discernibly spiritual its orientation will become. For the sake of parity with others it will acquire similarity. All it can really say at this point is that it is following the directives of the Church it presumably serves. Pope John XXIII and the Council he summoned into being said nothing more frequently, or with greater zest, than that the order of change, the technological order, is the realm in which the Church's mission must henceforth be conducted. Obviously therefore the Catholic university must live within that order, and train young people to do so with ever increasing skill.

That there are grave risks here may not be as evident as perhaps it should be. Being in the public domain—being chained, where research is concerned, to tasks which are of direct, immediate interest to the body politic—can act as a curb, or even as a stone around the waist. Let us state the problem at a low level of materialistic concern. A private university always needs more money than it has. After having dealt with the student as a tax-collector does with the citizen, it passes the collection-box around to the corporately or individually wealthy. Then, of course, there is always the state. The university which agrees to do things just because money is available may well be venal. Must the galleon always reach port with the gold? Or should one be squeamish about the blood on the gold? No kind of prostitution could be worse than the prostitution of the university, for this is the real treason of the clerks. Accordingly one must say that although the Catholic university should not shirk its duty within the public domain, it must never be for sale. It is a holy place. It must for weal or woe bear witness. I am convinced that the Catholic people sense this deeply, no matter how like other universities institutions those such as Louvain or Notre Dame may become. For this reason, the *real,* abiding reason why a Catholic university should exist, the university comes alive and stays alive. It grows mysteriously out of the experience, the desire, the affection, and the awe of people who are the Church.

It is often said, and the observation is pertinent and important, that the existence of a Catholic university will depend on whether academically gifted young people continue to want to come to it even though the financial sacrifice involved is necessarily great. Certainly if they did not, if they wished rather to "escape," the Catholic university would be in considerable peril and there would be no point in trying to conceal the fact. But if the question of finance has been deprived of its sting by increased provision for student scholarships, there is no basis for pessimism on this score, if the university vigorously realizes its opportunity. It is true that there is now a conflict between generations which comes closer to the edge of actual combat than any we have previously had to reckon with in this country. The present situation, at least in the eyes of those of us who must look at it from a distance, seems to derive from a very real awareness of the weight of numbers and the babel which has so little room for one voice.

It seems to me that this feeling should prove less bitter on the kind of Catholic campus I have been describing than elsewhere. But it is true that the traditional environment, which was based on a set of rules designed to provide a discipline making holiness possible, cannot long survive. The rules are, in the minds of undergraduates, enforced *in loco parentis;* and it is precisely the parent from whom the young man or woman seeks to break away. To build a university community will therefore not be easy. It never has been, especially when a major part of the job has been bringing the colleges and the graduate or professional schools into some kind of interlocking relationship. But if those, religious and lay, who give the university its scholarly depth and breadth can reach out to young people with respect, hope, and affection, a measure of contagion will be provided. Only this kind of contagion has ever called a Christian community into being.

Just a word in summary of the argument. When one says that an educational institution needs constantly to bear in mind the relationship between its activity and the life of the total community in which it finds itself, one is talking in peculiarly contemporary terms. Probably eighteenth-century Oxford could not have cared less, and a good case could be made in favor of its position. We cannot make that for ourselves. We are modern and therefore mobile, and in this context there is need for centers of higher learning in which Catholics can muster their strength and gradually acquire that measure of casual certainty about their purpose in the nation which is the indispensable complement of maturity. There is no need to make glowing phrases about the matter. It will be quite sufficient if some generations hence the American Catholic scholar can be nonchalant as he walks about the intellectual scene. He will be as little of a prig, we hope, as Colonel Newcombe was, and as much of an adventurer as Daniel Boone. He will wear the hairshirt of his religious commitment but after washing it he will not hang it on the line. Men will know without being told that there is a place in his heart to which he withdraws, but realizing that will not lead them to think that there is any kind of pride in him. He will understand that his scholarship, however impressive it may be, is only a segment of the total scholarly endeavor, and that its deep purpose is to sense more acutely the blessing which lies on all Being, all truth about Being, because it is of God.

8
The
Climate
of Change

There is a text for this chapter, taken from the Conclusion of the *Pastoral Constitution on the Church in the Modern World*, promulgated at the close of the Second Vatican Council:

> *Drawn from the treasures of Church teaching, the proposals of this sacred synod look to the assistance of every man of our time, whether he believes in God or does not explicitly recognize Him. Their purpose is to keep men gain a sharper insight into their full destiny, so that they can fashion the world more to man's surpassing dignity, search for a brotherhood which is universal and more deeply rooted, and meet the urgencies of our age with a gallant and unified effort born of love.*
>
> *Undeniably this conciliar program is but a general one in its several parts—and deliberately so, given the immense variety of situations and forms of human culture in the world. Indeed, while it presents teaching already accepted in the Church, the program will have to be*

further pursued and amplified, since it often deals with matters in a constant state of development. Still, we have relied on the Word of God and the spirit of the gospel. We entertain the hope that many of our proposals will be able to bring substantial benefit to every one, especially after they have been adapted to individual nations and mentalities by the faithful, under the guidance of their pastors.*

It would be difficult to conceive of a more "open ended" theological declaration. Note that whenever the teaching of the Church on doctrinal issues was under consideration the authority of the Holy See and of the bishops was carefully defined by the Council, no matter how thoroughgoing and even startling the innovation. Thus, in the *Constitution on the Liturgy*, it is recognized that adaptations might conceivably go far beyond merely translating the liturgical texts into vernacular languages, but it is affirmed that such adaptations must first be "carefully and prudently" considered by the bishops or bishop concerned, and then submitted to the Apostolic See for approval. In the *Pastoral Constitution on the Church in the Modern World*, however, no such specific limitations are discernible. And yet this is the document which deals with all things which are the proper concern of education, except in so far this treats of the Church, the study of Scripture, and the organization of the "family of God." Here we also find proposed a grant of freedom in terms of intercultural discussion which is quite extraordinary: ". . . let it be recognized that all the faithful, clerical and lay, possess a lawful freedom of inquiry and of thought, and the freedom to express their minds humbly and courageously about those matters in which they enjoy competence."** This is virtually the language of the first statement on academic freedom issued by the American Association of University Professors! That pioneer declaration also stressed both liberty and competence.

* Walter M. Abbott, S.J. (ed.), *The Documents of Vatican II* (New York: Guild Press, 1966), p. 305.
** *Ibid.*, p. 270.

In other words, Catholic education is henceforth committed to participation in the world-wide discussion of the arts and the sciences as well as of theology. All the shades are up and the windows open. Many people, not accustomed to being in this kind of public thoroughfare, feel a little as if they had suddenly been whisked off to a town in the Near East where everything is done in the street, from haircutting to having one's blood pressure taken. Of course, a contemporary Catholic is not obliged to agree with every view expressed in this text because (as the authors say) it was written against the background of the vast and far-reaching changes which have taken place in human society and in the knowledge that other changes will undoubtedly occur. But a Catholic now seems necessarily committed to the basic guidelines of the constitution, which are in essence those spelled out in the Johannine encyclicals, *Mater et Magistra* and *Pacem in terris*: the proper norms of human society are peace, freedom, justice, and love. Catholics acting in concert with all men of good will are bidden to help transform these norms into social realities.

What does all this signify in terms of the educational mission of the Church? What does it mean to the religious in particular, for whom this is of both missionary and professional concern? How is Christ's kingdom, which is not of this world, to be established in the world, and, what is more, with the help of the world? These are questions which many are now exploring, often in a mood of bewilderment . . . and bewilderment will not be altogether absent from the comment which follows. Undoubtedly what has been happening recently in the Church can only be understood as a new Pentecost— a fresh outpouring of the Spirit in a world to which science has been giving such vast instrumentalities of change that literally nothing human can remain as it has been. But Science knows only too well that what it provides so lavishly, namely the resources of nature harnessed to human use, does not alter the fact that man has knowledge of both good and evil. Only God knows how great man's potentiality for evil really is. History, even contemporary history, merely offers samples. Therefore the language of the Holy Spirit, speaking through the Church, calls for a release of all the forces which can be unleashed from mankind's knowledge of the Good.

It is, for example, not necessary that men slay each other in meaningless holocausts like those we have witnessed during this century, or could witness on an unimaginable scale of terror almost any evening. The time has also passed when the vast majority of human beings must live with practically nothing to eat or to wear. Science could, for instance, create a system of irrigation in Latin America which would increase the production of food there a hundred fold. It is also no longer inevitable that countless millions of people must remain illiterate. And though city life will henceforth be the lot of the majority of human creatures, that life can be freed from the inhumanity which is now the appalling lot of very many. All that is called for is that man increase his knowledge of the Good and resolve to take advantage of every opportunity to put it to use. The Church ardently believes that such an awareness can be maintained only in union with God, who has been made manifest to it through Christ. But in its vision of the new Pentecost it is moved to say, in essence: "Many of you who are our companions in human history, do not possess the gift of faith. But we revere the knowledge of the Good that is given you through the natural order and your desire to use that knowledge. Together we can substitute freedom for bondage and terror, justice for lawlessness, tranquility for war, human welfare for human rapine. Let us do so!"

Yet very many of us are rooted in the soil of the Church as it was before the New Pentecost. This does not mean only that we may not like what is happening and regret, bitterly perhaps, a whole catalogue of innovations, from the loss of the Latin Mass and the chant which traditionally accompanied it, to ecumenism and modern scriptural exegesis. It may be that few adult Catholics in the United States do not, when they are entirely candid with themselves, deplore the tossing aside of something or other which seemed to them precious. But having roots in the soil of the Church as it was can also lead to just the opposite result. We can cut off the tree from those roots and attempt to graft it on others. We can say that even the Council was only a beginning, and then project doctrine and conduct of a kind which seems to us desirable, or, as some would have it, "honest." Because the talk here is about education, we can reflect for a moment on scholarship and see what is happening to it in terms of conservatism—of strong and lasting opposition to change—as well as in terms of almost unrestricted interest in innovation. At stake doubtless are the "values" which governed the development of learning and research during the eighteenth and nineteenth centuries. What were they? To answer very simply: they were tirelessness, meticulousness in finding out as much about events and texts as was humanly possible, and the creation of many forms of "Historicism." Therefore a scholar was for the most part looking at the past, and so the sharp differences between humanistic studies and the natural sciences of which we are now so much aware came into being. The scientist grew more and more concerned with the "next step" toward the gaining of insight into nature, while the humanist toiled over Dionysius or the Gospel according to St. Matthew. Catholics generally were, in terms of the intellectual life, historically oriented; and though one said that there was not, could not be, a conflict between religion and science, it was clear that the gulf between the two yawned ever wider. Perhaps what is really happening now is that some of us are clinging to the scholarship of the past, while others no longer care about it.

First, let us look at the laity in this context. The call for more active participation in and responsibility for the mission of the Church has been sounded. It has been said with some basis (though perhaps not without some malice), that pamphleteers for innovation in the United States are often ex-seminarians. Involvement in this discussion does, of course, demand considerable preparation. When the average earlier American Catholic's commitment was at all sincere he was normally content with having the bishop and his clergy rule the Church. He grumbled, often a great deal. Indeed the more ardently religious the household, the more attentive its members would probably be to the foibles, mannerisms, and alleged autocracy of the pastor. It was a way of conjuring up unprinted (sometimes unprintable) editorials on the conduct of the Church. But at least everyone knew pretty well what he was expected to do. The "laws of the Church" were plainly spelled out; and though one did not always observe them, one felt that it was highly advantageous for mankind to have in its midst a *magisterium* speaking with authority. One did not very often quote the French historian Hippolyte Taine, speaking of Christianity:

Always and everywhere, for eighteen hundred years, wherever those wings fail or are broken, public and private morals are degraded. In Italy during the Renaissance, in England under the Restoration, in France under the National Convention, man seemed to become as pagan as in the first century. He became at once as he was in the times of Augustus and Tiberius, voluptuous and hardhearted; he misused others and himself; brutal or calculating egoism regained ascendancy, cruelty and sensuality were openly paraded, and society became the abode of ruffians and the haunt of evil.

But this is what one deeply and earnestly believed. The Church existed in order to make sure that the wings did not fail.

We should not hesitate to say that this certainty has to a certain extent been undermined. It is not the modification of various laws and rules which really counts. If the Church can decree that not eating meat on Friday is what every Catholic is commanded to do, then it can also say that this form of abstinence is no longer required. The Mass said in the vernacular and not in Latin is still the Mass. But when the Church proclaims that it is penitent for past errors and weaknesses, and hopes to obtain absolution at the bar of

Christian public opinion, when it announces that it respects the intellectual integrity even of atheists, the average American Catholic, brought up as he has been brought up, watches a log which has burned in his hearth for generations crumble into ashes. He had thought that the Church possessed the "truth" and that everybody else was in error. There can be no doubt that it was absolutely necessary that the Council and the Church say what has been said. All of us have to realize that the resolve to reform, expressed so auspiciously at the Council of Trent, had petered out abysmally by the middle of the twentieth century because so many had once thought that remedying the evils of the French Revolution implied being indifferent to any other evils. But the road from Trent to Pope John's Council is a long and tortuous one, and we cannot expect the American layman to walk down it in a hurry—though walk he must. Here there are no cars doing a hundred miles an hour, nor will a helicopter help at all.

Note also how peripheral to the Church the quest for that sincerity in religion which is holiness has been during recent times. The religious have, to be sure, had their own quest and fulfillment, and to it ample reference will be made later. But what I shall call the "creative saints" of recent centuries have frequently lived and moved (except for the Curé d'Ars, who was a law unto himself) in the courtyard of the Church. Let us, making no mention of the living, name a few—Pascal, Dostoevski, Kierkegaard, Simone Weil, Charles Péguy, Dietrich Bonhoeffer, Martin Buber, and, for a long time, Newman. Who can doubt that anyone who wished to write the history of religious insight in terms of recent Western culture would have to be concerned primarily with these? In a time which knows of the enthusiasm, the elation, of scientists entering the "space age" it is clear that the quest for holiness, in religious terms, has its counterpart in the laboratory. The Church must know about the laboratory, but its task is always to reveal its own dynamism.

The layman in Catholic education will therefore inevitably be caught up in a process of re-education. What the course of study is to be remains for the moment obscure. It does not seem possible that it will reflect all the subtleties of current theological speculation. If we persist in straining religious faith through the sieve of philosophy, rather than taking the opposite course, as has been traditional, it seems inevitable that men will in the end cry out for what is simple because it is ultimate. But on this cloudy landscape one guess is quite as good as another. All we really know is that the future of Catholic education will be to an unprecedented extent in the layman's hands. Just how he is to construe the intellectual mission of the Church henceforth will depend on how he is enlightened by the grace of God, and how industrious he is in the pursuit of wisdom.

What, then, of the counsels of perfection? On one level we took it for granted that the life of a religious was an act of shutting out finite things—of dying with and through Christ.* The virginity of religious women was, when well understood, not a way of dying to the world, but rather an anticipation of the resurrection that is to come.** And yet often the rule set such store by the fact that the religiously committed virgin could be tempted, was tempted, that to all intents and purposes she was excluded from the company of adults except in so far as her own community was concerned. The spiritual director was likely to counsel the avoidance of companionship with the male sex. Though it was necessary to have a priest serve as its confessor and chaplain, the community so thoroughly neutralized him that even if he had in some moment of weakness looked upon Sister X as a woman he would have been yanked back into the rigors of reality immediately by the sheer fact that the wall

* It is regrettable that in what follows the emphasis will be almost exclusively on communities for women. But we lack both the data and the commentaries which would make a fruitful discussion of the communities for men profitable.
** See "The Meaning of Virginity in Religious Life," by Sister M. Elena Malits, C.S.C., in *The Changing Sister*, edited by Sister M. Charles Borromeo Muckenhirn, C.S.C., pp. 89–126 (Notre Dame, Ind.: Fides Press, 1965). This is a very effective presentation, in the contemporary mode.

of habits about him was not only impenetrable but overwhelming. He was likely to feel in the end like an overgrown and overfed baby.

Until very recently the life histories of distinguished women in the religious life were very much alike except when they were mystics. In these cases the biographies or autobiographies are of course among the great books of all time. It has, for example, been almost impossible to write a thoroughly bad life of St. Teresa of Avila. Her personality and her immersion in the stream of divine affection are so completely real and convincing that even a skeptic is likely to end writing good prose. Friedrich von Hügel's account of St. Catherine of Genoa is, despite the learned reflection in which it is encased, one of the most remarkable of all stories of a soul. And the *Autobiography of St. Therese of Lisieux*, though it may perhaps (as has been said) reflect desire more than it does realization, is nevertheless a very persuasive and illuminating statement of authentic holiness. Although being a mystic is wonderful if one can manage it, most nuns have been too realistic about themselves to try. They have merely wanted, in response to what they believed was a "calling," to do something they termed "giving myself to God," which exacted of them poverty, chasity, and obedience. For this they were reverentially honored at least collectively by the Church and the Catholic people.

Now we have moved into a time when sex has become not only a good thing (which it has always been for anybody who had his wits about him) but a treasure of such worth that one has to enter something like a brief for not taking advantage of it. Some of the newer quasi-theologies about sex and marriage seem a bit bizarre even to people conjoined in holy wedlock for decades. What must they appear to be to a teaching sister who is expected to expound them to the young lovers of the immediate future! That coitus is not primarily a release of pent-up biological energy but a bridge which lover and beloved can cross with the whole of each one's spiritual baggage, including their sense of the presence of God, makes it a special kind of "sacrament" in some people's eyes. This total commingling supposedly takes place with spiritual jubilation on both sides, far outdistancing anything Coventry Patmore wrote about the analogy between human and divine affection.* Yes, is not this "sacrament" so genuinely spiritualizing and satisfying that it takes precedence over marriage itself? For marriage, after all, is only a contract. Therefore it may be that the sole sexual reality that counts is union of the kind described, matrimony or no matrimony.

Naturally the bewilderment which this commentary is beginning to reflect should not be taken as meaning any sort of power to summon the new theology of sex (or any other theology) before the bar of justice. For that, the reader is invited to look up writers like Ida Goerres.** Here we are only trying to gain some idea of the fix a teaching religious, formed in the traditional manner, finds herself in when she tries to do just this part of her educational job. Perhaps she has been taught to believe that going to see a Bardot film or reading *Playboy* magazine was wrong because it might lead to an "occasion" of sinning, at least in terms of "bad thoughts." But if coitus is so wonderful an enterprise even in the spiritual sense, then perhaps the more one thinks about it, even with the help of Bardot, the holier one is becoming. On the other hand, the religious of yore often entertained odd notions about the sexes. The convent girl who, having been kissed tenderly on the brow by a boy friend, was sure that she was going to have a baby really existed some decades ago, as did the practice of not letting a boy talk to a girl in the convent parlor unless a chaperone was present with or without her knitting.

Enough of that. The sister who tries to explain why she is in a

* Conventry Patmore (1823–1896), distinguished poet, devoted the major part of his verse and prose to this theme. See *The Unknown Eros* and *Rod, Root and Flower.*
** Ida Frederike Goerres, nee Countess Coundenhove (1901–   ) may well be considered a forerunner of the *Aggiornamento.* Deeply religious, she has commented in many books on conventionalism in the Church. See, for example, *Die Leibhaftige Kirche* (1950). The comments referred to here appear primarily in her *Diaries.*

convent doing chores for the educational mission of the Church confronts a whole series of other questions.

Thinking American Catholics, moreover, are unimpressed with a defense of virginity based on its assets to the Church's institutional life. Sensitive to the deficiencies of parochial education, to take but one example, they are not inclined to judge contributed service necessarily as an asset. The vocation to consecrated virginity will never justify itself to twentieth-century people on the grounds of organizational profits. Too often the operations of religious communities in our highly skilled, professionally-managed society appear pathetically ineffectual and incapable of competing with institutions powered by means other than "dedication." Even when successful the race to keep up with secular institutions exacts a price so high that the effort risks destroying the objectives. Involved in a type of administrative work which appears only remotely apostolic to them, religious women could turn into cold functionaries instead of witnesses to Christ. Pressured by impersonal circumstances, their very sense of living a consecrated vocation could be endangered.*

There is a truth here. Putting all our energies into a college and still not managing, say, to keep up with Monteith or Antioch can be a frustrating experience, especially if one is being "dedicated" to a chore which is about as inspiring and invigorating as ironing overalls—at least, if one looks at it in a certain mood.

The religious woman of older days, however strongly she might feel the tedium of life (from which we are, alas, none of us emancipated but which can, God knows, get hold especially of a lonely woman made as all women are for affection), could always find strength in the fact that she lived in a special way in the presence of God. The world was never to be too much with her. Life was regulated, always regulated, but there were hours when she could

* Sister M. Elena Malits, "The Meaning of Virginity in Religious Life," *op. cit.*, pp. 94–95.

find an Augustinian refuge in God. Today, in the reality of a Church facing a world of change, is it not better that one be about one's apostolic task early, fortified, to be sure, by the Mass of the people? At all events, one must see to it that one is not what everybody calls a "mouselike creature." If the advice of Cardinal Suenens is followed, the sister will deal with young adults more than with children.* She must therefore, as the phrase has it, "get into the act."

The teaching sister is of course not alone in the world. In several respects, she is at least as well prepared intellectually as anyone in the American Catholic Church. In all communities (or nearly all) which have been engaged in education, training at the college and university level has not only improved scholarship but has taught the art of participating in discussion as full and equal participants. The sister who has run the gantlet of a Catholic or secular graduate school has now been "socialized" in a way older convent-centered forms of community-building did not imagine.

A reference to the male sex may now be appropriate. According to Father Greeley, there is also a "new breed" of young clergymen who proceed "with a cool and nonchalant competence that is often quite disconcerting. They want to be at the places where decisions are being made and to take their part in making them."** Perhaps the core of their ambition is to be not seminary graduates merely but academicians as well; and it is therefore not out of keeping with the trend that so many minor seminaries are being transformed into fully accredited colleges of liberal arts, and that young men in major seminaries are given leaves of absence to do scholarly work. "New Breed" priests no longer wish to be pastors who, as one mordant description has it, are seen at marriages and funerals and when the bishop comes to town. They take the social gospel very seriously.

* See his *The Nun in the World* (Baltimore: Newman Press, 1962), p. 118. This book by a prelate whose influence on the Second Vatican Council was very great, was a major source of the movement for change in the religious communities.

** Andrew M. Greeley, "A New Breed," *America* CX (May 23, 1964), 64 ff.

Whereas their precursors of a generation or so ago became interested in the more aesthetic aspects of the liturgical movement, the "New Breed" are concerned with the Negro, the migrant worker, and the mentally ill. They seem to place emphasis on courting "danger" rather than avoiding it. They worry not about chastity but about what they are being chaste for. What matters to them is living as other educated Americans do, participating in the life of inquiry, debate, and comment. Brash and inconsiderate at times, they nevertheless have pulses and blood pressures even as did the Master and his last apostle, St. Paul. But it always needs to be borne in mind that the "New Breed" is a platoon and not an army.

This change of attitude, surely more noteworthy and in many ways more startling than that which occurred when groups of immigrant clergy and religious settled in the United States and had to adjust themselves to a wholly different and far less tradition-bound environment, is in several major respects long overdue. Forty years ago a Catholic Negro of my acquaintance, newly arrived in Chicago, went to Mass in a church which at least outwardly did not seem to cater to a socially exclusive congregation. Nevertheless, poignantly enough, he was tapped on the shoulder by the pastor and told that he should promptly go elsewhere. One may hope that not even the "Old Breed" would act like that today. As for the elite of the clergy and religious of the United States, it is probably ahead of the majority of the laity in so far as Christian social action is concerned. But fifty per cent of all Catholic young people attend college, the gap will be closed, though not as quickly as the times may require.

What changes have actually taken place in religious communities whose mission is primarily educational? What we know in a general way is that the impact of the Sister-Formation Movement is very great and is central to the discussion. Records of the annual Notre Dame Conference of Local Superiors provide admirable documentation for a study of the changing mentality of community directors over a period of some years; and a great deal of scattered comment, much of it written by teaching religious themselves, reflects discussions taking place in mother houses or on missions. Some of this raises eyebrows, and perhaps, appears to be unrealistic and immature. As a whole, howeveer, it needs to be taken very seriously because it points the way from the recent past to that part of the future which we can, at least to some extent, foresee.

A careful review and analysis of these data would be a formidable undertaking, and we are a long way from being able to undertake the task. The major reason is the relative immaturity of Catholic graduate schools of education. One such school could be well staffed if it could be established in one place, or if lines of communication were adequate. We know, for instance, that the teaching of the natural sciences in Catholic secondary schools is far better than it used to be, but no adequate survey of the development has been made. It is also clear that some Catholic colleges are resisting overdue reorganization and reorientation, but the process of intelligent upgrading is going on in a many places.

In view of lagging research, we shall limit the present discussion to an admittedly impressionistic characterization of changes in the orientation of teaching communities, utilizing an unpublished doctoral dissertation by Sister Roseanne Murphy, S.N.D.* The study is concerned with examining the development of decision-making in the teaching communities of the United States—an original and difficult undertaking. The central part of it is a comparison between three religious communities, all of them founded in the United States and so without lies to Europe. The co-operation given in terms of supplying information and comment left nothing to be desired, so that the profiles are doubtless as realistic as could be hoped. In addition a questionnaire directed to a sample of community superiors in the country as a whole was answered by 77 per cent

* *Organizational Stance and Change: A Comparative Study of Three Religious Communities* (unpublished dissertation; Notre Dame, 1965). Described in a mimeographed report, by William T. Liu (Notre Dame, 1966).

of those who had been invited to do so. Members of ten communities were also interviewed and the interviews were taped.

On the basis of the data and analysis provided by Sister Roseanne, it is possible to conclude that change is taking place and that much more is to come. The most difficult area to explore is no doubt that of "community identity" on which so much stress has traditionally been laid. Members of the group need to feel that they have a corporate individuality which can be recognized at least by themselves. It is for this reason, for instance, that the question of the habit is of genuine concern. If all religious dressed alike, would they end by *being* alike? The question is certainly more important for women than it is for men. Male religious wear a habit when they are "at home," but in the United States at least put on the familiar Roman collar in dealing with the world at large. This is not a possibility many female religious (or those who set the stamp of approval in Rome or elsewhere) seem willing to consider. Accordingly the changes which have been made so far are toward simplifying or streamlining the traditional garb. And at least for those of us who are not couturiers the results are often aesthetically more satisfying than are some abbreviated modern creations.

But there is much more to identity than its outward symbol. The community rule, the daily communal prayer (a remnant, however small, of the multicolored fabric of medieval monasticism), the discussion of the special mission to which the community is dedicated, the life and ideas of the founder—all these create a feeling of belonging. Right now these do not seem important to a great many young people, but the "crisis" in regard to religious vocations may hopefully be regarded as temporary. Although the kind of identity which meant so much in the past is very likely to have less appeal now, it should be remembered that, since the close of the feudal period, convents and monasteries have not been places in which one locked up the unwanted; they have rather been havens to which men and women like Ignatius Loyola or Elizabeth Seton went with the last desperate leap of their souls. Only those too immured in the here and now will doubt that many others will do so in the future. It is highly likely, however, that the search for religious community by a young man or woman will henceforth depend primarily on choice; one may safely predict that the postulants of the years to come will shop around.

At any rate, the changes which have been or are taking place in religious communities seem, when they do not have to do with "identity," likely to cluster around three considerations. First, how shall the rule of obedience be interpreted? In some earlier times, a superior may have thought and said, as did the Feldwebel in *All Quiet on the Western Front*, that he was to command while the others obeyed. The leadership charisma attached not to the individual but to the office. No one will question that this code reflected a kind of wisdom. The individual was relieved of responsibility for deciding what God's will was; and this emancipation is still quite all right when it is desired. But in our world a soldier is no longer in a phalanx but in a foxhole; and a student brought up on literature about scientific experimentation thinks in concert with his classroom no more than half the time. The comunity rule is therefore now a code with which to conform, of course, but not silently or blindly. In this respect, too, the Second Vatican Council has made its indelible mark. Expressed in sociological terms, the tendency is to move from external to internal social control.

Second, granted reappraisal of the rule, the trend is toward participation in discussion by all members of the community. The structure therefore resembles that of a college or university faculty in the sense that there are instrumentalities for participation through committees or through meetings of all community members having tenure (that is, those who have been professed). Self-studies will be pursued, having to do with the whole of the comunity effort or with some part of it. Indeed, in communities which are now actively engaged in appraising their present and future organization and activities, large and probing questionnaires are distributed, individual and group interviews are arranged, and the whole "product" is then appraised in the most approved sociological style. It is of course understood that in the final analysis the decisions must be made by those in charge—that is, the general chapter acting in prudent concert with Rome—just as in the university decisions are made by the president conjointly with the board of governors or trustees. Perhaps all this constitutes the most startling, even "radical" change in the history of the Church in the United States. There are, to be sure, contemplative orders in which nothing like this will occur, but it seems improbable that any community which is engaged in the "active" life will not achieve some such revamping of its basic social structure.

Third, it is evident that once "participation in discussion" has been instituted, "decision-making" will take on a different character. At present it is impossible to secure agreement about what this means or will mean. The exercise of authority by the general is defined in terms of canon law and varies according to the rule proposed and approved by Rome. Modifications of the rule are not always readily endorsed, even when they are desired. Sister Roseanne's study deals with important aspects of the problem. One community she examined has a greatly cherished monastic tradition. Even such modifications of the rule as would make it possible for the sisters to meet quite normal requirements of the teaching profession (such as matriculation in universities near which the community does not have a convent, or attending professional meetings) will be interpreted by some as a "watering down" of the monastic commitment; and yet unless such modifications are made, the sisters will begin to seem "old-fashioned" and hampered by "authoritarianism." In such circumstances the mother superior must perforce gingerly walk a tightrope; and "democratizing" the "decision-making process" might make matters much worse. A second community examined operates schools and hospitals scattered over a wide area. The headaches suffered by its mother-general are caused primarily by trying to make the far-flung enterprise operate as a unit, at least in the religious sense. A considerable amount of "problem solving" must be delegated to local superiors who have no or little advance training and who must because of canon law be relieved of their responsibility at the end of six years. When that law was "reformed," a highly commendable effort was made to enable the community to decide who should exercise authority over it as well as to make that authority flexible. But—and quite naturally—it did not deal with administration or with how to prepare persons for it. As the units to be supervised grow larger and more complex, the need for efficient administration likewise increases. This the community in question realizes and is trying to meet.

The third community investigated is one which probably has gone further in the direction of democratizing decision-making than any other.

The mother-general has said to the community:

We must ask if our present customs and practices further the development and expression of adult forms of behavior. Do they, for example, allow maximum scope to the power of personal decision? I believe that if we answer these fundamental questions honestly the changes called for will be thorough-going and numerous.

What is needed here is a fearless restructuring of communal forms of living in such a way that a rich and varied emotional experience becomes accessible. Community structures must be critically reevaluated from the point of view of truly adult interpersonal relationships.*

This exhortation has been taken seriously. Discussion takes place almost constantly; the selection of sisters for leadership positions is given careful consideration; and efforts are made to provide training. While it is true that this community consists of women with

* Sister Roseanne Murphy, op. cit.

marked professional qualifications who can look back on a tradition of distributed authority, its current thinking is advanced to a point which others cannot easily and speedily reach.

The basic issue is "institutionalizing" versus "de-institutionalizing." There are those among the clergy and the religious who think and say that the people of God will be able to comfort the whole human family most successfully if the apostolate abandons the institutional forms of the past.

Such discussion is certain to affect commitment to the educational mission. If religious generally were seriously to doubt that the Catholic school offers them the best opportunity to express themselves in terms of service to Christ, it would be a sanguine prophet indeed who would not think that the heart had gone out of the enterprise. In what follows an attempt will be made to state the argument for and against the doubt, though in this case—as the chapters which preceded have indicated, if they were at all successfully written—I entertain a bias against the doubt.

Unquestionably not a few religious, including some of the most deeply devoted among them, no longer accept the educational mission if it necessarily equates teaching religion and teaching secular subjects. This group argues that mathematics or even history can be expounded by persons without any concern whatever for the Christian life as well as, or perhaps even better than, by the devout. On the other hand they say no one can so well initiate the young, or the old for that matter, into the "mystery of the Church," to use De Lubac's term, as one who has given himself utterly to the Church. Nor should one limit the process of initiation to the exercise of academic intelligence. The teaching, guiding, exemplifying can also be carried on as part of the social mission. Indeed, this kind of activity may prove most successful when it is not identified with any visible agency of the Church, or even any building which bears a Catholic name or symbol. For in this way we personalize the Christian mission and so make it more meaningful.

No one ought to disparage such convictions, which in different social contexts were those of St. Francis of Assisi and St. Vincent de Paul. But it may be that criticism of them is more than just an expression of conservative opinion. First, one may wonder whether some current enthusiasm for "dialogue with the world" does not reveal a considerable amount of wishful thinking about the race to which we belong. This has a history which on the whole is pretty shoddy. For example, enabling Negroes and Mexicans and Puerto Ricans to attain to full stature in American life is clearly one of the most imperative duties of our time. But is not the absence of strong social institutions one of the central difficulties? Those which have developed have made a deep impression on public opinion generally and deserve great credit for helping to bring about the removal of iniquities and inequalities. But to anyone who studies the situation with some care, their outlook has not reached down into areas in which effective institution-building is needed. The responsible poor are as powerless to deal with the irresponsible poor as are responsible affluent citizens. What we have come square up against is the *anomie*, the normlessness, of a population which has lived so long without norms that the very language it uses is one in which it can communicate only with itself.

No one will wish to disparage any Christian apostolate which is basically an extension of Catholic Charities, provided it is professionally oriented and ethically dedicated. Every good example given, every act of kindness, each hour of effective counseling, is precious. But it is at least highly probable, for example, that creating and maintaining institutions in the inner city, both with and without physical habitats, remains a contribution to the common good. The Church already has an appreciable number of schools in blighted areas which have been kept open long enough to make the evidence concerning what they have accomplished significant. If they have been successful, we should all know about it. The last thing anybody in a slum should be is romantic. It is hard for some people living in one even to wish to escape. They have gotten used to their own purveyors of sex, liquor, dope, and hatred. We will have to sell them something else, and that is no job for anyone with his or her head in the clouds.

Still, one can dream of schools taught by persons with a strong religious motivation in which effective work is done in job-training after school hours. In New York, for example, Frank Cohen, in behalf of the Louvenburg Foundation, has devised and tried out a pattern where space is provided for a two-fisted community organization, and where race hatred is countered with unflagging professional determination that it will give way to respect and even affection. Maybe, if such institutionalized activity were seriously tried, in the light of experience already obtained, it might point to a way out of an ever gloomier bog. Expensive? Of course. But we who seek to write another chapter in salvation history should not balk at the stenographer's fee. Is it not too often jauntily assumed that if sisters go out of their convents and their schools, where they have been serving the affluent middle class, their apostolate would take on a new radiance? Maybe that is true. No harm will be done if some experimentation is tried to see whether it is really true.

Too much talk about the "affluent middle class" seems prone to discount sociological fact, while reflecting theological presuppositions not as yet clearly formulated. True enough, it has been pointed out over and over again in this book that the most tragic fact about Catholic education in the United States is that so many young people cannot take advantage of it (although their parents ardently wish they could); admission is often contingent on ability to pay tuition fees, as well as on pupil aptitudes more likely to develop in households where education has been cherished. We have therefore underscored the necessity for finding better ways of sharing religious concern with all Catholic parents and children. But is it regrettable that the American Catholic population should to so notable an extent have been emancipated from its menial status?

Do we really think it a pity that the trade union has put some butter on the skilled worker's bread, so that his children can now think seriously about a college education? If we do not, why should we talk as if educating them were somehow, from the spiritual point of view, like playing bridge on Capri? Surely we cannot mean that second-class citizenship should be established the other way around—that teaching "affluent" children as well as one can is reprehensible because their parents can afford to pay? Cannot one rejoice in the desire of many young religious to participate in the war against poverty without wishing to associate the effort with a holy war against the rich?

The theological presuppositions, though it is still difficult to formulate them clearly, are of genuine interest. They are based on Scripture, which makes assistance to the needy—in every sense in which the term "needy" can be used—a basic obligation of the religious mission. In the Old Testament responsibilities are outlined, often in detail. For example, the farmer is ordered to leave something in his fields for the poor. In the New Testament, however, they are open-ended. The counsel of perfection suggested to the rich young man was that he give everything he had to the needy so that he might follow the Master. The sternest of Christ's admonitions is simply that there is no room in the Kingdom for the man who cannot spare a cup of water for the poor. On such counsels of perfection the monastic life has been founded, so that obedience may flower in the soil of selflessness. But one must not oversimplify. The Christ whose words are only in part recorded in the New Testament is so awesomely, sublimely great because in him and by him all the paradoxes and dichotomies of the life of the human spirit are recognized. That a man comes to the love and the service of God only through neighborliness is not true, since it is said that Mary has chosen the best part. A theology which is not also mystically, ascetically oriented toward God cannot be a complete theology; and assuredly historical experience indicates that the radiant warmth of such an all-embracing doctrine can transform both an institutionalized and a de-institutionalized educational mission.

However diligently and sympathetically a religious community regards the changes which now virtually compel every form of human society to find new moorings, success cannot be hoped for unless in arriving at decisions there is taken into account with complete sincerity the views and aspirations of the whole community. This will be not at all easy to do. Every sounding so far taken reveals that the conflict between generations in the community is far more significant than it has previously been in this country. Young and old may be at odds not only over relatively superficial matters, such as the form of dress or the quality of spiritual reading, but over the interpretation of the counsels of perfection themselves. The postulants and novices come from high schools of a kind their elders could not know—high schools in which the impact of the sciences and the social sciences is more keenly sensed, the quality of instruction improved, and student participation in the affairs, if not the government, of the school taken for granted. They will therefore expect to find that these forces, which have shaped their attitudes during four years, often gained in schools conducted by members of the community they have chosen to join, will also make themselves felt during the process of religious formation. From my participation in three self-studies by religious communities, it is clear that young men and women expect religious formation to be challenging and difficult. Indeed, there seems to exist a genuine hunger for discipline—a hunger which has its counterpart among abler and more serious college students as well. But they want to understand the methods and objectives of religious formation. They repudiate doing things just because they have "always and everywhere" been done. And so one thinks that they must have ample and continuing opportunity to find out what the things they are doing mean.

When one goes on to say that the conflict extends to the "interpretation of the counsels of perfection themselves," one is of course taking it for granted that the candidate for the life of religion has at least the maturity reached by a high-school graduate and is not a mere child. Indeed, it is likely enough that during the years which lie ahead a goodly number of those trained for the priesthood will be mature and perhaps even elderly, and that the practice of admitting older men and women into the teaching communities (once quite normal in the United States) will be resumed. Chastity is not something which greatly bothers the ardent, religiously oriented young man or woman. It seldom occurs to them to reflect at length on the fact that the state of life they are entering is "unnatural." Such considerations are much more likely to loom up large later on, when life in the monosexual community is felt to be not that of a happy home, made so by a wife and children . . . or when the beauty of a young woman kindles the fantasy of an older man. And so those who have all this behind them may be needed.

Obedience and poverty are far more controversial. Although the Council strongly reaffirmed the nobility of the religious life by stressing the value of tradition, of the rule and of the counsels of perfection, it nevertheless decreed a number of reforms which, while perhaps not as far-reaching as those advocated by Cardinal Suenens, do make change a goal toward which communities must strive. The superior's authority to arrive at decisions and to require that they be carried out is not to be weakened, said the Council, but he is enjoined to "give the kind of leadership which will encourage religious to bring an active and responsible obedience to the offices they shoulder and the activities they undertake." This means that the superior must listen to the members of the community over which he presides and discuss matters of moment with them. More generally, in so far as the total community and not the particular house is concerned, the general chapter or similar organization is bidden to "express in its own way the fact that all members of the community have a share in welfare of the whole community and a responsibility for it." But doubtless the most notable of all the reforms proposed is that which provides for adequate training, not only for the religious life and the apostolate but for the work to be done and the leadership to be exercised. Endorsing the Sister-Formation effort, the Council Fathers said: "Therefore religious men other than clerics, and religious women as well, should not be assigned to apostolic works immediately after the novitiate. In suitable residences and in a fitting manner let them continue their training in the religious life and the apostolate, in doctrine and technical matters, even to the extent of winning appropriate degrees." •

Obedience is now obviously quite different from what it was some decades ago. Theoretically, to be sure, a superior might still order his subordinates about in a fairly arbitrary manner, since he retains the power to make decisions. But the community knows that he must listen and discuss, bidden as he is to realize that all those in it share the responsibility for its welfare. As soon as talking things over becomes the normal prelude to decision-making, this loses its arbitrary character but also becomes vastly more difficult. It used to be that in many a college the department chairman made all the decisions concerning appointments, promotions, and the course of study. If he was a wise, farsighted chairman, what he decided to do was usually beneficial to all concerned. When he was not endowed with these qualities, things could become very messy. But as soon as he was saddled with a faculty committee which was to share the responsibility, the wise, farsighted chairman often found that he was wasting a good deal of time and that the results obtained were not always better. On the other hand, the martinet found himself on a tether. Something analogous will take place henceforth in religious communities. Years of experimentation will be needed. Each community is likely to have its "new breed" and its "old breed" between which a long series of truces will have to be worked out.

• Walter M. Abbott, S.J. (ed.), *The Documents of Vatican II*, pp. 478–479.

The vow of poverty is perhaps the most difficult of all the counsels of perfection to be practiced by the religious in our society. The Council dealt rather fleetingly though prudently with the problem. It said that the religious were of course to have everything they needed but that they were not to be ostentatious about their wealth or to aspire to amass possessions. Since members of most communities own nothing of their own, and despite accumulations of real estate, cash in the till is usually conspicuous by its absence, there would appear to be little to worry about, at least from a spiritual point of view. But communism has suggested a dimension wholly different from that of sputnik. Practically every community now sends some of its members to places like the *barriadas* of Lima, the slums of our own inner cities, the human wasteland of East Pakistan. Compared with the life encountered there, that which falls to the lot of even the farthest-down-the-line brother or sister in the United States is affluent. He may eat—if the fare is simple— chicken with rice, and drink milk. Should he be ill, doctors and nurses will be on duty; the nutritionist will be on hand with trays. Finally, in old age, he will look resignedly and comfortably at the changing miracles of nature from a window in a home for aged members of the community. The dweller in a *barriada* could not conceive of such bliss even if he conjured up dreams of Paradise. And it is this fact which leads many, especially among the younger religious, to wonder what the vow of poverty means. There are those in the prosperous Catholic laity who ask whether these moods are not inspired by Marxism-Leninism. Alas, it would appear that they have not read the gospels, say young religious.

They listen to words like these, written by Archbishop Helder Camara of Brazil:

The Holy Father surely feels that, just as in moments of acute crisis and threat to public security, God has always raised up pastors to liberate populous cities or regions from slavery or death, the en-

tire Church must be mobilized today, when injustice can be measured on a world-scale, when the masses suffering from hunger and on the threshold of revolt are increasing daily, when universal peace is menaced as it has never been before.

Only the Highest Pontiff's authority will be able to stop exploitation by people who, in an attempt to avoid co-operating with the Church in the maintenance of public welfare, excuse their self-interest on the pretext that our only duty is to think of eternal salvation. As if eternal life could be isolated from life on earth, or love of God from love of man. As if the Scriptures did not say that a man who claims to love the God he cannot see, without loving his neighbor whom he can see, is doing sleight-of-hand.

Sometimes the best of our younger clergy, like the young or old laity, may be imprudent or impetuous. But the Church in the United States may be witnessing something like what happened in Italy when a young man burned his clothes in the market place and set out to serve the Lord. Nevertheless, it need not stifle the Catholic educational mission—or the Protestant and Jewish educational missions, for that matter. These are bound to continue, and, I think, to deepen in awareness and service. The plain fact of the matter is that the United States cannot save other people unless it saves itself, and it cannot educate youth in far-off lands unless it schools its own young people.

There remains the difficult and perhaps equally central problem of how to identify the lay teacher as more than a name attached to a digit in the budget. Can the inevitable separation between him and the religious community be made no more of a barrier than a fence between neighboring houses? Is it possible that having laymen teach religious and ethical subjects will someday be just as normal and natural as having them give instruction in chemistry or English? Will these laymen have a genuine, continuing interest in the special purpose and atmosphere of the Catholic schools?

Other questions remain, and they are also not easy to answer. One can assume that non-Catholic teachers will be invited to join the staffs not simply because Catholics are not available. But will the reason be a hope that dialogue with them will begin at an early age in the student's life? Will the meaning of the idea of the "family of mankind" be made manifest in the schools through example and personal commitment? All this is certainly desirable, but it will require of those in charge of the schools some reorientation of attitudes which are not so much traditional as rooted in the special American experience of the past.

It is, nevertheless, the concept of service, based on reverence for the dignity of every human person and in devotion to the special Christian mission, which bids fair to make such co-operation fruitful. Of course, the educator must be careful not to rely too heavily on the pedagogy of action. What is needed above all is understanding, the primary target in all American schools from this day forward.

I shall close this book with reflections which perhaps summarize everything in it. The era when education beyond the elementary school has become almost universal has created a new religion. This has its own great basilicas, which are the universities. They profess conflicting doctrines, but subscribe to subtly formulated, widely accepted dogmas based on the assumed infallibility of science. Cults spring up around them, probably more hedonistic than those of antiquity. Above all the new religion has its miracles, which inspire awe and dread alike. The principal saints on its altars are those who have performed the miracles. Seen in its totality the creed seems to dwarf Christianity in terms both of power and meaning. The Christian sees of course that it rests on recognition of the fact that Nature, once created, was made autonomous by its Creator. He is not within but outside of it. Man is its master and can enrich himself from a treasury which is in fact rather pitifully meager but can seem almost unbounded when compared with the resources ancestral generations had to draw upon. What can Christian, or specifically Catholic, education do but stand in line for its share of the wealth?

Can it do even that? Is not the queue of rich depositors so long that Christian education can do no more than wait patiently at the end of the line? Would anything special happen if it boarded up its house and told its clients to go elsewhere? Sometimes it seems so clear that the answer to the last question must be No that a chill of resignation settles on its spokesmen. But let us see a little of what might happen if they succumbed to that temptation. First of all, the Christian teacher must remember that when God created Nature he saw that it was good. From that divine vision none of us should distance himself, though it be true that Nature pairs its benignity with barbarous cruelty and thereby achieves renovation. Man can ape it by combining his virtue with his bestiality, but in this he only achieves his deterioration, and perhaps his destruction. His creative freedom can uncreate him. This is the knowledge with which Christian teaching begins so that the hope of redemption may be kindled. The mystery of Evil, which is always a human mystery, can be overcome by the no less unfathomable mystery of the Good. Such are the insight and the desire which fashion the core of Christian education—namely, the counsels of perfection. The Christian teacher can accept them in whole or in part. It may be that he will only reverence and not realize them. They are not in Nature. They exist only in man. But they cannot any longer be impressively defined in rationalistic terms. To say that one who has neither family nor possessions is "free" for service to religion merely raises the question, "free for what?" To escape from the world? But what is the world? It cannot be Nature because God named man master of that. Nor can it be the world of man because man is God's son. Let us turn the rationalistic view upside down. The "perfect" Christian is he who is completely in bondage. He is the pane of glass through which the light can shine, the beggar who in begging gives alms, the soldier who is struck down for his enemy's sake. Through knowing in the innermost part of his being that he has been created, can he direct human creativity to its destiny? Such a hope is made more real wherever there is a school, however humble, in which the counsels of perfection are cherished.

Appendix:
Enrollments in Catholic
Educational Institutions

Enrollments in Catholic Educational Institutions in the school year of 1965–66 were reported as follows:

Elementary Schools	4,465,000
Secondary Schools	1,095,000
Colleges and Universities	417,115
Seminaries	49,957
Total	6,027,072

The number of institutions was reported as follows:

Elementary Schools	10,936
Secondary Schools	2,460
Colleges and Universities	314
Seminaries	454
Total	14,164

Enrollments in Catholic Elementary Schools, as of the opening of the 1966–67 school year were reported as follows, for Elementary and Secondary Schools:

Elementary Schools	4,245,786
Secondary Schools	1,107,767

The number of institutions in these two categories were thus reported:

Elementary Schools	10,427
Secondary Schools	2,417

It should be noted that the new secondary schools are larger and better equipped.

The number of teachers reported for the same school year was:

Elementary Schools	112,786
Secondary Schools	55,783

Against these figures one may place the Notre Dame Study's projection of potential school enrollments as of 1968–69, if the percentage rate of admissions in effect in 1962–63 was to be maintained:

Elementary Schools	
pupil increase	758,700
teacher increase	18,966
Secondary Schools	
pupil increase	329,363
teacher increase	12,315

Selected
Bibliography

Listed are twelve currently available books which seem most likely to give the reader a realistic impression of the history, aims and achievements of Catholic education in the United States. There are many others having genuine merit, and attention has been called to some of these in footnotes.

1. A History of Catholic Education in the United States, by James Burns, C.S.C., and Bernard Kohlbrenner (New York: Benziger Bro., Inc. 1937). A pioneer survey, unfortunately never revised, which is still the best available terse summary of stages in the development of Catholic education.
2. Catholic Education in America: A Documentary History, by Neil G. McCluskey, S.J. (New York: Teachers' College, 1964). A compendium of important documents bearing on the development of Catholic education, from the Pastoral Letter of Bishop John Carroll (1792) to the Pastoral Letter of the Bishops and Archbishops of the United States (1919), it has a very effectively written introductory essay, which the reader will find at least as significant as any of the documents reproduced.

3. *Religion and Career*, by Andrew M. Greeley (New York: Sheed & Ward, 1963), utilizes data gathered by the National Opinion Research Center, University of Chicago, in order to examine the question as to whether Catholic career expectancies have been actually lower than those of other social groups in the United States. The conclusions drawn were so optimistic that some critical comment contended that they simply could not be correct. But Father Greeley has stood his ground well. The question and the answer are important because one should know in what sense Catholic education provides an "upward bound" program (using the term in no racial sense).

4. *The Education of Catholic Americans*, by Andrew M. Greeley and Peter H. Rossi (Chicago: Aldine Press, 1966), uses data supplementary to those which formed the basis for *Religion and Career*, and is concerned primarily with (a) the results of the Catholic effort to teach Religion in the schools and (b) with attitudes towards Catholic schools on the part of the Catholic public. This book should be seen as supplementary to the Notre Dame Study, and not as competitive with it. The Greeley-Rossi study is concerned with persons who have graduated from Catholic schools, while the Notre Dame study deals with pupils in attendance. The conclusions drawn are comparable, though G.-R. is somewhat more optimistic.

5. *Parochial School*, by Joseph Fichter, S.J. (Notre Dame, Ind.: University of Notre Dame Press, 1958), is a sociological study of a Catholic school in the Midwest. Indicted for being relatively sentimental (as it probably is), this book is nevertheless a warm, human, sociological document of great value to anyone who desires to catch the spirit of Catholic education.

6. *A History of Catholic Education in the United States*, by Edward J. Power (Milwaukee: Bruce Pub. Co., 1958), is a valuable survey of this segment of the Catholic educational situation. There are several interesting impressionistic books dealing with Catholic collegiate and university campuses, but none of them seems sufficiently comprehensive.

7. *The Making of a Sister-Teacher*, by Sister Maria Concepta, C.S.C. (Notre Dame: Fides Press, 1965), is especially valuable because of its analysis of the financial problems which confront a religious community which is dedicated to the educational mission.

8. *Religion, the Courts, and Public Policy*, by Robert F. Drinan, S.J. (New York: The Macmillan Company, 1963), seems by far the best treatise on the subject with which it deals. Many books seem far too apologetic in tone.

9. *American Catholic Dilemma*, by Thomas F. O'Dea (New York: Sheed & Ward, 1958), is perhaps the most effective of the several analyses of alleged Catholic intellectual and academic inferiority. Even if, as Greeley believes, such studies are useful by reason of what has been rather than of what now is, it may be helpful to keep one stage of the evolution in mind.

10. *The Catholic Church and German Americans*, by Colman J. Barry, O.S.B. (Milwaukee: Bruce Pub. Co., 1953), is an admirable model for needed studies of Catholic ethnical groups in the United States.

11. *Are Parochial Schools the Answer?* (New York: Holt, Rinehart and Winston, 1964) is Mary Perkins Ryan's program for Catholic education reform in the post-Vatican Council II world. Its great value lies in the fact that it places in the forefront of attention the youngsters who receive little or no training in religion.

12. *The Shape of Catholic Education*, edited by Robert Hassenger. (Chicago: University of Chicago Press, 1967). The editor presents what can realistically be described as a compendium of short studies of Catholic higher education written by young scholars many of whom are well-trained sociologists. The book is particularly valuable because it summarizes a good deal of otherwise inaccessible research.

13. *Catholic Schools in Action: A Report, the Notre Dame Study of Catholic Elementary and Secondary Schools in the United States*, edited by Reginald A. Neuwien (Notre Dame, Ind.: Notre Dame Press, 1966).

About the Author

GEORGE N. SHUSTER grew up in southern Wisconsin, graduated from Notre Dame, and served in the trenches and in military intelligence during World War I. After the war he taught English at Notre Dame and wrote his first book, *The Catholic Spirit in Modern English Literature*. He received his Ph.D. from Columbia University; his doctoral studies also led to his most scholarly work, *The English Ode From Milton to Keats*.

Dr. Shuster was editor of *Commonweal* for several years, was made a Fellow of the Social Science Research Council to study German political history, and became President of Hunter College in 1938. His knowledge of Germany and his concern for international education led to a continuing relationship with the State Department, and he served as a member of the American delegation which assisted in the founding of UNESCO and as deputy for Bavaria in the post-World War II military government in Germany. In 1960 he retired from Hunter and returned to Notre Dame as Assistant to the President and organizer of the University Center for the Study of Man.

Among his other books are: *The Ground I Walked On, Education and Moral Wisdom, The Germans, Religion Behind the Iron Curtain*, and the widely known anthology, *World's Great Catholic Literature*.